Pliny's Women

Constructing Virtue and Creating Identity
in the Roman World

Pliny's Women offers a comprehensive consideration of the many women who appear in the letters of Pliny the Younger. Combining detailed prosopography with close literary analysis, Jacqueline M. Carlon examines the identities of the women whom Pliny includes and how they and the men with whom they are associated contribute both to this presentation of exemplary Romans and particularly to his own self-promotion. Virtually all of the named women in Pliny's nine-book corpus are considered. They form six distinct groups: those associated with opposition to the principate; the family of Pliny's mentor, Corellius Rufus; his own family members; women involved in testamentary disputes; ideal wives; and women of unseemly character. Detailed analysis of each letter mentioning women includes the identity of its recipient and everyone named within, its disposition within the collection, Pliny's language and style, and its significance to our perception of the changing social fabric of the early principate.

Jacqueline M. Carlon is Assistant Professor of Classics at the University of Massachusetts, Boston. In addition to awards for her teaching, Dr. Carlon has received the Rallis Award from the Boston University Humanities Foundation and the 2008 Barlow-Beach Award for Distinguished Service to the Classical Association of New England, of which she was president in 2005.

Pliny's Women

Constructing Virtue and Creating Identity in the Roman World

JACQUELINE M. CARLON

University of Massachusetts, Boston

CAMBRIDGE
UNIVERSITY PRESS

CAMBRIDGE UNIVERSITY PRESS
Cambridge, New York, Melbourne, Madrid, Cape Town, Singapore, São Paulo, Delhi

Cambridge University Press
32 Avenue of the Americas, New York, NY 10013-2473, USA

www.cambridge.org
Information on this title: www.cambridge.org/9780521761321

© Jacqueline M. Carlon 2009

First published 2009

Printed in the United States of America

A catalog record for this publication is available from the British Library.

Library of Congress Cataloging in Publication data
Carlon, Jacqueline M., 1953–
   Pliny's women: constructing virtue and creating identity in the Roman
   world / Jacqueline M. Carlon.
      p.   cm.
   Includes bibliographical references and index.
   ISBN 978-0-521-76132-1 (hardback)
   1. Women – Rome – History.   2. Sex role – Rome – History.   3. Pliny, the
   Younger – Correspondence.   I. Title.   II. Series.
   HQ1136.C367 2009
   305.48′871–dc22   2008044129

ISBN 978-0-521-76132-1 hardback

Contents

Preface

Since I first began research on women in Pliny's letters, nearly ten years ago, the work of Pliny the Younger has gone from abject neglect to hot topic, with an entire issue of *Arethusa* devoted to Plinian scholarship in 2003 and the publication of a number of books, including a consideration of Pliny's self-representation by John Henderson (2002). The latest contributions, alas, postdated the completion of this manuscript: Nicole Méthy's *Les lettres de Pline le Jeune: Un répresentation de l'homme* (Paris: Presses de l'Université Paris-Sorbonne, 2007) and Ilaria Marchesi's *The Art of Pliny's Letters* (Cambridge: Cambridge University Press, 2008). But the reinvigoration of Plinian scholarship is exciting, and it pleases me greatly to know that I have so many companions in my affection for Pliny.

The fundamental work on Pliny's letters remains the historical and social commentary of A. N. Sherwin-White (1966), which, although it has been superseded in consideration of certain individual letters, remains an invaluable resource and starting point for any researcher. The prosopographical sections of my work are particularly indebted to the monumental contributions of Werner Eck and Sir Ronald Syme, with whom I occasionally disagree but whose insights are always crucial to any understanding of Roman family structures, and of course to Marie-Thérèse Raepsaet-Charlier (1987), whose work on elite women of the early empire is seminal.

I am also grateful to the many scholars of the past forty years who have written on Roman women, most of whose work I read in preparation for this book and whose names are too numerous to mention. Without ingesting the fruits of their labors, I would not have ventured to ask the questions that provoked this analysis. Working on the margins and often in uncharted territory, those scholars have brought substance to Roman women who had previously lingered as mere shadows in our perceptions of the past.

Finally, I wish to thank my thesis adviser, Ann Vasaly, whose sharp eye and careful guidance helped me to complete the initial research on which this book depends. I also must acknowledge the anonymous readers of earlier versions of this book, whose insights and advice have been invaluable in the crafting of this final product. I am grateful to Beatrice Rehl, my editor at Cambridge, for her interest in and support of my work; to my colleagues Kenneth Rothwell and Emily McDermott for their willing ears and unending confidence in my abilities; and especially to Steven, my husband and best friend, whose support and loving care make all things possible.

List of Abbreviations

AE	*L'Année épigraphique.* Paris, 1888–.
CIL	*Corpus Inscriptionum Latinarum*, i–xvi. Berlin, 1863–.
ILS	*Inscriptiones Latinae Selectae.* Ed. Herman Dessau. Berlin, 1892–1916.
NP	*Der Neue Pauly: Enzyklopädie der Antike.* Ed. Hubert Cancik and Delmuth Schneider. Berlin, 1996–.
PIR	*Prosopographia Imperii Romani.* Ed. Edmund Groag, Arthur Stein, Leiva Petersen, and Klaus Wachtel. Berlin, 1987–.
RE	*Paulys Real-enzyklopädie der klassischen Altertumswissenschaft.* Ed. Georg Wissowa, Wilhelm Kroll, Kurt Witte, Karl Mittlehaus, and Konrat Ziegler. Stuttgart, 1894–.

Introduction

mihi nisi praemium aeternitatis ante oculos,
pingue illud altumque otium placeat.

Pliny, Epistulae 9.3

That life of rich and profound ease would be pleasing to me if the
reward of immortality were not before my eyes.[1]

As it became an institution in its second century, the principate
forever transformed the lives of Rome's elite, leaving little room for
dissent and an empire that would shortly cease to pine for the glory
days of the republic. Fame was not to be achieved by deliberating
legislation in the senate; great military victories on the battlefield
were few, and those became triumphs not for the general but for the
emperor, who celebrated them all, even if he had never appeared on
the battlefield. Indeed, what glory there was for a man lay in becoming a member of the senate, when the emperor chose to recognize
and reward his talent. Further honor might come in the awarding
of office, culminating in the receipt of one or more consulships, a
hollow office whose only assets were the cachet of the title and the
opportunity to offer thanks to the emperor in oratorical form – the
gratiarum actio. But the memory of a speech or of service to the state
was fleeting, easily replaced by that of the next powerful orator or
adviser. How then was a man to secure lasting fame?

---

[1] All translations are those of the author.

Pliny the Younger's literary models provided him an answer: his uncle and adoptive father, Pliny the Elder, whose deeds Tacitus immortalized in his *Historiae*,[2] and Cicero, whose political and rhetorical successes and whose service to the state were recorded in writing, both his own and those of historians. Pliny could secure his *aeternitas* through the publication of his speeches and through a new genre – a collection of letters, whose careful selection and arrangement would offer its readers a vivid portrait of Pliny and make him an exemplar of moral rectitude and proper comportment. Cicero had, after all, won lasting fame with his speeches (as well as his own proscription and execution) and had intended to publish a collection of his letters. So Pliny published his speeches, but alas, only the *Panegyricus* survives, a unique type of rhetoric that is hardly representative of Pliny's oratorical skill.[3] But he also set about to accomplish what his predecessor had not lived long enough to do, in a way that Cicero, known for his own persistent self-aggrandizement, would surely have appreciated – publishing a carefully polished collection of correspondence.

Modern sensibilities preclude the kind of open self-promotion in which the Roman elite so readily participated. While we quietly revel in kudos heaped upon us by others and even manipulate conversations to provoke praise, we are quite averse to open self-aggrandizement. But how could an orator establish his credentials in a court of law, as Cicero so often did, without informing the judges of his qualifications, his service to the state, his integrity? Pliny the orator merely extended the rhetorical technique of ethopoeia to epistolography, creating "correspondence" whose purpose may well have included the communication of ideas and the maintenance of relationships with its addressees, but which, when collected, refined, and published, became the medium through which Pliny created a lasting monument to his virtue.

Despite their intense focus on Pliny's character (or perhaps because he needs to set himself within a milieu that makes his self-characterization credible), his letters are filled with information about

[2] As the portion of the *Historiae* that would include the death of the elder Pliny is not extant, we can only assume from Pliny's letters to Tacitus regarding the eruption of Vesuvius that he would have appeared within its account.
[3] While Pliny's *Panegyricus* is not treated within this study except in passing, it does offer significant support to the analysis of the exemplary wife in Chapter 4.

social relations and economic concerns in Roman society of the late first and early second centuries c.e. As a result they have been mined extensively as a source for details not only of Pliny's life, including his relationships with Trajan and Tacitus, but also of the daily activities of the senatorial class, the mechanisms of imperial administration, and the workings of the Roman judicial system. Indeed, scholarship that focuses on this period of imperial history has long relied on the positive nature of Pliny's assessment of Roman society as a counterbalance to Juvenal's vitriol and Tacitus' overwhelmingly negative view of the principates of the Julio-Claudians and Flavians.

Nowhere has Pliny's upbeat and idealized presentation of his immediate milieu been more cited than in efforts to reassess the disparaging evaluations of female behavior offered by his contemporaries. Yet most citations of Pliny's work that refer to women are short passages, extracted from their generic context, which seemingly ignore the autobiographical nature of the *Epistulae* and the political and social capital that their publication might have produced for their author. Women in the letters have been referred to individually and in discussions of Roman marriage or motherhood, but little attention has been given to the importance of women in the wider context of Pliny's corpus.[4] The few works of scholarship that do focus on the appearance of women in Pliny's letters have been severely limited in scope, largely ignoring Pliny's purpose in choosing particular women for inclusion in the *Epistulae*.[5] This study presents a comprehensive examination of

---

[4] Articles by Bodel (1995) and Sick (1999) focus on Minicia Marcella (*Ep.* 5.16) and Ummidia Quadratilla (*Ep.* 7.24), respectively. Arria the Elder (*Ep.* 3.16) is possibly the most cited of Pliny's women in general works on Roman women (e.g., Königer 1966), and references to individual letters and characters abound in books that explore women's roles in Roman society (e.g., Dixon 1988). A comprehensive work on Pliny like Bütler's (1970) does include consideration of the women in Pliny but only as they pertain to the topics he discusses – illness, friendship, the power of the exemplum, among others.

[5] For example, Dobson 1982 and Vidén 1993: 91–107. Dobson offers a brief and somewhat naive discussion of Pliny's attitude toward women, reaching the conclusion that Pliny believes women to be the moral and intellectual equals of men. In this short article, Dobson cites thirty-six of Pliny's letters, virtually all of those in which women have any significant presence, but no letters are analyzed in depth. Dobson's analysis is hindered by piecemeal citation of the letters, the lack of any attempt to identify the women as individuals, and disregard for the autobiographical nature of the letters. Like Dobson, Vidén (in a chapter dedicated to Pliny in her survey of women in Roman literature) finds evidence of economic and social equality among

the women in the letters, focused particularly on their identities and the ways in which they serve Pliny's primary goals – preserving his *gloria* and securing *aeternitas*.

Pliny's Life and Career

As Anthony Birley (2000) notes, there is now scholarly consensus on most of the details of Pliny's biography. Birley recounts the facts, at length and with great attention to the salient sources, so thoroughly that repetition here is unnecessary. Although some pertinent facets of Pliny's life are examined more completely in the subsequent chapters, a brief sketch will suffice for the moment.

As Pliny makes clear from his letters to Tacitus regarding the eruption of Mount Vesuvius (6.16 and 6.20), at the time of the disaster in 79 C.E. Pliny was a young man of seventeen, living with his mother and enjoying the intellectual guidance of his uncle, the Elder Pliny,

the men and women of Pliny's time. Vidén mentions a number of letters in passing, focusing on a handful that offer somewhat developed depictions of women. Most notable among these are 7.19 (Fannia), 3.16 (Arria), 5.16 (Minicia Marcella), 7.24 (Ummidia Quadratilla), 4.19 (Calpurnia), and 7.11 (Corellia). While Vidén studies Pliny's financial and legal interactions with women and his putative *amicitia* with some of them, she fails to consider in depth the family connections of the women Pliny chooses to discuss or address in his correspondence. Without this prosopographical background, the reader cannot determine whether Pliny's relationships with individual women were independent from those he may have maintained or wished to cultivate with the men connected to them.

Only Maniet (1966) and Shelton (1990) have examined in any detail the appearance of women in Pliny, but their work, too, is limited. Both trace Pliny's concerted effort in his letters to present the positive attributes of Roman wives. Shelton examines a number of Pliny's letters in which the qualities of a good wife are discussed. Foremost among these are the three that Pliny addresses to Calpurnia (6.4, 6.7, and 7.5) and his letter to her aunt in praise of Calpurnia (4.19). Other letters that are important to her argument are 5.16, 6.24, 7.19, 8.5, 8.11, and 8.18. Maniet's concern is to demonstrate that Pliny's affection for his wife is genuine and distinct from that which he feels for his friends. Shelton (1990: 186) recognizes that Pliny intends for the women he mentions, particularly his own wife, to serve as exempla of proper feminine behavior, but she explores neither Pliny's motivation for such an optimistic portrayal nor the reflection that his characterization of his wife might cast upon his construction of his autobiographical image. Elsewhere Shelton (1987) does make clear the importance of her belief that Pliny published his correspondence in order to produce an autobiography and that each letter can be viewed as a segment of such an undertaking. Although Shelton's work is valuable, it considers only Pliny's presentation of women as wives, and it focuses, naturally, on one woman – his wife, Calpurnia – largely overlooking the other idealized women in the letters.

whose prolific scholarship Pliny discusses at length in *Epistulae* 3.5. The death of his uncle was but one in a series of losses that would strip Pliny of all his immediate family – father, sister, uncle, and finally mother – leaving him, by the time the letters were assembled (and likely even when they were written, if we may count them as "authentic" correspondence), with only far-removed memories of those who shaped his early life. Those early losses combined with the death of at least one wife, and perhaps two, leave Pliny with few easy options for creating in the letters a complete picture of himself as a proper Roman man, whose behavior needed to be open to scrutiny not only in service to the state and others but in the close company of his family. This dearth of kin is made even more acute for Pliny by his lack of children. Pliny the son, Pliny the brother, Pliny the father are all roles difficult to define in a script missing so many players. Honoring the few familial ties he has and creating new ones by assuming the places of deceased or ineffective men become critical avenues for Pliny's self-representation. It is not surprising, then, that women related to those men, as well as those related to Pliny by marriage or bound to him by *amicitia*, are key components for him in developing a comprehensive picture of his character.

Like many members of Rome's elite in the late first century, Pliny was of equestrian origins, elevated to senatorial status to help fill the dwindling elite ranks of Rome. His adlection to the senate, like that of his contemporary Tacitus, occurred during the reign of Domitian, before the dreadful concluding years of the emperor's reign. Pliny must have shown an early talent for accounting, as much of his career involved dealing with state finances in various capacities. In doubt is the timing of his first service in such an office, as prefect of the Military Treasury. Birley argues for a one-year term in the years 96–97 and appointment by Nerva, whereas A. N. Sherwin-White and Sir Ronald Syme prefer a three-year term in 94–96 and appointment by Domitian.[6] There is tenuous evidence on each side of the debate,

---

[6] A. Birley 2000: 10–15. Syme (1979c: vol. VII, 562) remarks that it is exceptional careers with rapid advancement that tend to appear in our sources and that "normal" intervals between terms of offices might vary substantially. Sherwin-White (1966: 73) comments that the office was of triennial duration and that Pliny himself remarks that he held no office in 97 – thus his preference for 94–96 for Pliny's service in the prefecture.

and its definitive resolution seems unlikely without new evidence. The difference between the two dating possibilities is not insignificant to an assessment of Pliny's character: if Domitian continued to reward him by choosing him for office, then Pliny's declarations of his own precarious position during the later years of the despot's reign and his condemnation of Domitian after his death are disingenuous at best. The issue of Pliny's peril and his actions on behalf of his "friends" who were executed or exiled in 93 is taken up at length in Chapter 1 and offers a reassessment of his involvement with the condemned.

Pliny's next treasury appointment is more securely dated, as he served with Cornutus Tertullus in the office of prefect of the Treasury of Saturn for the better part of three years from 98 to September of 100, when both men were rewarded by Trajan with the suffect consulship. Pliny's honors continued in the years that followed, culminating with a special assignment to represent the emperor as *legatus Augusti* in Bithynia-Pontus, where his financial skills were particularly needed to deal with what appears to be significant incompetence if not malfeasance in the province's prior administration. The tenth book of the *Epistulae*, which was not published by Pliny and so falls outside the scope of this study, offers remarkable documentation of the difficulties Pliny encountered in addressing both old and new matters in the province, as well as great insight into the burdens of imperial rule for both legate and emperor. Pliny did not live to return to Rome from this final service to the emperor.

To judge from inscription evidence and Pliny's own remarks in the *Epistulae* and the *Panegyricus*, his was a life of regular service to the emperor, to his hometown, and to justice in the courtroom as both prosecutor and defender – a life that was enriched by periods of withdrawal to the countryside and his villas, where he read, revised his speeches, wrote poetry, and corresponded with friends. Demurring to write history, he chose instead to supply Tacitus with historical accounts, to recall the settings of his speeches, and to explicate exempla of model Roman men and women in epistolary form.

The *Epistulae*

It is now universally agreed that the arrangement of Pliny's letters is far from incidental, as he claims in his first letter. Indeed, each of the letters is carefully located, and various types are distributed throughout the first nine books.[7] Only the letters of book 10, certainly published after his death and without his editing hand, can be said to remain unrevised and assembled without any purpose other than to juxtapose Trajan's responses to Pliny's inquiries.

Although there is little consensus as to the form of publication, whether in pairs or triads of books or even as single books, John Bodel (n.d.) has nicely demonstrated that a final nine-book structure was surely Pliny's intent for the handpicked letters, and thus any study of the corpus must take into account where letters appear in relation both to the work as a whole and to one another.

In comparison to the letters of Cicero, whose addressees are often prominent political figures of his time, the recipients of Pliny's missives are remarkably nondescript, with the obvious exception of the historian Tacitus. Fewer than half of the hundred or so addresses can securely be identified as of senatorial rank, and a substantial percentage remains unknown outside of Pliny.[8] It is considerably easier to identify the six women who receive letters from Pliny, as they are quite closely associated with him – his wife, her aunt, his mother-in-law, his mentor's sister and daughter, and a relative by marriage.[9] Letters addressed to women are widely dispersed in the first eight books, appearing in all but book 5. Their broad distribution suggests careful placement by Pliny. Despite the fact that women constitute so small a number of recipients, women do, in fact, have a substantial presence in Pliny's letters, appearing in 15 percent of the letters and all nine books.

---

[7] Sherwin-White (1966: 43–44) offers a typology for the letters in his commentary, assigning them to eight categories: public affairs, character sketches, patronage, admonitions, domestic, literary, scenic, and social courtesy. Like all such attempts, Sherwin-White's classification is somewhat arbitrary, but it does serve to illustrate the diversity of the letters, both within books and across the collection in its entirety.

[8] There is difficulty in securing a precise number of recipients, as the nomenclature Pliny uses is not consistent. By Sherwin-White's (1966) count there are 101, but A. Birley (2000: 21) suggests as many as 105. Jal (1993: 212) notes that, at 101, Pliny would have precisely as many addressees in approximately one-third as many letters as Cicero did. The potential coincidence of numbers is meant to point out the diversity of Pliny's recipients rather than to draw any direct correlation between Pliny's work and that of Cicero.

[9] Excluded from this group is Cottia, the wife of Vestricius Spurinna, to whom Pliny directs a letter of condolence on the death of her son (3.10). In this case, she is co-recipient along with her husband, and so the letter does not qualify as one addressed only to a woman.

In the complete corpus of 368 letters (a number that includes the correspondence with Trajan in which women have brief mention but no significant presence), 72 letters contain some reference to women. Thirty-four of those letters offer only passing mention of a wife, sister, mother, mother-in-law, stepmother, or daughter. There remain 38 letters, all found in the first nine books, which include 247 letters in total: of these, 18 focus upon women, 9 are addressed to women, and 11 include women prominently though not as their main subject. Still, the number of women constitutes less than 10 percent of the hundreds of individuals named in the letters, an indication that their particular identities are less important than their roles in the lives of their male relatives, almost none of whom go unnamed. Their relatively small number strongly suggests that the corpus as a whole presents a selective rather than comprehensive view of Pliny's relationships with women and that he has purposefully chosen the women he mentions and addresses.

The Question of Self-Representation

Scholars have largely abandoned further consideration of many long-standing questions regarding the *Epistulae* of Pliny the Younger, including efforts to determine their date or dates of publication or their "authenticity" – that is, were they actually sent to their addressees and, if so, how substantial was their subsequent revision – as well as attempts to reconstruct Pliny's villas. Instead, much recent work has focused on Pliny's letters as a vehicle for presenting himself as a model, both for his contemporaries and for posterity. While the reader must wait until the final book of Pliny's nine-book collection for the bald statement by the author that he desires nothing so much as to secure his fame by always having something *clarum ... et immortale* in mind (9.3), recent examinations have made clear that the function of the letters in his self-representation begins with the very first letter of the collection, where he asserts that the arrangement of the letters is entirely incidental, implying that they recount ordinary, everyday events in his life and thus properly represent his behavior and character.[10]

---

[10] Henderson (2003) has commented upon the impossibility of distinguishing between Pliny's dual roles of reporter and editor – giving the correspondence

Of course, the very nature of personal correspondence makes it an ideal medium for the presentation of its author's character. Through it, he can not only recall but also shape the events of his life and his interactions with friends, family, and the famous, revealing both by direct statement and by implication his innermost thoughts and feelings whenever he wishes to do so. Letters open a door through which the reader may look into the author's heart and mind, to know his nature by direct observation rather than oblique report. Yet even the most casual of written communication is fashioned to some extent by its author for the eye of his reader; even a simple note of thanks may express both real gratitude and the writer's desire to be seen as a polite and genuinely grateful recipient.[11] A collection of various types of correspondence by the same author can thus provide a series of vignettes from his life, each of which adds to a pastiche of his character traits.

As Elizabeth Meyer (1999) has demonstrated, Cicero fashioned his character in individual letters, as he had in his speeches, to suit the particular purpose of a letter and the nature of its recipient. As noted, Cicero had planned to assemble a number of his letters for publication – not, of course, without editing them: *eas [epistulas] ego oportet perspiciam, corrigam; tum denique edentur* (*Att.* 16.5.5). Although we cannot know the nature of the intended collection, Cicero's penchant for self-promotion surely would have assured that its contents highlighted only those traits that he considered worthy of a great statesman.

Despite some clear allusions to and echoes of his predecessor's letters in some of Pliny's corpus, just how extensive his contact was with Cicero's correspondence is open to debate and, with the exception of Pliny's letters to his wife (see Chapter 4), largely beyond the scope of this study. John Nicolson (1998), however, has nicely demonstrated that, while Pliny compares himself to the great republican orator repeatedly, references in Pliny's work to Cicero's letters are quite limited, suggesting that Pliny was familiar with only a few examples and possibly, even then, only excerpts from them.

Other literary predecessors had certainly employed the epistolary medium as a means of self-characterization, albeit with considerably

and Pliny's self-portrait layers of complexity that make the work a highly literary mosaic.
[11] See particularly Altman 1984.

more subtlety than Pliny. The *Epistulae Morales ad Lucilium* of Seneca most assuredly offer a portrait of their author's character, including justification of his role in Nero's reign and his accumulation of wealth, for both of which we may be sure he suffered severe criticism. Although Seneca's letters seem more apology than self-promotion, there is little doubt that they were intended to change the way in which his life and work were remembered – promoting his greatest strength as philosophical reflection rather than political manipulation. An author's character is evident even in verse epistles – Horace, steeped in philosophy, or Ovid, repentant in exile and counting on his missives to intercede for him with the emperor, to replace his absent person with their poetic power. Yet, with the poets the reader is always acutely aware of the literary nature of the hexameter and elegiac couplet. Pliny chooses a different approach, creating a new literary medium, clothed as everyday correspondence, to present his character.[12]

Although Pliny begins his collection of letters with the claim that they have been assembled randomly, as they came into his grasp (1.1), it is now widely accepted that Pliny's letters were at least edited before publication. Some may even have been written specifically for inclusion in the corpus. Indeed, the seeming anonymity of so many of his addressees makes such pretense easily believable, as he writes to so many ordinary people about everyday concerns. Pliny himself, moreover, acknowledges the letter's power to represent its author (4.13, 6.17), to oblige him (3.1, 7.1), and to offer a guide for others to follow (4.24). Pliny was also aware that even without the premeditation assumed in arranging an epistolary collection, letters were not exclusively a means of private communication. Individual letters might be intended for circulation or reading in an open forum, and some – though meant to be held in confidence – might well have been shared with others. The unplanned transmission of the contents of letters is well illustrated by Pliny's recollection of the reading of a letter before Domitian in which Modestus condemned Regulus and which caused the latter's

---

[12] On the letters as a literary enterprise whose intent was to create a persona like that of Horace, see Ludolph 1997. For an examination of the letters as an artistic construct, whose words shape Pliny's character like the hands of a sculptor, see Henderson 2002b. Both are a welcome break from the traditional scholarship on Pliny with its historical focus, and each compels readers of Pliny to be more aware of the many ways in which Pliny crafts his self-presentation.

unremitting enmity toward its author (1.5.14).[13] Pliny knew well the witness a letter could offer to the inner recesses of its author's character.

Letters, then, were a potent means of manipulating the images of the author and could be equally effective in portraying an addressee and others about whom the author wrote. Self-representation is particularly apparent in letters of recommendation and obituary, in which Pliny praises his mentors and exemplary Romans and defines his relationships with those individuals, but every letter in the collection can be read as part of a subtle program to paint Pliny's own character.[14] In fact, the great advantage of the medium of epistolography was the opportunity it provided for the author to highlight his virtues and those of others indirectly – that is, through what seems to be natural communication in customary social intercourse. Pliny can present his mentors, the emperor, and particularly himself without seeming to indulge in public self-aggrandizement or sycophancy.

Although the study of Pliny's letters offers the opportunity to explore his social, political, and personal relationships with those he addresses, because the collection includes only Pliny's letters and none from his correspondents, only cautious conclusions regarding the reality of those relationships may be drawn. In spite of the limitations imposed upon the reader by Pliny's overwhelming presence in the letters, they *can* be analyzed for Pliny's delineation of the roles he played in the lives of his addressees and they in his. In addition, it is sometimes possible to uncover Pliny's expectations of his interaction with his correspondents – that is, what political or social advantage or reciprocity he may be seeking. Most accessible to analysis by his readers is Pliny himself, in the guise he creates for his reader to see.

---

[13] Cicero's letters range from intimate missives for the eyes of the addressee only to formal communication sent to public figures and meant to be circulated. In addition, Cicero often reminds us that he must find a loyal courier for his letters to ensure that they will not fall into the wrong hands or that he sometimes conveys private or sensitive information orally through a messenger rather than entrusting it to the written word. It is clear that he expected some of his letters to circulate even if they were not intended to do so. For Cicero's concerns regarding reliable couriers, see *Fam.* 1.7; *Att.* 1.18, 8.1, 10.11, et al. Regarding oral messages carried by couriers, see *Fam.* 3.5; *Att.* 11.4, et al. For a comprehensive treatment of the subject, see Nicolson 1994.

[14] In his study of Cicero's letters, Hutchinson (1998: 22) notes that even in letters to Atticus, Cicero's concern that his friend understand and approve of his actions is a dominant force.

How women contribute to that image defines their importance to the letters, and thus an understanding of Pliny's self-representation must underlie any consideration of the women therein.

Methodology

My approach to Pliny's self-representation is indebted to work that has undertaken examination of the autobiographical process employed by Pliny. Chief among these is Jan Radike's consideration of book 3 of the *Epistulae*. He reads each of the twenty-one letters of this book with particular regard to how its subject and certain aspects of his use of language reflect upon Pliny and argues convincingly that every letter contributes to Pliny's picture of himself.[15] Jo-Ann Shelton, too, considers the idea of self-fashioning in Pliny, analyzing the structure of a single letter, also in book 3 (3.11), as it pertains to Pliny's activities in the final years of Domitian's reign.[16] With her thorough consideration of Pliny's diction and his arrangement of material, Shelton demonstrates that while the letter claims to be an encomium of Artemidorus, Pliny's true intent is to present a record of his own laudable actions.

To these I must add the work of Eleanor Winsor Leach (1990), who also argues that Pliny manipulates the material in his letters to enhance his image. Leach's analysis is useful because it sees Pliny's self-representation as an attempt to display his consistently virtuous behavior, both within the inner circle of his family and community and in the wider sphere of Roman politics. Leach compares

[15] Radicke 1997: 461: "Die Einzelinterpretation der Briefe läßt deutlich werden, daß Plinius über das ganze Buch hin ein umfassendes Selbstbildnis entwirft, indem er nach und nach viele verschiedene Facetten seiner Person vorstellt." Book 3 of the letters is also the focus of Henderson's (2002b) book on Pliny's self-representation. Hoffer (1999) in his study employs a similar thesis in examining book 1 of the letters. He attempts, with some success, to delineate the underlying tensions of Pliny's life and to identify those anxieties among the senatorial class as a whole. According to Hoffer, women in the letters serve as indicators of Pliny's private world, separate from the political sphere. Although such a conclusion is intuitively plausible, in his brief treatment of women Hoffer focuses strictly on their domestic presence and ignores the question of their connections to politically influential men.

[16] Shelton (1987: 125–127) highlights Pliny's careful construction of *Ep.* 3.11 and the rhetorical manipulation that allows him to make his courage and generosity central to the letter while appearing modest and reluctant to reveal them.

the idealized portrait of Pliny produced by a reading of his letters with the idealized imperial sculpture of Pliny's time and points out that, with his own behavior in the letters, Pliny offers not only a self-portrait but a prescription for the proper comportment of others in positions of authority. In light of her conclusions, it is not hard to imagine that to fashion an image for himself that aligned properly with the idealized *optimus princeps* Trajan, so highly praised in the *Panegyricus*, Pliny must have felt compelled to explain and perhaps recast his actions in the senate under Domitian, focusing his "historical" accounts on occasions when he chose to act independently in accordance with his personal values, and even to invent political alliances where they either did not exist or were tenuous. If he is to offer himself as an example for his readers to follow, Pliny must purge his past and reshape his present.[17]

Finally, Andrew Riggsby's work notes the importance to Pliny's image of not only his own actions and character but the ways in which he portrays those with whom he associates.[18] Riggsby successfully argues that Pliny's inflation of the reputations of those who surround him is a means of adjusting his own standing in his community. Such an interpretation strongly supports the notion that Pliny's selection of women to include in the letters as part of his social sphere and his idealization of them are important elements in his program of self-representation.

While an awareness of the tools at Pliny's disposal for portrait making – the characters of others, the Roman penchant for idealized images, the subtext of individual letters or books – contributes to the reader's understanding of his autobiographical intent, only a methodical and comprehensive examination of themes as they are considered throughout the entire nine-book corpus can illuminate the full scope of their importance to Pliny's presentation of his own character. Pliny's meticulous care with diction and syntax extends equally to *dispositio* of the letters. His immediately apparent commitment to *variatio* – with letters on trivial matters and even love letters

[17] See especially *Ep.* 4.24.7, 6.11.3, 7.11.8.
[18] Riggsby's (1998: 87) comment that "Pliny seems to devote less energy to controlling himself and more to controlling what others think about him" effectively separates Pliny's personal behavior from his presentation of it. Riggsby (1995) also considers Pliny's *aemulatio* of Cicero.

interwoven with obituaries and court cases – tends to obscure his painstakingly careful positioning of letters to create meaning and manipulate interpretation. In addition, Pliny's characterization of the individual actors in the letters must be compared with what is known from other sources for a clear understanding of his intent. Even the identity or anonymity of a letter's recipient can color its value to Pliny's wider purpose.

Thus, four of the five chapters of this study begin with an exploration of the familial and political connections of the women under consideration. These sections include prosopography and historical background where appropriate. Identification of each woman herself and of her affiliations provides critical context for assessing her inclusion and the value to Pliny of his relationship with her. Even a superficial survey of the letters indicates that many of the women whom Pliny mentions are closely related to men of power and prominence. Others are difficult to identify beyond their roles as wife or mother, yet they, too, add elements to Pliny's self-portrait, particularly in regard to his life away from the political arena. The fourth chapter begins with a brief analysis of the idealized wife as she was conceived by the Romans before Pliny's time. Such a consideration provides context for the main focus of the chapter: evaluation of Pliny's response to and expansion of long-held concepts of feminine excellence in his presentations of Minicia Marcella; his own wife, Calpurnia; and Clodia Fannia.

Finally, central to each chapter is the close analysis of key letters with careful consideration of each one's *dispositio*, recipient, and letter type, in addition to its rhetorical structure, diction, and content and how each letter, considered both individually and together with those to which it is thematically linked, contributes to the creation of Pliny's character.

Classification of Pliny's Women

Most of the thirty-three identifiable women in Pliny's letters fall into five distinct groups that are defined by family and thematic ties: those associated with the so-called Stoic opposition to the principates of Nero, Vespasian, and Domitian; those connected to Corellius Rufus, long recognized as Pliny's patron; those who receive Pliny's loyalty or benefaction; those who contribute to his portrayal of the ideal wife;[19] and women whose behavior Pliny judges to be unseemly.

Eleven, a full third, of the identifiable women of the first nine books of Pliny's letters are closely associated with members of the Stoic opposition to the principate. The Arrias, elder and younger, and Clodia Fannia, each appearing in five letters, are especially notable within this group. The prominence of these women in the letters compels close examination and reveals that Pliny is trying to connect himself through them to those who resisted the regime of the emperor Domitian, whom Pliny does not openly criticize until after the tyrant's death. That Pliny's intent is political rather than philosophical identification with the Stoics is demonstrated in these letters by the fact that he discusses senatorial action by the Stoics rather than their beliefs. Although Pliny's interest in the Stoics of his time has prompted a number of attempts to analyze his personal philosophy, most studies have concluded, in fact, that Pliny cannot be identified as an adherent of Stoic philosophy.[20] Rather, the actions of the Stoic opposition that Pliny admires are those that support their identification as bold and forthright public figures, exemplary Romans.

Pliny praises a number of men as models of proper comportment, including Verginius Rufus and Cornutus Tertullus, but there is no question that it was Corellius Rufus whose political guidance Pliny chose to follow. Corellius is dead before the publication of any of the letters, but the importance of Pliny's relationship with Corellius long outlasts the latter's death, as Pliny apparently remains in close contact with both Corellius' sister and daughter. In fact, Corellia Hispulla and her niece Corellia are two of the six women to whom Pliny addresses correspondence, while the remaining four are members of his own

---

[19] Clodia Fannia and her grandmother Arria the Elder are important members of both the first category, women associated with the Stoic opposition, and the fourth, ideal wives. For a complete listing of all Pliny's women and the letters in which they appear, see Appendix B.

[20] Although Pliny's "philosophy" is beyond the scope of this work, it is generally agreed that his personal philosophy is just that – both personal and somewhat eclectic, containing elements of Platonic and Epicurean doctrine and a substantial dose of Stoicism. André (1975: 247) concludes that the philosophy in the letters is one designed to fit Pliny's daily life and cultural surroundings without effort and "sans méditation intérieure," an accurate and well-supported conclusion, though hardly flattering.

family. His continued association with these women allows Pliny the opportunity to characterize both his relationship with his mentor Corellius and his own political behavior, which Pliny himself declares was profoundly affected by Corellius' advice.

A third group of women, those who receive Pliny's assistance or devotion, includes members of his family and women embroiled in disputes concerning testaments. While some of the latter have close ties with politically prominent men, ties that might have been of great value to Pliny, these women are important to his image not so much for their connection to elite men but because their financial or legal situations offer Pliny a forum in which to discuss his own moral convictions. Through his interaction with them and his fidelity and concern for family members, Pliny has the opportunity to display his integrity and personal ethics.

No study of women in Pliny would be complete without consideration of his presentation of ideal wives. Like all Roman wives, Pliny's wife, Calpurnia, was crucial to his reputation – that is, her behavior reflected directly on Pliny's ability to control his private life. The more his wife resembled him and conformed to his precepts, the more credit would accrue to him, particularly as Calpurnia came to him as a maiden, waiting to be molded into the ideal wife he required. As noted, other scholars have examined some of the qualities that Calpurnia and other model wives possess, but no one has attempted to analyze Pliny's portrait of Calpurnia in the context of his depictions of other women in the letters. Such an approach, in fact, reveals that the exemplum Pliny offers is considerably more complex than previously presented, constituting not merely a simple depiction of his wife's character but rather a triple image of the model wife in different stages of life: the bride, the young wife, and the matron. While Calpurnia is the model young wife, the reader must look to the maiden Minicia Marcella and the matron Clodia Fannia to complete Pliny's portrait of the ideal. Most illuminating to an assessment of Pliny's self-representation is that Pliny weighs the merits of each of the three women against the characters of the men with whom she is associated.

The final chapter focuses on women who are not ideal models of female behavior – a relatively rare category for Pliny's overwhelmingly positive character portraits. Each has failed to reach her potential as a proper Roman woman in some way – involved in unseemly, immoral, or illegal behavior with profound repercussions for the men to whom she is related. These few negative examples serve to reinforce the models that Pliny creates and to assure the reader that, while he prefers to offer positive exempla, he is quite aware of, although not personally touched by, the behavior of the debased women that his contemporaries Juvenal and Tacitus recall in vivid detail.

Each group of women permits Pliny to set forth elements of his character and episodes of his past actions in particular social and political settings: the turmoil in the last years of Domitian's reign; the patron-client relationship and *amicitia*; legal and financial dealings with family members and the vulnerable; the inner sanctum of married life; and even the personal lives of dishonorable women, whom he views always, of course, from an appropriate distance.

1

Pliny

Enemy of Tyrants

> *tot circa me iactis fulminibus ... mihi quoque impendere*
> *idem exitium certis quibusdam notis augurarer.*
>
> Pliny, Epistulae 3.11.3
>
> With so many lightning bolts thrown around me ... and with certain
> sure indications, I should have anticipated that the same type of
> demise loomed also for me.

This study of women in Pliny begins with a particular group
associated with one bloody episode during the reign of Domitian –
the trial and conviction of seven defendants in 93 C.E. – Helvidius,
Senecio, Mauricus, Rusticus, Arria, Fannia, and Gratilla – and their
subsequent execution or relegation. Pliny's involvement with the
prosecution and its aftermath frames his nine-book collection of letters and offers unquestionably the most patent example of his intent
to recast his past political activity. There are eleven women in this
category, by far the largest number of women who are connected
with one another, and the events that Pliny discusses are far from
ordinary. In fact, the treason trials of 93 must be considered the
marquee event of Domitian's "reign of terror," the final years of his
principate during which many of senatorial rank were put to death.
The condemned were part of the so-called Stoic opposition to the
principate, closely associated with philosophy and literature, who
with their demise became for the authors who wrote about them
symbolic of the powerlessness of the senate and the vulnerability

of its members under the worst of emperors. Indeed, one portent of Domitian's impending murder, Cassius Dio reports, was a dream that the emperor had in which Rusticus, one of those executed, approached him with a sword (67.16.1).

As fellow senators, both Pliny and Tacitus witnessed the trials of 93, and both use the signal event of Domitian's reign to tar the tyrant's behavior, but each paints a drastically different picture of his own involvement in the outcome of the prosecutions. Tacitus declares that Helvidius was led to prison by the "hands of the senators," that he and his fellow senators were "tormented by the sight of Mauricus and Rusticus," and that "Senecio drenched them with his innocent blood": *mox nostrae duxere Helvidium in carcerem manus; nos Maurici Rusticique visus adflixit, nos innocenti sanguine Senecio perfudit* (*Agr.* 45.1). Tacitus offers no excuse for his own complicity beyond the need for survival and for someone to remember the event and to tell the truth *sine ira et studio*. While he may not have participated actively in the destruction of the Stoic opposition, Pliny's silence, like that of his fellow senators, assured their condemnation, but Pliny offers us no inkling of whatever role he played in their trials, no mention of his presence or absence, avoiding entirely any appearance of bitterness or regret. Instead, he presents us with a carefully constructed image of himself as closely tied to five of the seven defendants, including all of the women, and subject at any moment to the same grave danger as that which befell them.

The wide distribution in the corpus of thirteen letters that concern members of the Stoic opposition not only is a testament to Pliny's commitment to *variatio* – as they appear in each book except the eighth – but also serves to highlight their importance to Pliny's wider purpose. In his unpublished monograph, *The Publication of Pliny's Letters*, John Bodel argues convincingly for the unity of the nine-book collection and furthermore demonstrates that Pliny carefully arranged the letters in each book, including those in the final book, whose plan long preceded its apparently sudden assembly before Pliny's departure for Bithynia.[1] Bodel proposes that Pliny

---

[1] The ninth book of the collection has often been criticized as containing short, rather trivial letters, the remnants of what remained in Pliny's unpublished supply, supposedly assembled with great haste so that the collection would be ready for publication before he left for the East. But Bodel demonstrates nicely that its

published a series of volumes, both singly and in pairs, and that, in later books, Pliny assumes his reader's knowledge of earlier ones. In light of this persuasive argument, the ordering of the letters that concern the Stoics should be viewed as a major pathway through which Pliny cultivates his relationship with the defendants and his image as the Stoics' avenger.

Indeed, Pliny expends great effort in defining and expatiating upon his friendship with the Stoic opposition and aligning himself with its political leanings. The women in the group, who are the focus of four letters and appear in a total of nine of the thirteen, are crucial to Pliny's association with Arulenus Rusticus and the younger Helvidius Priscus. Indeed, as all of the men with the exception of Mauricus were executed long before the composition or publication of any of the letters, Pliny's relationships with the women become the only means by which he may present his association with all of the condemned.

There was much for Pliny to gain in either creating or elaborating a friendship with the Stoics. Not only could he highlight the integrity of his conduct in the face of grave danger, but he could also align himself with a senatorial faction that had a long history of opposing the principate, men who saw themselves as inheritors of the same hatred of tyranny that Cato Uticensis expressed in his refusal to accept the rule of Julius Caesar. With the executions of 93, the faction was destroyed; and with the accession of Trajan, the *optimus princeps* with whom Pliny established an apparently strong working relationship and who took care to differentiate his behavior from that of his arrogant predecessor, there was "no need" for enmity with the emperor. Pliny is, of course, careful to downplay the highly political nature of the background and actions of those condemned by Domitian, stressing instead their philosophical and literary activities, thus making them seem harmless victims, persecuted by a paranoid and bloodthirsty villain. Their true nature and intentions were clearly much more complex than Pliny would have us believe.

---

arrangement echoes the books that precede it and that it contains several letters of great import to Pliny's career, including 9.13, the final letter regarding the Stoics, both of which arguments belie any such slapdash construction.

The Stoic Opposition to the Principate

There is little doubt that all of the emperors during the first century of the Roman principate faced opposition from those of senatorial rank who resented their own diminished importance and restraints upon their speech and actions. Writing after Domitian's death, both Pliny and Tacitus make clear that political expediency had severely limited their opportunities for frank expression under the tyrant's rule, especially during his "reign of terror" when incautious statements might mean condemnation.[2] It is primarily through these two authors that our knowledge of one particular nexus of senatorial opposition to the principate emerges. The group consisted of senators in three consecutive generations, serving under Nero and the Flavian emperors, who were bound to one another by familial ties or *amicitia*. All, particularly Nero's nemesis Thrasea Paetus, were associated by ancient sources with Stoic practice – especially Stoic martyrdom – and its teachers.[3] As a result, they are frequently, though debatably, referred to by modern scholars as the Stoic opposition to the principate.[4]

Although "Stoic opposition" suggests that its members were bound by their philosophical leanings, the group can scarcely be assigned any tenets that would securely identify its partisans as adherents of Stoicism. Neither Pliny nor Tacitus directly calls any of its members Stoic. They are so characterized by their connections with Stoic philosophers like Musonius Rufus and by derogatory remarks made by their accusers.[5] As part of the standard practice of attacking the

---

[2] See especially Pliny, *Pan.* 76 and *Ep.* 8.14, and Tacitus, *Agr.* 2 and *Ann.* 4.32.

[3] In our sources, Thrasea Paetus never declares himself to be a Stoic. Indeed, according to Tacitus, when he was seized by the authorities, he was in deep discussion with the Cynic Demetrius (*Ann.* 16.34).

[4] While Brian Jones (1992) and Wistrand (1979) use the phrase "Stoic opposition" to describe the extended family of Thrasea Paetus, other scholars have called the actions of the group resistance rather than opposition and may include in their discussion some reference to Stoic concepts or philosophy in general. See also Raaflaub (1987). Discomfort with the term "Stoic opposition" clearly arises from the absence of a direct connection between the philosophy's principles and hostility toward the emperor. Yet, the ancient sources clearly tie Stoicism to the persistent opposition on the part of the group. Consequently, the phrase is now in general use.

[5] Pliny, *Ep.* 1.5 and 3.11; Tacitus, *Ann.* 14.57 and 16.32.

character of the accused,[6] the *delatores* may have hoped to blacken the defendants' reputations by associating them with philosophers, a group that was always suspect in Rome; but, of course, none of the opposition members was prosecuted simply for being a Stoic. Subversive or treasonous political activity, sometimes expressed through literary works that seemed to betoken nostalgia for the republic, seems to have been the foremost charge. Thus, it is not unreasonable to see in their anti-imperial activities more than just an echo of Catonian Stoicism. For the purpose of this examination, the term "Stoic opposition" will serve as a convenient designation that is meant not to describe the philosophical beliefs of its members but rather to encapsulate their political allegiance to resisting imperial authority and restoring senatorial power.

Intransigent republicanism combined with open criticism of the principate is common to literary portrayals and historical accounts of the most prominent member of the opposition during Nero's reign, Clodius Thrasea Paetus. Tacitus, in particular, presents him as committed to promoting the position of the senate and to reclaiming at least some of its power. In the *Annales*, Thrasea argues for the dignity of the senate (13.49), refuses to participate in the obsequies customarily offered to the emperor by that body, walks out of the senate when it moved to declare Agrippina's birthday ill omened (14.12), and ultimately decides to abstain entirely from public business (16.20), while still participating in the political life of his native Patavium.

Throughout the Neronian books of the *Annales*, Thrasea is Tacitus' model for proper Roman behavior offered in opposition to the uncontrolled desires of Nero and the excessive honors required by the emperor from a servile senate.[7] Though his Stoic leanings were surely revealed in his writing a life of Cato, he seems to have suffered no punishment for doing so. What threat Thrasea actually posed to the principate is obliquely suggested by Tacitus in Capito's speech against him;[8] Thrasea had gathered a following, called "courtiers"

---

[6] That such accusations were pro forma is well illustrated by Cicero when he declares openly that the prosecution was expected to impugn the character of the accused without particular regard for what was true: *ut illos [accusatores] lex magis quaedam accusatoria quam vera male dicendi facultas de vita L. Murenae dicere aliquid coegerit* (*Mur.* 11).

[7] *Ann.* 13.49; 14.12, 48, 49; 15.20, 23; 16.21, 22, 24–26, 28–29, 33–34.

[8] In the speech that Tacitus assigns him, Cossutianus Capito also warns Nero that Rome now speaks of Thrasea's opposition to Nero as it had of Cato's to Caesar.

by Capito – *habet sectatores vel potius satellites* (16.22.10) – whose opposition to Nero and support of Thrasea's disposition might lead to Nero's demise and Thrasea's elevation to the principate. It was not his admiration for or biography of Cato that indicted Thrasea but rather his Catonian actions.

Imperial perception of a threat posed by the Stoics may be further illuminated by Tacitus' account of the downfall of Rubellius Plautus, a grandson of Germanicus and, for that reason alone, someone who posed a potentially significant menace to Nero's throne. In his condemnation, Nero's henchman Tigellinus comments that Rubellius had strong republican leanings and had taken up with the Stoics, whom Tigellinus describes as arrogant and ambitious (14.57) and, therefore, potentially dangerous. Although Thrasea did not have the Julio-Claudian connection that made Rubellius' presence so perilous to the emperor, Nero might have been persuaded that his Stoic tendencies made Thrasea equally dangerous, particularly if his affiliation with other prominent protesters made him a desirable candidate for rule.

While Tacitus downplays any sedition that Thrasea might have either initiated or inspired, choosing instead to present him as a symbol of senatorial liberty and thus as Nero's ultimate victim, Pliny's approach ignores the political side of Thrasea almost entirely. Instead, Pliny casts Thrasea in the role of wise adviser, quoting his sayings in two letters, 6.29 and 8.22. In the former, Thrasea explains the three types of cases that are worthy of being undertaken by an advocate, a list to which Pliny adds a fourth.[9] In the latter, Pliny includes a *sententia* that he attributes to Thrasea, who believed that men should be forgiven their failings, *qui vitia odit, homines odit* (8.22.3). As a model

Support or condemnation of Cato's views became symbolic of divergent political positions at the end of the republic with the appearance of Caesar's *Anticato*, written in response to Cicero's *Cato*. The excessively hostile tone of Caesar's pamphlet virtually ensured that Cato, an adherent of Stoic philosophy, would become enshrined as the model to be followed by those who longed for an idealized version of the lost republic. Indeed, a virtual cult of Cato prospered among members of the senate with republican views in the first century of the empire, but generally his acolytes did not seem to suffer prosecution unless they threatened the emperor's security either through treasonous conspiracy or verbal attacks.

[9] Thrasea's list included cases in support of friends, those which no one else would undertake and those which would establish a precedent. Pliny adds to these such cases as might bring *gloria et fama* (6.29.3).

of proper mores, Pliny's Thrasea is nonthreatening, someone who can safely be imitated even by those wishing to retain imperial favor. In fact, all of Pliny's Stoics are filled with wisdom and self-restraint, suitable for cultivation by an emperor, not for execution.

Sir Ronald Syme (1958: 557) has commented that Thrasea could have been charged with perpetuating a "hereditary feud" with the principate. Indeed, Thrasea had married Caecina Arria (the Younger), the daughter of Arria the Elder and Aulus Caecina Paetus, who was consul suffectus in 37 and became involved in 42 in the rebellion of the seventh and eleventh legions in Dalmatia, led by L. Arruntius Camillus Scribonianus. The revolt was short-lived, lasting only a few days. It is mentioned in passing in Tacitus' *Annales* (12.52) and used in the *Historiae* (1.89, 2.75) only as an example of the quick resolution of past military instability in contrast to the extended unrest of 69, but the historian's cursory treatment of the revolt belies the symbolic importance of Arria the Elder and Paetus; their joint suicide became a model for both noble death and marital devotion.

Pliny recounts several episodes from the elder Arria (I)'s life, all centered around her commitment to her husband, Aulus Caecina Paetus, and focused on the chief event of her life, the arrest and prosecution of her husband for treason against the emperor Claudius. But Pliny has little to say about the revolt of 42 for which Paetus was condemned, citing it only as context for Arria (I)'s actions.

The death of Arria (I) achieved legendary status in the decades that followed it, extolled by Pliny, Tacitus, Cassius Dio, and Martial. She is remembered by all of them for the courage she displayed at the end of her life.[10] According to Pliny, Martial, and Cassius Dio, when her husband, Caecina Paetus, wavered in his resolve to kill himself, she emboldened him by seizing the dagger, plunging it into her breast and declaring, "It does not hurt, Paetus" (*Paete, non dolet*). Even the little knowledge we have of Arria (I)'s agnate line is centered on this immortal act of *pietas*. In the *Vita Persii*, Arria (I) is described as a *cognata* (30–31) of the satirist Persius, her only known relative apart from those gained by her marriage to Paetus. He is said to have written in his boyhood a few verses for Arria (I) who "had killed herself before her husband" (*Vita Persii* 45–47). Persius himself was closely

---

[10] Pliny, *Ep.* 3.16; Tacitus, *Ann.* 16.34; Cassius Dio 60.16.5–6; Martial 1.13.5.

connected to the Stoic opposition to Nero through links with Thrasea Paetus and his teacher, the Stoic philosopher L. Annaeus Cornutus, who was himself a relative of the younger Seneca and Lucan. Praise of Arria (I)'s dramatic suicide elevated her to virtual "beatification" as evidenced by a later gravestone inscription on which the deceased, a certain Oppia, is commended to Arria, the Roman, and Laodamia, the Greek, among the *numerus sacratus*.[11] There is no question that, in choosing to accompany her husband even in death as Laodamia had her beloved Protesilaus,[12] Arria (I) became an enduring symbol of womanly courage and devotion. Furthermore, both she and her husband had died "Stoic" deaths in opposition to the tyranny of the principate.

If Syme is correct in his suggestion that Thrasea took his father-in-law's cognomen Paetus into his own nomenclature as a means of honoring him,[13] it is more than likely that the two men shared an antagonistic view of the principate and that Thrasea carried on, albeit by political rather than military means, his mentor's independent and rebellious attitude. But Thrasea's wife, Arria (II), does not live up to the precedent set by her legendary mother. According to Tacitus, when her husband, Thrasea Paetus, was condemned by Nero, Arria (II) desired to follow her mother's example and die with him, but Thrasea prevented her by reminding her that their daughter, Clodia Fannia, would then be left alone.[14] Arria (II) clearly did not

[11] *ILS* 6261: *Exemplum periit, castae, lugete, puellae. / Oppia iam non est, erepta est Oppia Firmo. / Accipite hanc animam numeroque augete sacr[ato] / Arria Romano et tu Graio Laodamia. / Hunc titulum meritis servat tibi fama superstis, / sibi suis posterisq. eorum.*

[12] Protesilaus, the first Greek killed at Troy, was so beloved by his wife Laodamia that she killed herself in order to be with him. Variants have her stabbing herself after he is brought briefly back to her from Hades by a pitying Hermes (Apollodorus, *Bibl.* 3.30) or throwing herself on a pyre her father had made in order to burn a statue of the now-deceased Protesilaus with which she had become obsessed (Hyginus, *Fab.* 104). Other sources for the story include Ovid, *Her.* 13, and Catullus 68.73-130.

[13] Syme 1982a: 105. The question of nomenclature in this period is a complex one that Syme deals with at length in a number of articles. It was not unusual for men to take names from both their paternal and maternal lines or, as in this case, to add cognomina based on marriage ties. The determining factor was likely the social and political prominence of the family with which the name was associated. The freedom to modify or expand one's name often produced incredibly long combinations, making the task of disentangling an individual's familial connections an extremely complex and uncertain one.

[14] Tacitus, *Ann.* 16.34. Syme (1982a: 105) has suggested that Fannia had her name from the name of Thrasea's mother and that C. Fannius, Pliny's friend, was,

enjoy the same elevated reputation as her mother, and although Pliny includes her in three of his letters, he merely mentions her name in 3.11 and 9.13; in 7.19, she is described with little elaboration simply as the mother of a great woman, *tantae feminae matrem* (7.19.9), Pliny's friend Fannia.

Sherwin-White (1966: 243) remarks that Fannia had inherited from Arria (I) "a tiresome obstinacy and a traditional republican-ism that made [her a] fit mate [for her husband]," and obstinacy or persistence, at any rate, is certainly a hallmark of Fannia's devotion to her husband, a *constantia* that is highly reminiscent of her grand-mother's actions. As the second wife of the elder Helvidius Priscus (Helvidius I), Fannia accompanied him twice into exile, in 66 under Nero and again in 74–75 under Vespasian, before her own exile in 93, almost two decades after Helvidius (I)'s execution. While Pliny is the only source of specific information regarding Fannia's life – in fact, the only one that includes her name – he offers no details of her first two exiles nor does he mention the revolutionary actions of her husband, and so we must turn to Tacitus and Suetonius for some of the missing information.

In 66, Fannia and Helvidius (I) were apparently caught up in the charges against her father, who, Tacitus reports, found solace before his execution in the fact that his son-in-law was to suffer only exile (*Ann.* 16.34–35). But the exile did nothing to suppress Helvidius (I)'s recalcitrant behavior toward the principate. According to Tacitus, while Thrasea had provoked the emperor's enmity merely by his with-drawal from civic life, his son-in-law was wont to affront Vespasian openly.

Undaunted by the exile he endured at the time of Thrasea's con-demnation, Helvidius (I) returned to Rome in 69 under Galba and was a prime mover for the restoration of the Capitol in 70, when, as praetor and in Vespasian's absence, he purified the ground before the rebuilding of the temple began (Tacitus, *Hist.* 4.53). Whether the emperor was vexed at this seeming usurpation of his authority cannot

perhaps, Fannia's uncle. Syme further includes Fannius as one of Thrasea's *nomina*. Though such an assertion is only theoretical, it does seem credible that C. Fannius, who wrote three books of an unfinished work about the fate of those killed or exiled under Nero, was related to Thrasea's family (Fannii appear with some fre-quency in *CIL* v, numbering at least sixteen individuals).

be determined. He may even have approved Helvidius (I)'s actions as symbolic of his own intention to honor the senate, as Nero had not. Another episode that Tacitus reports is perhaps more indicative of Helvidius (I)'s republicanism. Helvidius (I) apparently wanted to send a handpicked delegation of senators, rather than the one customarily chosen by lot, to meet and to hail Vespasian as emperor. In the speech that Tacitus assigns to Helvidius (I), the praetor clearly recalls Vespasian's *amicitia* with Thrasea and then continues with the statement that good government is served by good advisers, implying that the emperor would do well to choose new friends with republican leanings similar to those of Thrasea (*Hist.* 4.7).[15]

Helvidius (I) seems to have followed further the exemplum offered by Thrasea in his treatment of the emperor – though, as Alexander Gaheis notes, his was a revolutionary spirit rather than one of passive resistance (*RE* VIII, Helvidius 3). Suetonius reports that Helvidius (I) was the only man to greet Vespasian upon his return from Syria *privato nomine* rather than to hail him as emperor. During his praetorship, moreover, Helvidius failed to include the customary honors for Vespasian in his edicts. Eventually, Helvidius (I)'s continued treatment of the emperor as an ordinary citizen became more than Vespasian would bear; Helvidius (I) was first exiled, accompanied for the second time by Fannia, then put to death, although apparently the emperor had second thoughts and tried too late to rescind his order (Suetonius, *Vesp.* 15).

It is evident from our sources that his father's execution and stepmother's exile under Vespasian had little effect on the progress of the career of the younger Helvidius (II), who reached the office of consul suffectus before 87. The same is generally true for other opposition members whose careers seem to have thrived under the emperor Domitian. As their political progress extended even to the consulship, it may reasonably be asked whether the successful careers of those associated with the opposition were owed to Domitian's attempts at conciliating his detractors. But, in fact, no evidence exists

---

[15] Pigoń (1992: 236), pointing also to Helvidius (I)'s further attempts to restore the senate's authority on financial matters, believes that his determination to send a select group to receive Vespasian might reflect Helvidius (I)'s desire to provide the new emperor with a council of senators who were committed to strengthening the role of the senate.

of a concerted effort by the group to disparage Domitian until 93. Helvidius (II) does not seem to have inherited his father's political outspokenness, as there is no mention in our sources of any action taken by him while he was in the senate or serving as a magistrate. What Sherwin-White (1966: 242) calls his "cautious retirement" may simply have been quiet participation in civic office or the avoidance of the emperor baiting in which his father had reveled. Nevertheless, either the year 93 brought a marked change in Helvidius (II)'s disposition toward the emperor, prompted perhaps by the often-cited decline in Domitian's treatment of the senate, or Helvidius (II)'s supposed reticence is a modern fiction created to fill the lack of information regarding his political activity.

Whatever Helvidius (II)'s political demeanor might have been, his demise came in the trials of 93. Suetonius writes that Helvidius (II) was charged by Publicius Certus for mocking Domitian's divorce in a stage farce he had composed. In it, the biographer says, Domitian and his wife were thinly disguised as Paris and Oenone (*Dom.* 10.4). Given his family's history of openly anti-imperial activity, there is doubt whether Helvidius (II)'s literary activity was the sole reason for his condemnation, but any other subversive activity he might have engaged in remains obscure. Indeed, while Pliny refers repeatedly to the defense of Helvidius (II) that he offered several years after Helvidius (II)'s death (and, of course, after the murder of Domitian), his readers remain unenlightened as to any details of Helvidius (II)'s public career or even the specific cause of his condemnation. In the three letters that recall the speech given by Pliny on behalf of Helvidius (II) – *Epistulae* 4.21, 7.30, and 9.13 – Pliny is intent upon explicating the qualities of his oration and its reception not only at its first delivery but in its subsequent written form as well. The speech's content, which must have included the charges against Helvidius (II) and a defense of his actions, receives no treatment in the letters. Without the details of the indictment, only Suetonius' account of Helvidius (II)'s literary offense remains.

Whether the presentation of a defamatory play was the cause of action against Helvidius (II) or not, he was surely complicit with his stepmother, Clodia Fannia, in encouraging or even commissioning a biography of his father, for which its author, Herennius Senecio, was condemned at the same time as Helvidius (II). In *Epistulae* 7.19, Pliny recounts in great detail Senecio's testimony in his own defense in which he stated that he had written his life of Helvidius (I) at Fannia's request. Pliny adds that Fannia had readily admitted not only to commissioning the biography but also to providing her husband's diaries to Senecio, without the knowledge of her mother, Arria (II) (7.19.5). Senecio was condemned. Convicted as well was Arulenus Rusticus, who had eulogized Helvidius (I) and written a biography of Thrasea. All three men were executed, while their female relatives, Fannia, Arria (II), and Gratilla (Arulenus Rusticus' wife), were banished along with Iunius Mauricus (Arulenus Rusticus' brother).

Apparently untouched in the accusations and condemnations was Anteia, the wife of Helvidius (II). Little is known of her beyond the smattering of information offered by Pliny's letters in which she is mentioned by name only once, in 9.13, while her offspring appear in 4.21. She bore Helvidius (II) at least three children, a son and two daughters, none of whom is identifiable with any certainty. Sherwin-White (1966: 493) remarks that she was likely from a consular family, but he is reluctant to connect her directly with P. Anteius Rufus, who was forced to commit suicide during the reign of Nero. In fact, it is entirely possible that Anteia not only was related to this Julio-Claudian consular but was his daughter, and perhaps a sister of Anteia Rufina, as identified by Marie-Thérèse Raepsaet-Charlier (1987: 69). R. S. Rogers (1960: 23) associates her with three condemned Anteii of this era: one Anteius, perhaps the father of Anteius Rufus, who commanded a fleet under Germanicus and was banished and executed by Caligula (Tacitus, *Ann.* 2.6); a second, proposed as the brother of Anteius Rufus, who was killed by Caligula's bodyguards after the emperor's murder (Josephus, *AJ* 19: 125–126); and, finally, Anteius Rufus himself who was linked with Ostorius in allegations about their use of astrology and horoscopes to determine their own and Nero's destinies (Tacitus, *Ann.* 16.14). It is not hard to believe that Helvidius (I), a vocal opponent of the obsequious attention to the emperor that was expected of senators, had chosen as his daughter-in-law the child of a man whose family was so closely associated with opposition to the principate.

Arulenus Rusticus' choice of Thrasea as a subject for praise in politically dangerous times certainly suggests that he, too, was dissatisfied with autocratic rule. That Rusticus and Thrasea's stepgrandson Helvidius (II) are prosecuted at the same time implies a substantive connection between the families. Evidence of a familial bond tying Rusticus and Iunius Mauricus to the family of Thrasea Paetus rests on a single letter of Pliny in which he mentions that Thrasea's daughter Fannia had been looking after the Vestal Iunia, who had fallen ill and who was, therefore, entrusted to Fannia's care by the pontifex. Fannia received this charge because Iunia was *adfinis* (7.19.1). While it might be argued that Iunia's name is hardly sufficient evidence to connect the two families, Arulenus Rusticus' praise of Helvidius (I) and the prominence of both Rusticus and his brother Mauricus in literary references to the Stoic faction opposed to Domitian strongly suggest a close alliance between the two families. Although it is impossible to reconstruct the details of the alliance, Rusticus and Mauricus were swept up in the prosecutions of 93.[16]

Whereas Tacitus refers only obliquely to the events that signaled the end of Stoic opposition, Pliny recalls the prosecutions early in the corpus of his letters; *Epistulae* 1.5, for instance, is a letter in which both Iunius Arulenus Rusticus and Iunius Mauricus are mentioned. The brothers appear in a total of seven letters, a second in book 1 – 1.14 – and one in each of five other books: 2.18, 3.11, 4.22, 5.1, and 6.14. Although Mauricus is mentioned in a total of six letters, Rusticus receives much more attention from Pliny, possibly because his execution effectively made him a martyr to those sickened by Domitian's actions; indeed, Pliny's references to Rusticus are emotionally charged, particularly in the concern he expresses for the future of Rusticus' children (1.14, 2.18).

Arulenus Rusticus is considerably more prominent in Roman literature than his brother Iunius Mauricus. Rusticus' death frames Tacitus' *Agricola* (2, 45); as mentioned previously, his specter appears to Domitian before the emperor's death in the work of Cassius Dio (67, 16); and he is called the Stoics' ape (*simia Stoicorum*) by the *delator* M. Aquilius Regulus in Pliny's letters (1.5.2). Although Rusticus had been praetor in 69, it was apparently not until 92 that he reached the suffect consulship. Some scholars have assumed that the long delay was due to his devotion to Thrasea Paetus and Helvidius (I) in their roles as defenders of senatorial *libertas*.[17] Such an explanation,

---

[16] For stemmata illustrating the familial connections, see Appendix A, Figures 1–3.
[17] For example, Sherwin-White 1966: 95.

however, would imply that Rusticus' association with the Stoic opposition and its assumed threat to the principate had stymied *his* political progress but had not had the same negative effect on the career of Helvidius (II). Furthermore, such a scenario requires an abrupt and inexplicable change of disposition by Domitian, with the emperor granting to Rusticus a presumably long-withheld consulship at the beginning of the very period in which the regime declined into increasing injustice and cruelty. Rusticus' identification as consul in 92 seems secure, because, as Syme (1982a: 105) makes clear, his cognomen Arulenus, which appears in the Fasti of Potentia for 92, is extremely rare and used elsewhere in Italy only of freedmen. Thus, it is more reasonable to assume that Rusticus had not been involved in open opposition to the principate before Domitian's grant of the consulship. Perhaps he had lived in the same kind of quiet retirement as Helvidius (II), only to reemerge on the political scene in the early 90s when Domitian's rule began to deteriorate.[18]

It is even more difficult to discern the involvement of Iunius Mauricus, the only man to survive the trials, in opposing the emperor. He appears briefly in Tacitus' and Plutarch's treatments of the events of 69, as he tries to quash the spate of violence against those who engaged in prosecutorial activity under Nero (*Hist.* 4.40 and *Galb.* 8), and Martial comments on his *aequitas* (5.28.5), but it is Pliny who remains the chief source of information on him.

While Iunius Mauricus is one of Pliny's addressees and is mentioned in a number of letters, even Pliny provides little concrete information about him. Two of the letters that Pliny addresses to Mauricus concern personal matters, as Pliny responds to requests from Mauricus to find a tutor for the sons and a husband for the daughter of his brother Arulenus Rusticus (1.14 and 2.18), and so they offer no details of his political life. Pliny insists in *Epistulae* 1.5 that he must await the arrival of Mauricus and his approval before acting against Regulus for his role in the prosecution of Arulenus Rusticus. Whether Pliny was motivated by courteous respect for Mauricus or by close personal ties to him is

---

[18] Pliny makes clear in *Ep.* 1.14.5 that it was entirely acceptable for individuals to eschew a senatorial career, choosing instead to live in relative obscurity outside of the city of Rome. Such a choice might well have little to do with an individual's political leanings but might instead be predicated on financial concerns arising from the restraints on commercial activity among members of the senatorial class.

impossible to say, but Pliny's admiration for Mauricus' wisdom and courage is plain. Pliny offers him as an exemplum of an honorable man who survived Domitian's reign.[19] While Pliny places Mauricus securely among those prosecuted in 93, he provides no inkling of Mauricus' role or the depth of his involvement in opposition activities.

Like his brother Arulenus Rusticus, Iunius Mauricus seems to have attained the suffect consulship sometime during the reign of Domitian, although the date is far from certain and much contested.[20] That he escaped execution in 93 may indicate the peripheral nature of his association with any organized resistance, or it may reflect Domitian's hesitation to take harsh action against a man who was so highly esteemed. Having endured exile rather than execution, Mauricus was recalled after Domitian's death and served as a counselor to both Nerva and Trajan, enjoying an impeccable reputation as a man of influence and wisdom, a man who was known for his fairness and was considered to be one of the best men in Rome.[21]

The women of the Iunii receive rather superficial treatment by Pliny. Although Gratilla, the wife of Arulenus Rusticus, is listed among the seven Stoic friends of Pliny in 3.11, her further identification is elusive in his corpus, with only brief mentions of her name in two letters (3.11 and 5.1). She may well be the Verulana Gratilla who Tacitus says was in the camp of the Flavians on the Capitoline Hill when the Vitellians besieged it (*Hist.* 3.69). Sherwin-White (1966: 243) goes so far as to suggest that it was by her association with the Flavians and her intercession that the Iunii were spared when Helvidius (I) was prosecuted under Vespasian. Because there is no evidence of their complicity in any action taken by Helvidius (I), her intervention on behalf of the Iunii can hardly be surmised. If Pliny's Gratilla was Verulana Gratilla, she was likely a daughter of L. Verulanus Severus, a legionary legate under Corbulo in Armenia in the early 60s and consul suffectus before the death of Nero.[22]

[19] See particularly Pliny, *Ep.* 1.5.16 and 4.22.3–6.
[20] Proposed dates range from as early as 81 to as late as 96, with Rogers (1960: 20) favoring a consulship served under Titus in 81, Groag assigning 92 as the most likely date (*RE* X, Iunius 94), and Brian Jones (1979: 110) proposing either 81 or 96.
[21] Pliny, *Ep.* 1.5.16; Tacitus, *Hist.* 4.40; Martial 5.28.5; Plutarch, *Galb.* 8.5.
[22] Nichols (1978: 126–127) picks up Sherwin-White's assertion and the identification of Gratilla as the daughter of Corbulo's commander. He further claims that she kept in contact with her father's Corbulonian friends, joined the Flavian party,

After her exile in 93, Gratilla disappears from Pliny's letters; he fails to say that she was recalled in 97 when Fannia and Arria returned to Rome. It is evident, in fact, from Pliny's letters to Iunius Mauricus that her children, more than one son and at least one daughter, were exclusively in her brother-in-law's care after his return from exile. While Mauricus' tutelage of his brother's children is not unexpected, we might hope for some mention in Pliny of her ongoing interest in their welfare, particularly in letters that pertain to the selection of significant figures in their lives – tutor (2.18) and husband (1.14). Perhaps Gratilla did not survive her banishment, though one would expect Pliny to use her death to condemn her accusers. It seems more likely that Pliny's relationship with Mauricus served well to connect him to the Iunii and abrogated any need for him to cultivate Gratilla.

One final woman associated with the Stoic opposition appears early in Pliny's letters. In *Epistulae* 1.5 – as Arulenus Rusticus had enjoined him – Pliny defends Arrionilla against the vile prosecutor Regulus. Her identification is limited to her status as wife of Timon (1.5.5), but because of Rusticus' apparent interest in protecting her, Arrionilla and her husband were probably associated with the Stoic opposition, although no corroborating evidence exists that might confirm their participation. Timon, her husband, cannot be identified. Sherwin-White (1966: 97) comments that Arrionilla's name suggests that Timon married into the family of Arria and Thrasea and that Timon "must" be one of Arulenus Rusticus' philosopher friends.[23] His speculations await substantiation, but this identification would place Arrionilla neatly within the extended family of the Helvidii and Iunii. While such a connection makes for tidier history, it is by no means required in connecting her with the Stoic opposition. Although the extended family of Fannia constitutes a large majority of the opposition group, nonfamily members like Rubellius

---

and used her influence with Vespasian to save the Iunii. But I find it hard to imagine under what circumstances Verulana Gratilla might have become so close to the emperor as to affect his decisions. Her father receives only passing mention in Tacitus and seems to have no connection to Vespasian.

[23] The chief argument against Sherwin-White's proposal is that one would expect that if Arrionilla's name were derived from Arria, it would appear as Arrianilla, just as Arrius becomes Arrianus.

Plautus, Barea Soranus (prosecuted at the same time as Thrasea), and Herennius Senecio are also well attested.

Which circumstance in 93 had prompted what appears to be a sudden cascade of incautious literature that was sufficiently hostile to the principate to provoke executions is puzzling, especially as Arulenus Rusticus had just served as consul in 92, an indication at least of Domitian's tolerance and likely even of his favor. It is not unreasonable to posit that opposition members were compelled to more strident vocal resistance by the emperor's increasingly threatening behavior and that they were involved in subversive activities beyond the publication of irritating literature. That the prosecutions included not just the three authors but four other family members suggests a threat to Domitian that was more substantial than mere words. While Fannia might have been punished for her endorsement of Senecio's work, there is no indication in the sources of the involvement of her mother, Arria the Younger, and no clear cause for the inclusion in the charges of Gratilla or Iunius Mauricus. The reasons for their prosecution remain obscure but are highly suggestive of wider anti-imperial activity in the extended family of Thrasea Paetus, an opposition that died with the executions of 93.

The murder of Domitian opened the way for the return from exile of those banished in the final years of his reign. Apparently, many of the accusers who carried out the emperor's campaign of attacks on members of the senate were themselves prosecuted after his demise. When Fannia and Arria (II) returned to Rome, Pliny says that he sent for Anteia to tell her that he intended to avenge her husband's death by speaking against one of his accusers and to offer her a share of the glory that would ensue from Pliny's success (9.13.4–5), insisting that he was not seeking nor did he require her support. Indeed, she had evidently remarried after her husband's execution within the two-year period required by the law *de maritandis ordinibus*.[24]

Pliny reports earlier in the collection (*Ep.* 4.21) that both of the daughters of Anteia and Helvidius (II), known only as the Helvidiae, had died in childbirth. At least one of them had been entrusted to

[24] In *Ep.* 9.13.16, Pliny tells his reader that Cornutus Tertullus was appointed as guardian for one of the Helvidiae at the request of her mother and stepfather.

the guardianship of C. Iulius Cornutus Tertullus who, though as much as twenty years older than Pliny, served as his colleague both in the prefecture of the Treasury of Saturn and the suffect consulship. Identification of the spouses of the Helvidiae remains obscure, but on the basis of the name of a proposed daughter of one Helvidia – Herennia Helvidia Aemiliana – J. Devreker has posited that M. Annius Herennius Pollio was husband to one (*AE* 1975: 21, 131). Pollio was consul suffectus in 85,[25] and Werner Eck suggests that he might be identified with the Herennius Pollio (*RE* 14S, Herennius 35b) whom Pliny names as his colleague in his account of the prosecution of Bassus for extortion while the latter was proconsul of Bithynia (4.9). Pliny's close relationship with Tertullus and collegial relationship with Herennius Pollio make the identification of Pollio as husband of one of the Helvidiae tantalizing, but, as it is based solely on nomenclature, insecure at best.

While the names Helvidius, Priscus, and Thrasea do appear in epigraphic evidence later in the second century, the family seems to have lost all significant political presence after the death of Domitian. Indeed, were it not for the immortalization by Tacitus and Pliny of their prosecution in 93, the entire family might well have fallen into obscurity.

The future of the Iunii is equally dubious. While Pliny recommends a suitable husband for Gratilla and Arulenus Rusticus' daughter in 1.14, the young woman herself remains unnamed and unidentifiable, though she would presumably have been called Iunia. Pliny responds eagerly to Mauricus' request that he look around for a likely bridegroom (1.14.1–2). He recommends Minicius Acilianus whom, we may safely assume because of the letter's publication, she married. Pliny is our sole source of information regarding the young man who, Pliny says, is only a little younger than he (1.14.3). He was the son of Minicius Macrinus, an *eques* who refused praetorian status offered to him by Vespasian, preferring instead to live a quiet life removed from struggles for status. Acilianus' mother goes unmentioned in the letter, though it is likely that she is referred to in 8.5, a letter that extols the virtues of the wife of Macrinus, who, Pliny says, spent her life in

<hr>

[25] If M. Annius Herennius Pollio is the son of P. Herennius Pollio, as Devreker assumes, father and son served together as colleagues in the suffect consulship in 85.

devotion to her husband.[26] Mentioned also in Pliny's description of Acilianus is his grandmother, Serrana Procula, evidently known for her *severitas*, who is a model of propriety even among the Patavians, distinguished by their adherence to traditional behavior. Pliny further details Acilianus' *cursus* up to the date of his recommendation, by which time the young man had reached the office of praetor. No record of any consulship exists, and it is likely that Acilianus died young, especially if he is to be identified as the deceased in Pliny's letter 2.16, in which Pliny is heir to part of Acilianus' property. Of his young wife, Iunia, who, through Pliny's selection of her husband, offered Pliny some link to her father Arulenus Rusticus and uncle Mauricus, we hear no more.

The Letters

As this summary of the Stoic opposition to the principate has shown, Pliny's letters are a vital source of information concerning its female members. With the exception of Arria (I), whose noble death is recalled in a number of sources, little mention is made of any of these women elsewhere, nor are we given details of their actions in defiance of the principate except by Pliny. But in his corpus they appear in all but books 2 and 8, leaving little doubt as to the importance of the Stoic women within Pliny's epistolary program. The following chart lists the nine letters and the names of the women who are mentioned in each.

Letter	Women
1.5	Arrionilla
1.14	(Iunia)*
	Serrana Procula
3.11	Caecina Arria the Younger
	Clodia Fannia
	Verulana Gratilla
3.16	Arria the Elder
	(Vibia)**
	Clodia Fannia

---

[26] *PIR²* M 617 remarks that it cannot be determined whether this Macrinus is Minicius Macrinus, but considers it probable.

Letter	Women
4.21	(Helvidiae – two sisters)
5.1	Verulana Gratilla
6.24	Arria the Elder
7.19	Caecina Arria the Younger Clodia Fannia Vestal Iunia
9.13	Anteia Caecina Arria the Younger Clodia Fannia

* Names in parentheses indicate that the woman is identifiable though unnamed by Pliny.
** Vibia cannot be included in the ranks of the Stoic opposition but is, in fact, related to the family by marriage.

Not all of these women are equally prominent in the letters. Of the eleven women who are mentioned, seven – Arrionilla, Iunia, Serrana Procula, the two Helvidiae, the Vestal Iunia, and Anteia – appear in only one letter each. Verulana Gratilla is named without elucidation in two letters. But the remaining three women – the Arrias, mother and daughter, and granddaughter Fannia – appear in a total of five of the nine letters, and they are crucial to our understanding of Pliny's relationship with the Stoic opposition and thus to his epistolary revision of his political affiliations and activity in the later years of Domitian's reign.

The importance of the Stoic women in Pliny's letters is marked by their early appearance in the corpus in *Epistulae* 1.5, the first letter that describes any of Pliny's political activities. Over the course of the nine-book collection, Pliny reveals and illuminates his relationship with these women, who offer him unique opportunities to express his disgust with what he presents as the persecution of the group and to align himself with them both as a close personal friend and as an ally in their resistance to the tyrant Domitian. Careful examination and discussion of seven of the nine letters[27] in the order of their

[27] Letter 5.1 is omitted from this discussion. While it mentions Gratilla and Rusticus, it does little to expand the reader's perception of Pliny's relationship with the family. It does, however, reiterate the climate of fear surrounding the prosecutions of 93 as in it Pliny mentions fellow heirs who were friends of the Stoics and therefore

appearance in the corpus reveals the purpose each serves in Pliny's careful construction of his association with the Stoic opposition.

LETTER 1.5: ARRIONILLA. Arrionilla is the first of the Stoic women to be mentioned by Pliny, and although she seems to be an insignificant (almost incidental) addition to Pliny's account of past events, she plays a crucial role in the delineation of his relationship with Arulenus Rusticus. She makes just a fleeting appearance in a letter that sets a firm foundation on which Pliny will build a lasting image of himself as closely tied with opponents of Domitian, although the chief event of the letter postdates the tyrant's death in 96.

As he awaits the approval of Iunius Mauricus to pursue the prosecution of M. Aquilius Regulus for his role in the treason trials of 93, Pliny writes to Voconius Romanus a scathing account of his prior battles with Regulus. While many of Pliny's addressees are either unidentifiable or seemingly insignificant to the topic at hand, Voconius Romanus is Pliny's lifelong friend and protégé – one of a number of men whose social promotion Pliny takes on as his charge. Some of the beneficiaries of his assistance are noble young men like Ummidius Quadratus and Fuscus Salinator, destined for the senate and consulship, for whom Pliny serves as adviser; others, like Voconius Romanus, Romatius Firmus, and Rosianus Geminus, are friends whom Pliny considers worthy of promotion to equestrian or even senatorial rank. Pliny writes to these commendable associates, offering suggestions for study, sending copies of his speeches, giving advice on a number of topics including courtroom behavior and the value of virtues like tolerance and generosity, and often drawing upon his own experiences as exemplars. That the recipient of letter 1.5 is one of Pliny's cultivars signals the importance of the letter as one that defines character and proper comportment, one that offers Voconius Romanus Pliny's actions as a model and begins, for Pliny, the process of reshaping his past political identity.

In the letter, Pliny expresses his vehement anger provoked by Regulus' prosecution of Rusticus and Regulus' public reading of a

---

feared any attention they might attract by appearing in court (5.1.8). In the same letter, considered in Chapter 3, Pliny naturally exhibits no such disinclination to take legal action to secure his inheritance and the wishes of the deceased. Nor is 6.24 included in this analysis, because it mentions Arria's suicide only in passing as a measure by which an anonymous woman's similar act might be assessed.

The Letters   39

speech against Rusticus after the latter's execution (2–4). Pliny notes that he himself was not invited to the reading of the speech and suggests that Regulus had excluded him because he feared Pliny's retribution for a potentially deadly (*capitaliter*) trap that he had laid for Pliny during an earlier court proceeding. Here Pliny introduces Arrionilla, wife of Timon, whom Rusticus had asked Pliny to represent in that earlier case. There follow Pliny's accounts of his verbal sparring with Regulus, which he would have his reader believe put him in grave danger, and of Regulus' desperate attempts to reconcile with Pliny after the death of Domitian because he feared that Pliny would do precisely what he tells his reader he is waiting for Mauricus' approval to do – that is, to bring charges against Regulus for acting as Domitian's henchman.

Pliny provides no further information about the cause of the earlier action against Arrionilla or the outcome of the proceedings. It seems at first glance that Arrionilla's trial simply offers the opportunity for Pliny's recollection of his victorious war of words with Regulus. In fact, Pliny's naming of Arrionilla and her benefactor offers the only direct link in the letters between Pliny and Rusticus while the latter was alive, because it was Rusticus who had called upon Pliny to defend her: *aderam Arrionillae Timonis uxori, rogatu Aruleni Rustici; Regulus contra* (1.5.5). In other letters, particularly those addressed to Rusticus' brother Mauricus, Pliny will refer to his love for Rusticus and the influence his advice had on Pliny as a youth, but in no other narrative is Rusticus actually present.

The importance of a tangible connection between Pliny and Rusticus should not be underestimated in analyzing Pliny's efforts to portray himself as a supporter of the Stoic opposition. Without his defense of Arrionilla while Rusticus was still alive, Pliny would merely become another cowed senator, too afraid, until after Domitian's demise, to oppose the tyrannous regime and sycophants like Regulus. Without Arrionilla, Pliny's connection to Rusticus would have been limited to reminiscences of his affection for Rusticus, directed primarily to his brother, Mauricus. Through a discussion of his legal representation of Arrionilla, Pliny sets himself in the Stoic camp in direct conflict with the villainous Regulus long before the confrontation in 97 that is the chief theme of 1.5. While Pliny is left awaiting Mauricus' approval to proceed with a formal accusation against

Regulus, he has, through his retrospective account of his prior confrontation with the villainous *delator*, introduced the personal relationship between himself and Arulenus Rusticus that he will further
define in his letters to Mauricus.

LETTER 1.14: IUNIA. In the next letter that concerns one of the
Stoics, 1.14, Pliny presents to his addressee Iunius Mauricus a lengthy
recommendation of an appropriate spouse for Mauricus' niece. It
seems certain that Pliny had an ongoing relationship with Mauricus;
as Rusticus' brother and guardian of his children and as a recipient of three letters, Mauricus offers a contemporary link for Pliny
with the Stoic opposition and serves as a conduit through which Pliny
strengthens the reader's perception of his connection to Rusticus.

In fact, two of the three letters that Pliny addresses to Mauricus
are concerned with the care of Rusticus' children: 1.14, discussed
here, and 2.18, in which Pliny has been asked to look for a tutor for
Rusticus' sons.[28] Although in the latter Pliny expresses his delight
that Mauricus has solicited his help, the letter is chiefly an opportunity for self-aggrandizement as Pliny highlights both the respect with
which the *iuvenes* treat him and his personal devotion to the memory
of their father. The reader anticipates Pliny's diligence in the search
for an appropriate candidate, one who will see to it that the boys
become *digni patre* (2.18.4), but neither the tutor nor either of the
boys is named in the letter.

Likewise in 1.14, Pliny never names the future bride, presumably
called Iunia, who is known only by the phrase *fratris tui filia* (1), nor
are any details of her life given in the letter. Even her chastity war-
rants only an oblique reference following Pliny's description of the
fine physical qualities of her potential bridegroom, a *praemium*, Pliny
says, for the *castitas puellarum* (8). Pliny's focus in the letter instead
falls on his love for Rusticus, whom he calls *summus vir* (1). He is
effusive in the expression of his pleasure at being asked to select
the father of Rusticus' grandchildren. No task, says Pliny, could be
more important or pleasing for him to undertake than to choose
a suitable young man: *nihil est quod a te mandari mihi aut maius aut*

---

[28] The third letter, 6.14, is a note in which Pliny accepts an invitation to visit Mauricus'
villa at Formiae.

gratius, nihil quod honestius a me suscipi possit, quam ut eligam iuvenem,
ex quo nasci nepotes Aruleno Rustico deceat (2). He uses the opportunity to recommend Minicius Acilianus, who has both a companionable and respectful relationship with Pliny (3). For, Pliny says, the
young man wants to be guided by Pliny, as Pliny was by Mauricus and
Rusticus (4). The reader is left in no doubt that Acilianus will be a fitting spouse because he aspires to be like Pliny and, by extension, like
Mauricus and Rusticus, whose model Pliny claims to have followed.

In asking Pliny to recommend a husband for Iunia, Mauricus has presented Pliny with a forum through which to project his association with
the family both back in time through his indebtedness to and affection
for Rusticus and into the future during which, the reader imagines, he
will continue to enjoy relationships with Mauricus, Acilianus and his new
wife Iunia, and their children. Mauricus' acceptance of Acilianus as a
suitable bridegroom (safely assumed by the inclusion of 1.14 in Pliny's
corpus) will forge, for Pliny, a permanent connection to the family.

LETTER 3.11: CAECINA ARRIA (II), CLODIA FANNIA, VERULANA
GRATILLA. As we have seen, Pliny has already associated himself
both personally and politically with Arulenus Rusticus and Iunius
Mauricus and their family in *Epistulae* 1.5 and 1.14. The names of
three women associated with the Stoic opposition appear in 3.11,
and, at first glance, they seem no more than placeholders whose presence is not significant to the structure of the letter. Yet their mention
at this point in the collection is pivotal to the letters that follow, which
will highlight Pliny's friendship with two of them. In 3.11, Pliny makes
as open a statement about his association with the Stoics as occurs in
the entire collection of letters.

The letter is addressed to Iulius Genitor, a much-admired friend
of Pliny, who may have served as a tutor for Arulenus Rusticus'
sons. Genitor is the tutor whom Pliny has praised highly and rec-
ommended to Corellia Hispulla just eight letters earlier in 3.3, and
Sherwin-White (1966: 213) does not hesitate to connect Pliny's recommendation of Iulius Genitor in that letter with Mauricus' request
of 2.18. While he may have served both families, there is no compelling reason beyond the relative proximity of the two letters to assume
that Genitor served both the Iunii and Corellii; however, no other
candidates are mentioned in the interim, and Genitor's skills would

certainly fit the requirements set out in 2.18. If Genitor was tutor for
Rusticus' sons, he would certainly be a suitable recipient – someone
associated with the family of some of the prosecuted – for Pliny's discussion of the danger he courted by his actions in 93 and for Pliny's
praise of Artemidorus,[29] a Stoic philosopher.

Pliny begins 3.11 by extolling the generosity of Artemidorus, and
much of the letter would seem to focus on the characterization of this
philosopher. Yet, it is Pliny who becomes the center of the letter, as
he uses his own interaction with Artemidorus to illustrate the latter's
virtues. Pliny recounts at length how he had endangered himself by
lending money to the philosopher when no one else was willing to do
so, that is, following the expulsion of philosophers from Rome in 93.[30]
Then, Pliny fixes the time of the loan and expands upon the risk he had
taken in giving it. Not only had he lent money to an expelled Stoic philosopher, but he had done so at a time when seven Romans of senatorial rank with strong Stoic connections had been condemned to death
or exile – *atque haec feci, cum septem amicis meis aut occisis aut relegatis,*
occisis Senecione Rustico Helvidio, relegatis Maurico Gratilla Arria Fannia, tot
circa me iactis fulminibus quasi ambustus mihi quoque impendere idem exitium
certis quibusdam notis augurarer (3.11.3). Here, for the first time in the
letters, Pliny not only has connected himself directly as an *amicus* with
specific members of the Stoic opposition but also has set himself in the
midst of the peril experienced by Domitian's opposition.

Pliny continues the letter by denying that he is worthy of the *gloria*
that Artemidorus assigns him for his actions (thus making clear that
he has received such approbation), and then he proceeds to explain
what a close friend he is and to extol the philosopher for his many
good qualities. Pliny thus strengthens his connection with the Stoics
through his association with Artemidorus and becomes the recipient
of the admiration of a man of sincerity and integrity (6). In her examination of this letter, Jo-Ann Shelton (1987: 124–125) has argued
persuasively that 3.11 is highly rhetorical in structure, designed by
Pliny to make his support for the Stoics central to the letter and to
emphasize particularly the imminent danger that he faced because

---

[29] Artemidorus was also the son-in-law of the Stoic philosopher Gaius Musonius.
[30] Sherwin-White (1966: 763–771) fixes this date for the expulsion with his argument
that Pliny served as praetor in 93. Pliny notes that his service in that office at the
time of his loan to Artemidorus called attention to his actions (3.11.2).

of his friendship with its seven condemned members. There can be no doubt that with this letter Pliny wishes to align himself with the Stoic opposition, and the specific naming of his *septem amici* in the letter can be intended only to connect Pliny with the particular individuals who were condemned.

Rusticus was the best known of those executed, and Pliny does put his friendship with the Iunii on display, but the family of Helvidius (II), particularly through Pliny's association with its women, has a more significant presence in Pliny's letters than that of Rusticus.[31] The identification of the seven defendants is a pivotal point in Pliny's treatment of the Stoics as it introduces the Helvidii with whom Pliny has closer ties and through whom he can embellish his association with the opposition. Even before the reader is given any inkling of his relationship with the Helvidii, Pliny assures us that they are his friends by providing their names and by setting himself squarely on their side. The subsequent letters that concern the women of the family provide amplification of the relationship that Pliny only suggests in 3.11.

Lest his reader wonder who these women were or what the nature of Pliny's friendship with them might have been, just five letters later, at 3.16, Pliny places his longest letter focused on a woman, the famous Arria the Elder.

LETTER 3.16: ARRIA (I), CLODIA FANNIA, VIBIA. Pliny immediately states the theme of 3.16 – that individuals are often known for words or actions that are not, in fact, their most outstanding accomplishments, *facta dictaque virorum feminarumque alia clariora esse alia maiora* (1). He then launches into the presentation of evidence in support of his statement by recounting a conversation he had had with Clodia Fannia about her famous grandmother, Arria the Elder (Arria I). Although her suicide and last words became an apothegmatic means of sustaining her fame, her lesser-known actions make Arria (I) an ideal exemplum through which Pliny may support his statement regarding the relative fame and greatness of human words and deeds. Furthermore, the letter serves to draw Pliny into a close relationship with Fannia, as

---

[31] Sherwin-White (1966: 243) traces Pliny's connection to the family of Helvidius Priscus (II) to his association with Senecio in the trial of Baebius Massa (*Ep.* 7.33) and comments that Pliny's friendship with the Iunii was older. Yet Pliny makes much more of his relationship with the Helvidii, perhaps because Mauricus could act as a check on the accuracy of Pliny's accounts.

she recalls for him stories that must have circulated within her family but appear nowhere else in the historical record.

Before he begins his narration, Pliny remarks that he thinks his addressee[32] (and thus his reader) will marvel at reading about Arria's *obscuriora* acts in the same way that Pliny had at hearing about them. It is no surprise then that Pliny's narration is highly dramatic, heavily dependent on direct quotation of Arria's words. Pliny first reports that when both her husband Paetus and their son were gravely ill, Arria (I) chose to conceal the boy's death so as not to imperil her husband's recovery. Although she had arranged for and attended the funeral, when asked about their son's condition she would say to Paetus, *Bene quievit, libenter cibum sumpsit* (4). Pliny has begun his quotation of Arria's words with a truly ordinary statement with no aphoristic potential, yet the words are spoken in extraordinary circumstances. Pliny continues by recalling her calm demeanor in the presence of her husband in contrast to her open mourning after she left his room. Arria's ability to bear her loss appropriately marks her not only as devoted to the well-being of her husband but also as a Stoic *sapiens* in the tradition of the elder Cato, who, Cicero says, bore the death of his grown son with the equanimity expected of a wise man (*Amic.* 2).

Having told in painstaking detail the story of Arria's private and concealed grief, Pliny proceeds to offer, in stark contrast, a quick summary of her immortal act of suicide in a single sentence, composed of clipped phrases – *ferrum stringere, perfodere pectus* (6) – that ends with the words for which she was famous, *Paete, non dolet*. The reader is left in no doubt as to Pliny's assessment of the two episodes. With her heroic death, Arria envisioned *gloria et aeternitas* (6), but she could expect no fame or immortality for protecting her ailing husband. The greater act, Pliny makes clear, is the one done with no expectation of reward, *maius est sine praemio aeternitatis, sine praemio gloriae* (6).

Pliny continues his transmission of Fannia's account with details of Arria (I)'s actions before her suicide. She and Paetus were in Dalmatia with Scribonianus when the latter attempted to stir up a legionary

[32] Pliny's addressee is an acquaintance named Nepos, whose identity cannot be securely established. He may be Metilius Nepos, consul suffectus in 91, as suggested by Sherwin-White (1966: 146–147). Who he is seems to have little relevance to the content of the letter. Like many of Pliny's correspondents, Nepos has no tangible involvement in a letter whose purpose is to provide an arena for Pliny to expound upon a theme.

revolt against the emperor Claudius. Paetus was condemned for his involvement, but Pliny offers no details of his anti-imperial actions. Rather, his focus falls on Arria's behavior.[33] In five quotations joined by narrative sufficient only to provide appropriate context for each, Pliny presents Arria's words and deeds, known only by her intimates, in the aftermath of Paetus' arrest.

First, Arria (I) begs the soldiers that she be allowed not just to accompany her husband as he is transported to Rome but to care for him in place of his slaves, that is, to serve him his meals, dress him, and put on his shoes (8). The extent of her devotion to Paetus is remarkable, as she is willing to assume a servile role in order to remain with him. Furthermore, when her request is denied, Pliny reports that she followed along in a small fishing boat. Next, coming before Claudius, Arria encounters Scribonianus' wife, Vibia, who is offering testimony regarding the revolt. Clearly appalled by Vibia's duplicitous behavior, Arria says, *Ego . . . te audiam, cuius in gremio Scribonianus occisus est, et vivis?* (9). Pliny comments that this statement proves that Arria's determination to die a glorious death (along with her husband) was not sudden, and he offers Arria's critical assessment of Vibia's determined survival as a contrast to her own commitment to accompanying her husband even in death.

Lest the reader might wrongly believe that Arria (I)'s desire for glory was her sole motivation for determining to die with Paetus, Pliny proceeds to recall Thrasea's attempts to dissuade her and Arria's

---

[33] Pliny's portrait of Arria, an admirably forceful and headstrong woman, who accompanied her husband not only to Dalmatia but even to his death, seems somewhat ironic in light of the politics of her father-in-law, Aulus Caecina Severus. As a new man, Severus had been consul suffectus in 1 c.e. and proconsul of Africa between 8 and 10 c.e. Tacitus reports, in detail, Severus' proposal in the senate that no governor should be permitted to take his wife with him to his assigned province (*Ann.* 3.33). In the speech recounted by the historian, Severus warns of women as schemers and a magnet for extravagance and extortion in the provinces and among the soldiers. In Severus' speech, Tacitus recalls Livy's account of Cato's defense of the Oppian law (Livy 34.1–4). The parallel between Severus and Cato the Censor is particularly vivid, as Severus names the *Lex Oppia* as one being ignored, as if the law were still in force. Earlier in the *Annales*, Tacitus had highlighted the importance of Severus' military service under the command of Germanicus (1.29–2.5). There seems to be a marked contrast between Tacitus' portrayal of Severus as a staunch supporter of traditional views of women and the Arria of Pliny's letters, who neither stays at home nor heeds the pleas of her son-in-law, Thrasea Paetus, not to kill herself (3.16.10).

response – the third in this series of quotations – in which she refers
directly to her long and great *concordia* with Paetus as the reason for
her wish to die with him (10). Suspecting that her family might try
further to prevent her death, Arria declares, *potestis enim efficere ut
male moriar, ut non moriar non potestis* (11), then leaps from her chair
and bashes her head against the opposite wall. When revived, Pliny
reports, Arria said, *Dixeram ... vobis inventuram me quamlibet duram
ad mortem viam, si vos facilem negassetis* (12). Arria's perseverance is
unquestionable. She will die either a noble and beautiful death or an
ignoble and harsh one, but die she must.

Pliny concludes the letter by comparing Arria's commitment to her
husband before his condemnation with repetition of the immortal
words spoken at their suicide: *Paete, non dolet* (13). Those final words
were merely the culmination, Pliny says, of Arria's earlier statements
that he believes were greater than the immortal phrase that brought
her fame. Although Pliny does not use the term *constantia*, it is surely
this quality that he sees in her determined resistance to outliving her
spouse. Each of Arria's acts of devotion, whether to protect her ailing
husband from grief or to die with him even in a horrible or base way,
is ranked by Pliny as greater than her role as *consolatio et exemplum* for
Paetus in their final moments. In an example of ring composition
acknowledged by the author himself, Pliny closes the letter by declaring that he ends where he began as he repeats, *alia esse clariora alia
maiora* (13).

Critical to an accurate reading of 3.16 is Pliny's decision to use
direct quotations so extensively. In fact, there are fewer than a dozen
examples of letters in the first nine books in which Pliny employs such
quotations more than three times.[34] In eight of these, Pliny reports
his own conversations or quick retorts. Six letters that rely on direct
speech concern court actions in which Pliny was a participant. Most
notable among these are the first and last letters naming members
of the Stoic opposition, 1.5 and 9.13, not only because of their subject matter but especially because direct quotations are used more
frequently by far (fifteen and fourteen times, respectively) than in
any of the remaining examples. The preponderance of dramatized
speech enlivens the narrative of each of these letters and focuses the

[34] *Ep.* 1.5; 2.6; 3.9, 16; 4.11, 13; 5.1; 7.6, 33; 9.13, 23.

reader's attention on Pliny's courageous and forthright statements. After these two letters whose themes are so similar (Pliny's proposed prosecutions of those involved in the trials of 93), 3.16 has the most examples of direct speech.

What is even more remarkable about Pliny's use of Arria the Elder's words in 3.16 is that she is quoted a total of eight times. No other individual receives even marginally similar treatment by Pliny. Pliny chooses to let Arria speak for herself, connecting her words with his own to create a narrative, having first authenticated his quotations by assigning them to his conversation with Fannia. Some scholars have seen 3.16 as an excursion by Pliny into the realm of historical writing, a genre to which he seemed to aspire.[35] It is true that Pliny shows a similar preference for direct quotation in his historical account of the prosecution and execution of the Vestal Cornelia (4.11) with six examples in that letter (see Chapter 5). Indeed, Cornelia herself speaks twice, but Domitian and Senecio also are quoted. Furthermore, Pliny's historical letters contain a great deal of narrative. By contrast, Arria's story lacks all but the bare details of the historical events that surrounded and provoked her acts and thus cannot be seen as the kind of historical account Pliny is clearly capable of – for example, in his Vesuvius narratives (6.16 and 6.20).

Pliny's decision to present so many of Arria's words serves two major functions: first, it tightens his reader's perception of his bonds with Fannia and her family and, second, it elucidates his view that one's greatest deeds can easily be unknown outside of one's intimate circle. Through Fannia, Pliny has access to events that took place within Arria's household, as she recounts what amount to private stories and quotations from her famous grandmother; thus, Pliny can claim a palpable intimacy with the family. Although Fannia herself was surely known by anyone who was familiar with the events of 93, the

---

[35] Radicke (1997: 457–458) calls Pliny's account of Arria's brave deeds "ein Stück Historie im Kleinformat." He notes the importance of the letter to Pliny's elaboration of his personal connections with Fannia and the other members of the Stoic opposition but concludes that Pliny's self-characterization occurs only indirectly in this letter, as he shows approval of her beliefs through his clear admiration for Arria's Stoic stance. Thus, Radicke misses Pliny's concern with connecting Fannia to her famous ancestor and his further intention to offer proof that lesser-known or even obscure deeds and words may still constitute greatness.

elder Arria's fame was considerably more widespread, reaching well
beyond the bounds of senatorial politics. Pliny's friendship with her
granddaughter allows him to share with her in Arria's virtuous reputation. Arria (I) is clearly the exemplum upon which Fannia models
her own behavior, as her mother, Arria the Younger (Arria II), had
tried to do before her.

Pliny clearly intends his readers not only to accept the evidence he
offers concerning the lack of correlation between the notoriety and
the value of human actions but also to extend the application of this
concept to his own behavior. That is, Pliny's actions and words are
to be seen through the lens that he gives us in his examination of
Arria's unacclaimed deeds. Pliny, too, is the author of acts unknown
outside of the private circle of those who receive his letters. Through
the publication of his letters, however, he admits his reader into this
inner circle, in the same way that Fannia has drawn him into Arria's.
Pliny reveals to his audience in his own words his greater but obscure
deeds, particularly those on behalf of his friends in the Stoic opposition. That Pliny intends his presentation of Arria to reflect favorably
on his own behavior is reinforced not only by Arria the Elder's close
association with the Stoic opposition but also by the letter's placement so near Pliny's account of his "dangerous" behavior in support
of Artemidorus. The reader not only is left to wonder what other laudable yet unknown actions Pliny took on behalf of his friends but is
also encouraged to seek out indications of those lesser-known deeds
within Pliny's narratives.

Finally, Pliny's placement of 3.16 following the introduction of
Fannia and her mother Arria (II) in 3.11 serves as a strong indication
of the letter's importance to defining his friendship with opposition
members. Indeed, Fannia is the linchpin in Pliny's efforts to connect
himself with the Stoics both before and after Domitian's death. To
emphasize the ongoing nature of his relationship with Fannia – a
living remnant of the opposition – Pliny mentions early in the letter that their conversation about her grandmother happened "yes-
terday" (3.16.2). Thus, Pliny's involvement with the Stoic opposition
is contemporary, not just relegated to some distant past, and Pliny
may begin to expand upon his connection to the younger Helvidius
Priscus (Helvidius II) and reveal the depth of his relationship with
Helvidius (II)'s stepmother Fannia.

LETTER 4.21: THE HELVIDIAE. It is not Fannia but her stepson's daughters, the Helvidiae, who are the subjects of 4.21, the fifth letter that focuses on women associated with the Stoic opposition. Pliny writes to the otherwise unknown Velius Cerealis of his distress at the deaths in childbirth of both of the daughters of the younger Helvidius Priscus (Helvidius II). While the letter has some elements of a traditional *consolatio*, including the expression of its author's grief and his own need for consolation, none of Pliny's letters fits the chief requirement of a letter of condolence, that is, the author's intent to offer some relief for his addressee's aggrievement. Sherwin-White (1966: 42–45) assigns 4.21 to the list of obituaries in his classification of Pliny's letters, and the letter does share some of the characteristics of others in this category, but in no other example is Pliny's personal involvement so apparent. Even 1.12, Pliny's tribute to his mentor Corellius Rufus (see Chapter 2), although it includes the expression of Pliny's profound private grief, does not begin to approach the emotional intensity of 4.21. In fact, 1.12 is as close to a *consolatio* as Pliny comes in his letters. It expresses Pliny's grief and that of Corellius' family, and it offers a eulogy of the deceased and reasons to be resigned to his loss (he was old, ill, had lived a good life, etc.). It lacks only a recipient in mourning and is thus a vehicle for the revelation of Pliny's distress rather than a consolation for that of his addressee. By contrast, 4.21 offers no details of the lives of the Helvidiae, not even the names of their spouses. Instead, Pliny's letter centers on their father, the younger Helvidius Priscus, and the continued survival of his only remaining offspring.

It is not unusual for Pliny to begin an obituary letter with an expression of his own sadness, but 4.21 stands out for Pliny's extended lament. Some of the letters that report a death open with a simple statement of the person's demise and Pliny's sorrow, proceed with an account of the character and deeds of the deceased, and close with a restatement of Pliny's personal feelings or his view of the mortal condition.[36] When Pliny reports the deaths of Minicia Marcella in 5.16 (see Chapter 4) and Macrinus' wife in 8.5, he opens with a statement of his anxiety for the bereaved father or husband rather than expressing his own grief. Both 5.16 and 8.5 eulogize the dead by extolling their characters and offering

---

[36] See particularly *Ep.* 2.1, 5.5, and 8.23.

rather traditional solace, even though the letters are not addressed to those in mourning. Pliny closes 5.16 by encouraging Aefulanus Marcellinus, its recipient, to write a *consolatio* to Minicia's father, and it is the latter for whom Pliny mourns. By contrast, in 4.21 Pliny's grief for the lost women is pervasive and appears deeply personal, and in this respect the letter is drastically different from his other obituaries.

As the reader might expect, Pliny opens with an exclamation of the cause of his distress, the untimely death of the sisters, and then proceeds with an equally predictable expression of his own grief, *afficior dolore* (2). We might now anticipate some discourse on the character of the young women, but Pliny continues with extended expressions of his sadness, *supra modum doleo, mihi luctuosum videtur* (2), and ends with an anaphoric tricolon whose first member, *angor infantium sorte*, is expanded with a relative clause expounding on the loss of the infants' mothers at birth, *quae sunt parentibus statim et dum nascuntur orbatae.* For the second member, *angor optimorum maritorum*, Pliny offers no supporting clause but rather follows it abruptly with the third member, *angor etiam meo nomine* (2). The reader's attention is thus even more focused on the final lament than is customary in a tricolon, as Pliny's anguish for himself seems to have replaced the expected explanation of the grief of the bereaved husbands. Because Pliny has already expressed his own sadness and has given no indication of a personal relationship with the young women, his reiteration of his own sorrow is surprising. Indeed, the intimacy expressed by Pliny's personal sorrow is matched in the letters only by his grief at the loss of his mentor in 1.12.12: *doleo autem meo nomine.* More appropriate to ending Pliny's catalog of the bereaved for whom he is concerned would be the women's grieving parents, an addition that would complete the list of family members. Because their mother Anteia survived them, Pliny might at least have included her. Instead, with the unexpected *meo nomine* Pliny draws himself into the inner circle of bereaved family members as substitute parent. Their father Helvidius (II) is, of course, deceased, as Pliny reminds us in the next sentence. Yet Pliny not only continues to love him but, as he stresses with his pointed use of the superlative of the emphatic adjective *perseverans*, loves him with the utmost tenacity, *perseverantissime diligo* (3).

Pliny's statement of profound affection for Helvidius (II) is central to the letter and provides Pliny the opportunity to furnish evidence of his continued devotion. The proof lies in Pliny's defense of Helvidius (II) and Pliny's *libri* on his behalf, *ut actione mea librisque testatum est* (3). In letters that appear later in the collection, Pliny refers to a published version of his speech, presumably the *libri* he mentions here, delivered in vindication of Helvidius (II) (7.30). He also reports the events leading up to the speech's delivery as well as the accolades he received following it (9.13), but we have no inkling in 4.21 that Pliny's defense of his friend did not take place until four years after Helvidius (II)'s execution. Rather, Pliny's concern in the letter is to prove his ongoing love for Helvidius (II) and thus to provide justification for his quasi-paternal grief for the deceased young women.

Following his lament, Pliny shifts his attention to the one surviving child of Helvidius (II) and his hopes not only for his safety but also for him to be equal to his father and grandfather (4).[37] Pliny's sorrow will be assuaged by the boy's preservation and potentially fine character. Pliny concludes with further expressions of his anxiety regarding the future of Helvidius (II)'s line. It is important to note here that the letter tells the reader nothing about the children of Helvidius (II) beyond the state of their mortality. Their characters receive none of Pliny's usual treatment of the deceased in his "obituary" letters. While the deaths of the daughters of Helvidius (II) are sad for their husbands and daughters, Pliny stresses that their loss is critical to their father's line, as only one of his children remains. Likewise, Helvidius (II)'s son is defined solely by the importance of his survival to the preservation of the family and the hope that he will be like his forebears. Pliny's concern and love for the boy is thus an extension of his relationship with Helvidius (II) – a relationship whose survival is made all the more important by Pliny's abiding love for the boy's father. Although Helvidius (II) is long dead, Pliny's affection for him can now be expressed through his association with and concern for Helvidius (II)'s son, which are contemporary to the writing of the letter.

Thus, Pliny has assumed Helvidius (II)'s role both in his sorrow for the lost daughters and in his apprehension for the surviving son's

[37] Hope that a son grows to be his father's equal is, of course, a long-standing topos. Indeed, the desire of Sophocles' Ajax that his son be his equal, but luckier (*Aj.* 550–551), is a wish particularly suited to Helvidius II's son, whose family has been beset by disaster.

future. As a result, the letter centers on Pliny's feelings much more profoundly than his other obituary letters do and becomes a *consolatio* written to himself. He will be comforted by his great hope, *plurimum spero* (5), for the survival and good character of his surrogate son. We must lament here the loss of Cicero's *Consolatio* written to console himself on the death of his daughter Tullia, as it must surely have included his hopes for the future of his son and may well have influenced Pliny's treatment of the subject in 4.21. Cicero's letters do offer a model for how he presents his own anxiety through his expression of concern over the illnesses of both Tullia and his beloved scribe, Tiro. He is greatly aggrieved by his daughter's condition, as evidenced by his use of *excruciare* and *exanimare* (*Fam.* 14.19.1; *Att.* 11.6.4) to describe his feelings. Cicero even employs *angor* to describe his concern regarding Tiro's recovery (*Att.* 6.7.2), but the word is much more commonly used by Cicero to characterize his distress over matters of state and his standing therein.[38] We can only imagine the content of Cicero's *Consolatio*, but it is reasonable to surmise, on the basis of his treatment of Tiro's and Tullia's illnesses and his profound distress at her death, that it must have been filled with emotion. Pliny has no such claim to profound sorrow, and yet he portrays the deaths of the Helvidiae as a deeply personal loss. There is no doubt that, in doing so, Pliny speaks *in loco parentis*, leaving the reader of 4.21 with a strong impression of his close connections to and great concern for the family of the younger Helvidius Priscus.

LETTER 7.19: ARRIA (II), CLODIA FANNIA, THE VESTAL IUNIA. This sixth letter about the Stoic women offers a detailed portrait of Clodia Fannia, for whom, through his account of Arria (I)'s deeds, Pliny has provided the kind of ancestral distinction he generally reserves for the men he describes. Pliny addresses the letter to Priscus, who, although not identifiable with any certainty, is undoubtedly one of several Prisci who appear elsewhere in the corpus, none of whom seems to have had any apparent connection to Fannia's family. As in many of Pliny's letters, the obscurity of this letter's recipient enables Pliny to provide expansive characterizations of

---

[38] The verb *angere* appears thirty-seven times in Cicero's letters. In more than half of the cases, Cicero is describing his anxiety at personal political uncertainties. See especially *Att.* 5.10.3, 9.1.1, 9.6.4, 12.45.1; *Q Fr* 3.3.1, 3.5.1.

his acquaintances without the appearance of artifice, which would be marked were his recipient affiliated with the persons portrayed.

In 7.19, Fannia, who is critically ill, receives exceptional praise as wife and daughter. Pliny, in fact, not only voices his doubts that the future will ever offer such an exemplary woman, *eritne quam postea uxoribus nostris ostentare possimus* (7), but even extols her courage as an example for men, *viri quoque fortitudinis exempla sumamus.* Her role in Pliny's letters as the model of an idealized wife will be closely examined in Chapter 4, which is dedicated to that theme, but there is much in the letter that pertains to her role as member of the Stoic opposition and close friend of Pliny. In 7.19, for the first time in the letters, Pliny discusses Fannia's marriage to Helvidius Priscus (I) and provides some detail concerning the prosecutions of 93, highlighting Fannia's involvement.

Sherwin-White includes 7.19 among letters that provide character sketches, and it certainly does bear a number of features that justify that classification, including descriptions of Fannia's personal qualities and noble deeds, but Pliny's expression of his own grief and the great loss to the country that Fannia's death would bring make the letter as much *consolatio* as characterization. Although she has not yet departed, Pliny has written an obituary of Fannia and, in doing so, takes the opportunity to emphasize his affection for her and, through his concern for her, to draw himself closer to her parents and her husband.

Although Fannia, who was stepgrandmother to the Helvidiae, had received no mention in 4.21 and does not reappear after 3.16 until Pliny's great encomium of her in 7.19, there is no doubt that Pliny connects his feelings regarding her illness and decline with those he expressed concerning the deaths of the Helvidiae. *Epistulae* 7.19 opens with *angit me Fanniae valetudo*, clearly recalling the *angor* of 4.21 with which Pliny confronts his reader. The verb is little used elsewhere in the first nine books of Pliny's letters, appearing in only five other missives, twice to express his annoyance at being denied pleasurable pursuits because his duties press him.[39] Pliny also uses *angere* to voice

---

[39] *Ep.* 1.10.9 and 2.8.2. In 1.10 Pliny bemoans the fact that his duties do not allow him time to enjoy the philosopher Euphrates' company, while in 2.8 he cannot leave Rome to return to the pleasures of his native Comum.

his distress that Fannius had not made a new will before his death, to assure Annius Severus that he always tells him the things that upset him, and to brag that the people of Tifernum are always anguished by his departure from them (5.5, 5.1, and 4.1, respectively). Only in the letters about the loss of the Helvidiae and impending death of Fannia does Pliny use *angere* to convey his distress about the demise or illness of individuals.

Having expressed his anguish, Pliny explains the source of Fannia's illness as her diligent care for the ailing Vestal Iunia. This duty was prompted by Fannia's personal sense of obligation, first to her *adfinis*, Iunia, and later to the authority of the pontiffs, who, Pliny explains, regularly remanded ailing Vestals into the custody of married women (1–2). Pliny thus portrays Fannia as dutiful to both family and state, with her family ties given priority.

Pliny proceeds to describe her failing health and then comments that all that remains of Fannia is an *animus* and *spiritus* most worthy of her husband Helvidius (I) and father Thrasea (7.19.3).[40] While her physical, female body is wasting away, her intangible mind and spirit remain *dignissimus* of her two male models of behavior. She embodies their personal qualities and represents their values. In fact, after Pliny again expresses his fear and grief that she will slip away, he laments that so great a woman will be taken from the eyes of the state (4), a surprising statement and one that the reader might expect him to make of a prominent man whose death would impoverish his country.

With four loaded words, *castitas, sanctitas, gravitas,* and *constantia,* words that praise both private and public actions and have both moral and political significance, Pliny next begins a recitation of Fannia's political actions (4).[41] Pliny mentions only briefly the first two periods

---

[40] In seeking in 97, upon her last return from banishment, to avenge her stepson's execution, Fannia had followed the elder Helvidius' lead as, after his return in 69, he had attempted to impeach Eprius Marcellus, Thrasea's accuser. Tacitus (*Hist.* 4.6) reports that such a prosecution in 69 would have deeply divided the senate, many of whose members had served as *delatores* under Nero. Lacking the support of Galba, Helvidius withdrew his charge. Fannia, likewise, would not get satisfaction from Publicius Certus, though Pliny's attacks on her behalf clearly hindered the delator's career, keeping him from entering the consulship and stripping him of his treasury post and perhaps even contributing to his early death.

[41] See particularly Hellegouarc'h's (1972: 279–290) consideration of the political significance of *gravitas* and *constantia*.

of exile that she endured accompanying her husband. There is no evidence in Pliny's letters or elsewhere that Fannia was officially sanctioned either in 66, when Helvidius (I) was exiled for his connection with Thrasea, or in the mid-70s, when Helvidius (I) was again exiled and then killed under Vespasian. None of these details is mentioned in Pliny's letters. In fact, the lack of information suggests an attempt by Pliny to cleanse Fannia's actions of any treasonous intent, just as he does in his treatment of Thrasea, and to draw the reader instead to an assessment of her character based on familial devotion. Although she might have stayed in Rome while her husband was in exile, she chose instead to remain at his side. The effect in the letters is to make both Fannia and Thrasea seem motivated by *pietas* rather than sedition and so less deserving of the emperor's wrath.

Pliny does focus intently and at length on the details of Fannia's third exile, the one that she suffered long after her husband's death but still because of him (5), but again he provides no specific information of any subversive actions on her part beyond the literary activities of the defendants. Pliny explains that when Senecio was on trial for writing a biography of the elder Helvidius, Fannia admitted, when questioned, to asking Senecio to undertake the work and to providing him with her husband's diaries. Pliny quotes Fannia's answers to the prosecutor Mettius Carus as a series of terse, powerful, one-word responses, *rogavi, dedi, nesciente* (5). Thus, Fannia is presented as forthright, making no attempt to either explain or justify her actions, fearless in her responses. There is a sharp contrast between Pliny's presentation of the laconic utterances of Fannia and the aphoristic ones of her grandmother Arria (I) in 3.16. Arria (I)'s words, as Fannia relates them to Pliny, have power without her presence, but Fannia's presence has power that needs little justification in words. She is a fine representative of the revolutionary drive of Thrasea and Helvidius (I), a woman acting without male sanction in an effort to perpetuate her husband's memory, a task that might be undertaken by a son rather than a wife.

Pliny concludes his account of Fannia's actions in 93 with what he, as an author, likely considered to be her most valiant act. Despite the senate's order that the books that had apparently provoked the prosecution of Senecio be destroyed, Fannia managed to save them and took them into exile with her (6). That Pliny valued her defiance is apparent in the *figura etymologica* with which he concludes the section on her political acts: *tulitque in exsilium exsili causam* (6). Surely it was perilous for Fannia to have in her possession materials that the senate had ordered destroyed, but so determined was she to preserve Helvidius (I)'s *fama* that she even risked directly contravening a *senatus consultum*.

Pliny continues the letter by assigning to Fannia a few more personal qualities that suggest his intimate connection with her, as her charm and friendliness provoke both his love and respect (7). What follows would be surprising if Pliny had not already portrayed Fannia in rather masculine terms as an embodiment of her father and husband, for he holds her up as a model not only for *uxores nostrae* but for *(nos) viri* as well (8). As an exemplum, Fannia displays masculine qualities often used to describe men of rank, *gravitas* and *sanctitas*, virtues that Pliny assigns to Corellius Rufus and Verginius Rufus, by whose loss the state is diminished and by both of whom Pliny is greatly influenced.[42] Though still alive, she is ranked by Pliny among famous women of history, *illas quae leguntur* (8). Placed among the heroines of the past, Fannia's life takes on mythic proportions that her descendants cannot possibly match, prompting Pliny's fears that she will be the last of her line (8). Pliny makes clear that Fannia, like any great Roman statesman, deserves worthy offspring. It is surely no coincidence that here the reader is reminded of Pliny's concern for the survival and character of the only remaining child of Helvidius (II) (4.11). Fannia seems to have had no children of her own, and thus the child of her stepson Helvidius (II) must serve, if anyone can, to perpetuate her line.

In the final sections of the letter, Pliny returns to his personal angst at the thought of losing Fannia and discusses for the first and last time her mother Arria (II). Pliny is afflicted and tormented by the sense that in losing Fannia he is losing Arria (II) again. Although

---

[42] In the first nine books of the letters, Pliny confers the status of *exemplum* on selected men and women. Some, like Pomponius Bassus, an *exemplum pulcherrimae quietis* (4.23.4), are models in particular settings. Pliny presents only Vestricius Spurinna and his son Vestricius Cottius as unqualified models, the former for Pliny himself (3.1.11) and the latter for all young men (2.7.5). In total five men are presented as positive models. There are also two negative examples, Regulus and Pallas, and two *exemplaria* of former times, Verginius Rufus (2.1.7) and Cornutus Tertullus (5.14.3).

Arria (II) is mentioned together with the others executed or exiled in 93 and is named later by Pliny as he recounts his speech in vindication of Helvidius (II), Pliny's description of her here as the mother of a great woman is the only attempt he makes to portray her. Were it not for Tacitus' mention of her in the *Annales* as a courageous woman in the tradition of her own famous mother (Arria I), we would know her only as an appendage of her daughter Fannia. With an unassuming phrase, *rursus videor amittere*, Pliny evokes sympathy from his reader for his renewed bereavement, and subtly reinforces his presentation of his past close friendship with Fannia's mother, although there is no other evidence for such a relationship.

Pliny professes to have been grieved by Arria (II)'s death, yet she has no definitive purpose in the letter except to lengthen the duration of Pliny's association with the family. In fact, Pliny defines Arria (II)'s behavior strictly through the actions of her mother and daughter. In a reversal of their expected roles, Fannia is the model whom her mother follows. With the statement that Fannia had restored Arria to him through her own person, *quam [Arriam] haec [Fannia] ... reddit ac refert nobis* (9), Pliny makes it clear to his reader that Fannia represents the generation that preceded her. Pliny thus implies that his association with the women is long-standing, not simply cultivated in the less-treacherous times following Domitian's death. Added to Pliny's statements concerning her value to the state and her possession of the qualities of her husband and father, Fannia's role as re-creator of her mother makes her the key player in Pliny's presentation of his relationship with members of the Stoic opposition. Through his friendship with her, he reaches back to an imagined one with Arria (I), Thrasea, and Helvidius (I).

Pliny goes on to declare, as if Fannia were already dead, his equal affection for both Fannia and her mother. More important to defining his relationship with the Stoics, though, is his bold statement that he had been at their service at all times, even when they were in peril, offering support when they were in exile and serving as their avenger after their recall.[43] If Pliny's ties were as close to the family as he

---

[43] Having suggested that Pliny's relationship with Helvidius Priscus began in mid-93, Sherwin-White (1966: 426) comments on 7.19.10 that Pliny's connection with Helvidii family members is not clear. He offers the rather perplexing statement that Pliny owed a "Roman debt of gratitude to the family group" and then discusses

implies in both 7.19 and 4.21, his *officia* on their behalf could simply be considered an expression of his devotion to his *amici*. Obligation and reciprocity were, after all, the chief mechanisms for the maintenance of Roman social relations. But Pliny himself qualifies his relationship with Fannia by informing the reader that he is somehow indebted to the family to such an extent that her imminent death will make it impossible for him to restore equanimity in their friendship: *non feci tamen paria atque eo magis hanc cupio servari, ut mihi solvendi tempora supersint* (10). The nature of Pliny's debt is uncertain. Yet, judging by Pliny's emphasis on his own parsimony throughout the corpus, it is unlikely to be a monetary one. Perhaps Pliny has received the family's support in political or judicial ventures; perhaps, as Sherwin-White (1966a: 426) suggests, Pliny felt he needed to make up for his inaction in 93. Indeed, Pliny has made his encomium of Fannia one that focuses on the political nature and repercussions of her actions, on her public face rather than her private one. Whether Pliny's debt is tangible or metaphoric, as long as it is considered unpaid, it can remain the chief stated reason for his continued service to and relationship with Fannia, and its effect is to bind Pliny to her family. Therefore, the unpaid debt is invaluable to Pliny in perpetuating his connections with the Stoic opposition.

Pliny's recitation of his efforts on behalf of the women emphasizes his close relationship with both of them and prepares the reader for 9.13 in which Pliny, in a retrospective narrative, proves himself to be the avenger he calls himself, as he sets the scene for his speech in vindication of Helvidius (II).

LETTER 9.13: ANTEIA, ARRIA (II), CLODIA FANNIA. In this final letter, Fannia, Arria (II), and Helvidius (II)'s wife, Anteia, make brief appearances. The women are not integral to Pliny's narrative, and yet their presence lends credence to his account. He addresses *Epistulae* 9.13 to Ummidius Quadratus, arguably the most promising and closest of his young protégés, who will become Hadrian's consular colleague and will be connected to the imperial house through his son's marriage to a sister of Marcus Aurelius (see Chapter 5). In the

Pliny's association as a youth with Arulenus Rusticus. Sherwin-White has not captured the complexity of Pliny's presentation of these affiliations, nor does he separate the Iunii from the Helvidii, a division that is critical to understanding Pliny's supposed Stoic connections.

nine-book collection, the letter is also the last whose topic is Pliny's courtroom demeanor in the context of specific circumstances. Thus, the events described in 9.13 must be read as Pliny's exemplum for others to follow, and the defining moment of his career in forensic oratory, even though its subject is a speech given in 97, years before his consulship and the height of his service to the emperor.

Employing a common *topos* in which the content of a letter has been requested by its recipient, Pliny notes that Ummidius has been zealously reading Pliny's speech in vindication of Helvidius (II), and because of this, he has been pressing for a full account of the events surrounding its original delivery (1). Thus, most of the letter is devoted to Pliny's detailed recollection of the debate in the senate that preceded his speech for Helvidius (II); the enthusiastic response he received after its delivery; and the fate of Publicius Certus, whose prosecution for his role in the condemnation of Helvidius (II) was the subject of the dispute. Before he recounts the various speeches that preceded his vindication of Helvidius (II), Pliny delineates for his reader the reasons that, despite the advice of friends who were concerned with his future security, he had decided to attempt to bring charges against Publicius Certus. In fact, he takes great pains to justify his actions against Certus, most likely because, in indicting a senatorial colleague, Pliny risked exposing himself to the accusation that he had done precisely the same thing as Certus had in the prosecution of *his* fellow senator Helvidius (II).

Pliny reports that, after Domitian was killed, he decided the time was right to avenge those who had been harmed by the prosecutions that occurred during Domitian's regime, particularly those in which members of the senate had been attacked by their colleagues. The benefits of such an action, Pliny says, are threefold: to pursue the guilty, to avenge the wretched, and to promote oneself. He adds that Certus was particularly deserving of such a fate because he had made an attack on Helvidius (II) during the latter's trial, *manus intulisset* (2).[44]

---

[44] What role Certus had played in the prosecution of Helvidius is unclear. Sherwin-White (1966a: 492) comments that, because Helvidius was tried in the senate, all of the senators would have served as judges, and he suggests that Certus might have proposed the death sentence. As Pliny never calls him *delator*, we must presume that his role was somewhat peripheral to the actual trial.

Pliny next reveals his private motivation for attacking Certus –
his friendship with Helvidius (II), Arria (II), and Fannia. While he
states directly that he had an *amicitia* with Helvidius (II), he is careful to qualify the extent of their association, remarking that it was
"as substantial a friendship as [Pliny] could have with someone who,
because of the terror of the times, hid his great name and virtues by
living in retirement," *quanta potuerat esse cum eo, qui metu temporum
nomen ingens paresque virtutes secessu tegebat* (3). Pliny's admission is
rather shocking in light of his concerted effort to insinuate himself
into familial roles through his concern for the Helvidiae and Fannia
and to emphasize his love for Helvidius (II) in earlier letters. The
fact that Pliny himself sets a limit on his claim to a relationship with
Helvidius (II) before the latter's execution in 93 is clear evidence of
the tenuous nature of their acquaintance. To make an outright statement of *amicitia* with Helvidius (II) would surely have stretched the
truth beyond the bounds of exaggeration into falsification, as many
of Pliny's readers would have known the extent of his association
with the Helvidii before his condemnation. Pliny's explanation that
their relationship was limited because the "terror of the times" had
forced Helvidius (II) into retirement, preventing him from form-
ing a deep relationship, feels more like an explanation for Pliny's
superficial friendship than a true characterization of Helvidius (II).
It is particularly difficult to reconcile Pliny's description of Helvidius
(II)'s withdrawn existence with evidence of his consulship during
Domitian's reign and the production of the farce directed at the
emperor that provoked his demise.[45] There was no more prominent office than that of consul, and we must assume that Helvidius
(II) was politically active enough to receive such an honor, which
generally required significant service in other offices before it was
granted. Furthermore, he would hardly have provoked the emper-
or's ire if he were living in retirement. The *secessus* of Helvidius (II)

---

[45] Sherwin-White (1966: 243) sees the granting of "higher office" as Domitian's
attempt to placate members of the opposition, but it is impossible to determine the
emperor's motivation. As suggested previously, it is equally plausible that the members of the so-called opposition were not particularly vocal until the later years of
Domitian's reign, that his tolerance for their views waned in those years, or that
their prosecution was provoked by some more tangible conspiracy whose details
were not conveyed by our sources.

is surely devised by Pliny not only to excuse the superficial nature of their friendship but also to make Helvidius (II), a man living a quiet life and hiding his excellence, even more the victim of cruel and unjust prosecution. There can be little doubt that Pliny's persistent affection for Helvidius (II), so vehemently expressed in his lament over the deaths of the Helvidiae in 4.21, was almost exclusively posthumous.

The limit that Pliny sets on his association with Helvidius (II) does not seem to extend to his simple and direct statement of friendship with Arria and Fannia: *mihi ... amicitia ... fuerat cum Arria et Fannia, altera Helvidi noverca, altera mater novercae* (3). Pliny is careful to delineate their association with Helvidius (II), for they have a vested interest in avenging the death of their stepson/grandson and the exile to which they themselves were subjected. As discussed previously, 3.16 and 7.19 make clear that Pliny had a close relationship with Fannia and that *amicitia* alone might have given him cause for the prosecution of Certus.

Having introduced Fannia and Arria to the narrative, and thereby having suggested that his motivations are personal, Pliny immediately adds that he was compelled to action not by *iura privata* but by *publicum fas, indignitas facti,* and *exempli ratio* (3). Pliny explains that it was not his desire to attack his personal enemies as everyone else had after Domitian's death. He wished to deal with Certus not through the hatred of Domitian's time shared by members of the senate but on a charge appropriate to Certus' actions. Although Pliny downplays his private reasons for speaking against Certus, the reader can hardly forget his *amicitia* with Helvidius (II) and the women of his family. Pliny would not mention his *iura privata* were they not key to his vindication of Helvidius (II). It is his personal association with the family, in fact, that makes him a credible avenger. The inclusion of the universal *publicum fas* and *exemplum* serves only to elevate Pliny's actions from vendetta to justice. Pliny says as much, as he concludes the justification for his actions and his delay in seeking redress for Helvidius (II), noting that he waited for the first outburst against Domitian's henchmen to abate and "anger to be reduced to justice," *cum ... languidior in dies ira ad iustitiam redisset* (4).

Although Pliny has taken pains to emphasize that his desire to bring charges against Certus is motivated by his own sense of justice, the women of Helvidius (II)'s family appear immediately again in his narrative. When he determined that the time was right, he tells his reader, Pliny sent for Anteia, the wife of Helvidius (II), asking her to relay his intentions to Fannia and Arria, who had returned from exile. They were to consider whether they wished to be a party to the action Pliny was planning against Certus, and they were to act accordingly. Pliny offered the women a share of his glory, saying in effect that he had been prepared to act alone but did not begrudge them their participation: *ego comite non egeo; sed non ita gloriae meae faverim, ut vobis societate eius invideam* (5). If, as Pliny stated in 7.19, he had been in a long-standing relationship with the women, acting as a solace to Arria and Fannia in their exile, the plan to avenge Helvidius (II) might well have been part of the consolation he offered to the women. Pliny's directive to Anteia suggests that Fannia and Arria were unaware of his intentions, but it is hard to believe that they were not complicit in the plan to attack Certus from its inception. It is to Pliny's advantage to build an image of himself as so closely tied to the male membership of the Stoic opposition that, of his own accord, he spearheaded the campaign against Helvidius (II)'s persecutor.[46] In reality, his case would have been greatly strengthened by the inclusion in the action of those parties who were directly affected by the events of 93, of whom only the women, Anteia, Arria (II), and Fannia, and the children of Helvidius (II) survived.

Central to *Epistulae* 9.13 is the presentation in dramatic detail of Pliny's defense of his intentions to speak against Certus in the senate and the many objections raised thereafter, especially those that concerned the personal danger Pliny risked in charging a man of influence (11). Pliny, the *ultor*, replied to the opposition that he was prepared to pay the penalty for an honest act while avenging a disgraceful one. Pliny reports that a number of senators spoke in support of Certus and then Avidius Quietus and Cornutus Tertullus against him.

The argument presented by Quietus centered on the right of the aggrieved parties, Arria and Fannia, to be heard (15). It is interesting that Anteia is not included among the injured, although she surely

---

[46] The women would, of course, need a male prosecutor in order to bring an accusation.

suffered harm by the execution of her husband; however, she was not among those exiled, and she had remarried after Helvidius (II)'s death. Nor is Helvidius (II)'s son (for whose future Pliny is so concerned in *Epistulae* 4.21) mentioned among those harmed. Perhaps he was too young to be involved, though someone surely could have spoken on his behalf. Tertullus, closely associated with the family through his guardianship of one of Helvidius (II)'s daughters, does speak. Pliny reports that he set a limit on his own animosity and sought to comply with the moderate desire of the women, who wanted only to remind the senate of Certus' bloody sycophancy and to seek if not his punishment then at least his censure (16). Both Quietus and Tertullus emphasize that they are acting on behalf of Fannia and Arria.

Pliny's speech does not survive, but elsewhere in the letters we are told that it was compared with one of Demosthenes' speeches (7.39.4). Pliny does report the overwhelming congratulations he received from his fellow senators for reviving the custom of referring to the senate matters of public importance despite the risk of incurring the enmity of fellow senators (21). Pliny would have his reader see him as an old-style republican in the Ciceronian tradition, notwithstanding the fact that no subsequent charges were brought against Certus; he was, however, removed from office and never assumed the consulship assigned to him presumably by Domitian.[47] Certus fell ill and died a few days after Pliny's speech was published in somewhat revised form. Pliny is unwilling to take credit for Certus' demise, though he does seem to relish reporting it (25).

If, as Pliny's account of the content of Tertullus' speech suggests, Arria and Fannia were satisfied with Certus' political fall, Pliny might have considered his account with them to be paid. That he did not and wished for Fannia, as she was dying, to live long enough for him to provide restitution is surely Pliny's rhetorical fiction rather than an indication of the women's dissatisfaction with his actions. His unresolved indebtedness required a continued connection with Fannia, his only contemporary link to Helvidius (II). Before Pliny recounts the circumstances surrounding his vindication of Helvidius

[47] Pliny takes credit for Certus' fall from favor and quotes the closing demand of his speech: *Reddat praemium sub optimo principe, quod a pessimo accepit* (9.13.23).

(II), he has already established his close association with Fannia
and, through her, with generations of Stoic opposition. Although he
seems to minimize the importance of *privata iura* in his decision to
act as the family's avenger, those bonds are critical to the justification
of his actions: the women must be included in the attack on Certus,
for they are the injured parties, not Pliny. But in his determination
to prosecute, Pliny has assumed the role of the offended, as he might
perhaps have assumed the persona of Helvidius (II) himself in the
lost speech given in his vindication. There can be no question that
his desire to be closely associated with Helvidius (II) is the greatest
source of his motivation in pursuing Certus, or that his *amicitia* with
Fannia is meant to highlight that connection. Helvidius (II) and
Pliny cannot have been close friends, as Pliny himself admits. Not
only is there no evidence beyond Pliny's earlier attestation of any significant personal relationship between himself and Helvidius (II),
but there is every indication that Pliny, like Tacitus, was present and
watching when the prosecutions and executions of 93 occurred.

Conclusion

In our times, Pliny's modification of his past might be called "spin" –
the twisting of the facts just enough to make them reflect well rather
than poorly on the actor. But spin generally requires some recitation of what actually happened, however perverted causation and
outcome become in the process. Pliny gives his reader no account
of his own actions in the events of 93 but chooses instead to rewrite
his role through a carefully constructed tapestry of friendships, with
anxieties about and obligations to members of the Stoic opposition
and with his subsequent ineffectual efforts some years later to avenge
men long dead.

   Why this event, we might ask. There can be no doubt that, of all the
attacks made on the senate by tyrant emperors, authors of Pliny's time
viewed the executions of 93 as the most egregiously cruel, undoubtedly because Senecio, Rusticus, and Helvetius (II) are attacked for
what they write, or so our sources for the trials would have us believe.
The long history of anti-imperialist activities among the Helvidii
belies the nonthreatening character of family members presented by
Tacitus and Pliny. The truth is more likely that the elimination of any

Stoic political threat to the emperor makes the trials of 93 an ideal forum for the defense of writing as a valued elite activity. The Stoics become almost apolitical in their opposition, victims who represent the vulnerability of all men of great nobility and virtue. For Tacitus, who acknowledges that writing under the emperors has become a weak substitute for the political action of republican men of rank, the prosecution of authors, while potentially threatening to him, serves to ennoble his work.

Pliny's motivation for focusing on the Stoics is more complex but is surely centered on his speech in vindication of Helvidius (II), attacking Publicius Certus in a Demosthenic tour de force. While he often describes his courtroom activities and the acclaim that his speeches receive, Pliny pointedly refers to this speech in three separate letters. Pliny's personal outrage is a crucial element in the success of the speech, and so he must shape his relationships with the Helvidii in such a way that the reader sees his efforts on their behalf not only as justified but also as triumphant, rather than as a feeble attempt to undo his own inaction four years previously. Pliny's fury at his opponent has been building throughout the letters from his first one (1.5) about the prosecutions and his desire to punish Regulus. His disgust at Regulus increases thereafter with his treatment of Regulus the *captator* (2.20 – see Chapter 3) and Regulus the overwrought bereaved (4.7). It is surely no coincidence that in both 2.20 and 4.7 Pliny quotes Demosthenes' *De Corona*, when he criticizes Regulus for his ill-gotten gains (2.20.12) and histrionic oratory (4.7.7).

Pliny aims to be seen as acting from his own deep convictions, on behalf of close friends and in self-defense. Nowhere else in the sources that remain for us is Pliny even remotely connected with the Stoic opposition, not even as a proponent of Stoic philosophical tenets. It is left to Pliny to forge the bonds needed to glorify his own deeds. But this is no easy task, with only Mauricus surviving the trials and apparently opposed to taking actions against his brother's accuser. Whatever the nature of the friendship Pliny had with Mauricus, it did not extend to Pliny's appointment as the family's legal representative, and any independent action on Pliny's part would surely have been harmful to Pliny's stature, particularly considering Mauricus' apparent standing with the emperors Nerva (4.22.3) and Trajan (1.5.15). What remain for Pliny's use are the women, both those freshly returned from exile and those for whom Pliny is of service in the years before the publication of the letters, through whom Pliny may establish his history with the family and seek the glory he so desires.

Pliny relies on his mention of Arrionilla in book 1 to establish his association with Arulenus Rusticus and to serve as his sole personal contact with the condemned man. Pliny expands upon that tenuous relationship in his correspondence with Mauricus concerning Rusticus' children, especially in *Epistulae* 1.14 regarding the betrothal of Iunia. Mauricus himself might have offered the Stoic connection that Pliny seeks, except for the unclear nature of his involvement with the opposition and the lack of any delineation of his political views in Pliny's letters. Mauricus, moreover, surely knew the true nature of Pliny's involvement, or lack thereof, before the death of Domitian. The fact that he had only been exiled suggests that Mauricus remained a marginal figure in the Stoic threat to Domitian. Apparently denied the means to punish Regulus, Pliny never returns to the subject of his prosecution, and no formal charges can have been made, as Pliny would surely have relished reporting – as he does elsewhere – the decline of Regulus' fortunes. Pliny must instead transfer his indignation to another *delator* and his victims – the family of Helvidius (II) – to continue shaping his relationship with the Stoics.

Pliny's account in 3.11 of the danger he courted in visiting Artemidorus allows him not only to cast himself as heroic but also to introduce the idea that he too was a victim, though only liminally, of Domitian's wrath. Following the naming of all of the real victims, Pliny introduces his reader to his friend Fannia and her famous grandmother in 3.16, expands upon his love for Helvidius in 4.21 through his assumption of the role of mourning surrogate father, and forges unbreakable bonds with Fannia as her admirer and champion in 7.19. In this series of three letters, Pliny prepares his reader for 9.13, in which he proudly recounts the fulfillment of the vengeance he sought in 1.5. Pliny's target is Publicius Certus, Helvidius' nemesis, and not Regulus, the attacker of Arulenus Rusticus, but his intent is the same. As injured party and friend of the Stoic opposition, Pliny obtains satisfaction for the women of Helvidius' family and for himself, however much it may seem like a hollow victory.

While 1.5 and 9.13 treat events that must have occurred within months of one another following the return of the exiles to Rome, by the final letter Pliny's relationship with the Stoics has been transformed from a rather marginal association in 1.5 to an intensely personal one in 9.13, through letters that substantially postdate the beginning and end of the sequence. The process of revising the past is fraught with difficulties but eased considerably by the presence of Fannia, a strong, forthright woman from a family whose history had been greatly ennobled by its strong political and personal commitments. With Fannia, Pliny may legitimately maintain *amicitia*, without seeming to take advantage of her vulnerability as a widow. She is the stronger member of the friendship; he has a lasting debt to her. Through his interaction with Fannia, who is the embodiment of her father and husband, Pliny is able to reach back to the men, to what he wishes us to believe was a close personal relationship with Helvidius (II) and all of the opposition, and to affiliate himself intimately with the men whose execution he apparently had had neither the courage nor the means to oppose.

But in truth, with treatment of the Stoic opposition in his letters, Pliny does succeed in blackening the reputation of Domitian and his *delatores*, in portraying the prosecuted as loyal Romans of high moral character, and in securing lasting fame for Rusticus and Helvidius (II) and for himself. How many of those reading the nine-book collection published almost twenty years after the executions would have questioned Pliny's claim of quiet, behind-the-scenes support of the opposition? As Pliny reminded them all: a man's greater deeds are often less well known.

2

Pliny

Model Protégé

Quantum ille famae meae domi in publico,
quantum etiam apud principem adstruxit.

Pliny, *Epistulae* 4.17.7

The more he built up my reputation at home and in public, the more
he also built it up with the emperor.

While he labors to connect himself with the past and its righteous
opponents of bad emperors, Pliny's present and future political identity depends on his interaction with Trajan and those in close orbit
with the *princeps*. Pliny has no father after whom to pattern himself,
and his Uncle Pliny's career as an equestrian and military man was
not the sort of state service Pliny envisioned for himself. To ensure
access to the emperor and opportunities for advancement and recognition, Pliny needed to forge and maintain close ties with other
prominent and powerful men. If his letters are to serve his image
properly, they must illuminate for the reader Pliny's political journey
and must highlight the individuals who shaped and supported it.

Creating a political pedigree had been a requirement for advancement in the Roman world long before Pliny's time. Even the most
powerful Roman families during the republic relied for political support upon their close connections to other elite clans – obligations
forged through *beneficia* given and accepted in the name of *amicitia*.
Young men of promise from various families shadowed the powerful, both to learn political maneuvering and public speaking and to

secure their association with the ruling elite. Cicero makes clear in his *Pro Caelio* that he expects the praetors to assess the character of Caelius as superior, because as a young man he had been a follower of Cicero, his nature shaped by that of his mentor (9–10). The question of Caelius' guilt or innocence is subordinated to the importance of his rank within the elite network. As Cicero would surely know, breaking into the tightly woven fabric of Rome's elite was a formidable task, one rarely accomplished, and even when a "new man" succeeded, he still had to deal with his origins as an outsider.

In the principate when so many of the old aristocratic families were in sharp decline and young men of promise from equestrian ranks were regularly elevated to senatorial status and then to the consulship as new men, what mattered most in the political climb was to be noticed by the emperor. The ambitious needed to cultivate relationships with those men most closely associated with the *princeps* – those whose value had already been recognized by adlection to the senate, the granting of honors, or service on the emperor's council. New networks and alliances were created, based on the same system of reciprocal obligation that had always served Rome's elite.[1] Thus, Pliny's guardian Verginius Rufus supported Pliny's first candidacy for office and was present as he assumed his position;[2] he nominated Pliny for priesthoods repeatedly and chose his ward to speak to the senate on his behalf (2.1.8–9). Verginius was surely well known in elite Roman circles, but much more prominent in the letters is Pliny's association with Quintus Corellius Rufus, a somewhat obscure consular, who, like Verginius, was from the same area as Pliny, Transpadane Italy.

The importance of Corellius to Pliny's self-representation cannot be underestimated. Pliny leaves his reader in no doubt that Corellius was his most valued mentor, particularly in his support of Pliny's *cursus*. While Verginius voted for Pliny when he ran for office, Corellius not only voted for him but served as his adviser, guide, and companion in seeking offices, entering them, and serving in them (4.17.6). Pliny

---

[1] For consideration of the nature of *beneficia* given and received and the continuity of this elite system of exchange from republic to empire, see Griffin 2003.

[2] At what age Pliny became Verginius Rufus' ward is impossible to determine. Presumably, the appointment occurred after the death of either Pliny's father or his uncle. Verginius had made his name by defeating Vindex in 68 and thereafter twice refusing to be elevated to the principate (Pliny, *Ep.* 10, 9.19; Tacitus, *Hist.* 1.8.52, 2.49.51; Dio 63.23–25).

first mentions Corellius halfway through the first book (1.12), not long
after the first mention of the Stoic opposition, in a letter that showcases
Corellius' animosity for the villainous Domitian; Corellius is also present at Pliny's triumphant vindication of Helvidius (II) in the last book
(9.13). In between these two letters, Pliny carefully reinforces his relationship with Corellius, who, according to Pliny, survives Domitian just
long enough to be of service to the benevolent emperor Nerva.

Pliny could hardly have found a more suitable model for his own
political disposition – a man who despised the tyrant but served
the honorable ruler – but Corellius' contribution to Pliny's portrait
depends on both his characterization of his mentor and the careful
maintenance of his bonds to the man long after his death.

The Corellii

Quintus Corellius Rufus appears in seven of Pliny's letters, and in
each of these Pliny expounds upon Corellius' virtues and his own
reliance on the older man's advice and approval. Corellius is most certainly dead before the publication of any of the letters, as Pliny makes
clear in *Epistulae* 1.12. Furthermore, none of the letters that concern
him can be assigned a firm date earlier than the brief reign of Nerva,
during which Corellius met his end. Thus, Pliny's portrayal of his
affiliation with Corellius depends upon reminiscences of his mentor
and is furthered by his continued contact with surviving family members, Corellius' daughter, Corellia Hispulla, and his sister, Corellia.
Hispulla, the wife of Corellius, also appears in the first of the letters
concerning Corellius, but Pliny offers no evidence of an ongoing relationship between himself and Hispulla after her husband's demise.
The letters mentioning Corellius and these women are as follows:

Letter	Women
1.12	Corellius
	(Hispulla)* (wife)
	(Corellia Hispulla) (daughter)
	(Corellia) (sister)
3.3	Corellius
	Corellia Hispulla (daughter) – *recipient*
4.17	Corellius
	Corellia Hispulla (daughter)

Letter	Women
5.1	Corellius
7.11	Corellius
	Corellia (sister)
7.14**	Corellia (sister) – *recipient*
7.31	Corellius
9.13	Corellius

* Names in parentheses indicate that the woman is identifiable though unnamed by Pliny.
** Corellius is not mentioned in 7.14, but the letter is directly tied to 7.11 in which he is prominent.

Pliny's emotional lament for the loss of his mentor and his depiction of Corellius' character, particularly his fortitude in the endurance of lifelong illness, pervade 1.12.[3] The letter is the first of a series of letters that characterize and, in some cases, mourn the passing of those whom Pliny sets forth as models, both male and female, of proper conduct.[4] Pliny's political dependence on Corellius' advice and his assessment of the older man's *auctoritas* are apparent in *Epistulae* 5.1, in which Pliny consults with Corellius and Frontinus regarding a contested legacy Pliny has received. Pliny further defines his accustomed reliance on Corellius in 9.13 when he notes that before speaking out in defense of Helvidius Priscus and against Publicius Certus in the senate, he pointedly *avoided* consulting Corellius lest Corellius forbid him to proceed, even though Pliny always brought matters of concern to his mentor (6). In that same letter, Pliny describes Corellius as

[3] While Hoffer suggests that Pliny's expression of extreme loss may serve to mask any benefit that he enjoyed, politically or financially, from Corellius' death (146–147), such a conclusion seems to me unnecessarily harsh, because Pliny would expect to be acknowledged, perhaps quite generously, in his mentor's will. I believe Pliny's effusiveness is in keeping with other "obituary" letters in which he wants to reinforce his emotional identification with the deceased. Hoffer does outline an interesting argument that Pliny presents the course of his mentor's illness as parallel to the health of the state under both good and bad emperors (140–145). While there is no question that 1.12 is intended to juxtapose the deaths of Domitian and Corellius, more important to my reading of the letter is Pliny's determined and carefully drawn identification with his virtuous and defiant mentor.
[4] Foremost among these are L. Verginius Rufus (cos. 63, 69, and 97) in *Ep.* 2.1 and 9.19, Vestricius Spurinna (cos. 98) in *Ep.* 3.1, Arria the Elder in *Ep.* 3.16, Sextus Iulius Frontinus (cos. 73, 98, and 100) in *Ep.* 4.8, Minicia Marcella in *Ep.* 5.16, and Clodia Fannia in 7.19.

possessing "the greatest foresight and wisdom of our time," *providen-tissimum aetatis nostrae sapientissimumque cognovi* (6). Pliny's reverence for Corellius is especially prominent in his letters to and regarding Corellius' sister and daughter and nowhere more apparent than in *Epistulae* 4.17, where Pliny says that no one of his time was more influential (*gravior*), purer in character (*sanctior*), or more insightful (*subtilior*) than Corellius (4). Pliny's letters and two inscriptions are the only evidence for Corellius' career (*ILS* 1995; *CIL* xiv 4276.2), and, while Pliny makes his adulation manifest, it is considerably less clear whether his contemporaries shared his admiration for Corellius.

Q. Corellius Rufus was consul suffectus as a new man in 78 and served as legate of Upper Germany in 82. Although Sherwin-White (1966: 112) describes him as one of the officials "discarded" thereafter by Domitian, his disposal cannot be so easily deduced. Pliny calls him and Sextus Iulius Frontinus the two most admired citizens the empire had in the last years of Domitian's reign (5.1.5). Such a description hardly implies anonymity.[5] Although no further formal service is attested, Corellius was still of sufficient prominence at the death of Domitian to be appointed by Nerva to the land commission (4.17 and 7.31). While it is certainly to Pliny's advantage to extol the virtues of a man with whom he was so closely associated, it may be safely assumed that Corellius was well regarded. Nerva's recognition of Corellius was undoubtedly prompted by the latter's ability and by his reputation among his fellow senators, who had, after all, chosen Nerva as emperor.

Long after Corellius' death, Pliny maintains his connection to the family through his correspondence with two of its women. They appear in four letters, two concerning Corellius' daughter, Corellia Hispulla, and two regarding his sister Corellia. In *Epistulae* 3.3, addressed to Corellia Hispulla, Pliny recommends a tutor for her son. She appears again in 4.17 as Pliny discusses the reasons for his willingness to serve as her advocate. Pliny also continued to associate with Corellia after her brother's death. In *Epistulae* 7.11 Pliny discusses the sale of land to Corellia, who is also the recipient of 7.14 on the same topic. Pliny's closeness to these women is

---

[5] C. P. Jones (1968: 117) was quick to call attention to Sherwin-White's unwarranted assumption by pointing to Corellius' service as a consular legate. Pliny's pairing of Corellius with Iulius Frontinus, who reached the rare height of a third consulship, certainly speaks to Corellius' continuing political stature.

underscored by their unique position as his only female addressees beyond those in his immediate family, that is, his *adfinis* Calvina, his mother-in-law, his wife, and her aunt.

In recent years, prosopographical research on Corellia Hispulla has centered on the identity of her husband. Because Corellius is a rare *nomen*, L. Neratius Corellius Pansa is thought by many scholars to have been the son of Corellia Hispulla and either L. Neratius Priscus or his brother, L. Neratius Marcellus.[6] Pliny never names her husband, but in *Epistulae* 3.3 he remarks that her son has, on his father's side, an admired and respected (*clarus spectatusque*) grandfather in addition to a father and uncle who are *inlustri laude* (1). Both L. Neratius Marcellus and L. Neratius Priscus were well known, as the former held the suffect consulship in both 95 and 129, and the latter, consul suffectus in 97, was a much celebrated jurisconsult. The brothers may have been sons of L. Neratius Priscus, suffect consul in 87, although the late date of his consulship makes this identification somewhat suspect. Further confusion is added by yet another L. Neratius Priscus who appears as consul late in Trajan's reign or early in that of Hadrian. Syme (1957a: 491–493), picking up on the hypothesis first presented by Edmund Groag, proposed that Corellia Hispulla's father-in-law was not L. Neratius but M. Hirrius Fronto Neratius Pansa, who adopted L. Neratius Marcellus, her husband.

Werner Eck (1983) and Mireille Cébeillac (1982: 830) offer an alternative genealogy, suggesting that Corellius Pansa (Corellia Hispulla's son) emerged from a parallel branch of the *gens*. They propose that M. Hirrius Fronto Neratius Pansa was the father of L. Neratius Priscus and a daughter called Neratia Pansina. In their scheme, Corellius Pansa is the grandson of Neratia Pansina, who had married into a line of Corellii less distinguished than that of Corellius Rufus, one in which no one had yet achieved the rank of consul.[7] The strongest

---

[6] Those supporting this view include A. Balland, A. R. Birley, E. Champlin, J. Devreker, L. Vidman and M.-T. Raepsaet-Charlier.

[7] Torelli (1982a: 180–181) expands upon this theory, having Marcellus born of L. Neratius Priscus and adopted by M. Hirrius Fronto Neratius Pansa. He proposes that Pansa's line was a plebeian line, parallel to the line produced by L. Neratius L. f. Priscus, consul suffectus of 87, whose son was the noted jurist L. Neratius Priscus, consul suffectus of 97. In his construction, Hirrius' daughter, Neratia Pansina, married L. Varius Ambibulus, and their daughter, Varia Pansina, married L. Corellius Celer Fisius Rufinus, who came from a branch of the Corellii parallel to that of our

argument against this stemma is that Corellius Pansa became consul ordinarius in 122, an honor given almost exclusively to men from highly distinguished families and only rarely to *novi homines* unless they had offered exceptional service to the emperor.[8]

Raepsaet-Charlier (1987: 268 Corellia Hispulla) objects to Syme's choice of Neratius Marcellus as the husband of Corellia Hispulla on the basis of epigraphical evidence of his marriage to Domitia Vettilla. A quick divorce from Corellia would have enabled a second marriage, but it is difficult to imagine that Neratius Marcellus would have left his son in Corellia's care. Nor is there any reason to believe from Pliny's letter regarding his recommendation of Iulius Genitor as a tutor for Corellia's son that her husband was absent. Pliny is either merely responding to a request from the daughter of his friend and patron or, more likely, offering a recommendation that she did not solicit. The entry for Corellius Pansa in *Der Neue Pauly* (*NP* III, Corellius 1) merely makes him the son of Corellia Hispulla and *one* of the Neratii from Saepinum, either Marcellus or Priscus, the jurist. Either descent would fit the description that Pliny provides, and, because of the evidence regarding Marcellus' marriage to Domitia Vettilla, the jurist Neratius Priscus is more likely the husband of Corellia Hispulla.[9]

Additional evidence from Pliny may support the identification of Corellia Hispulla's husband as the famous jurisconsult. Pliny addresses five letters to someone named Priscus: 2.13, 3.21, 6.8, 7.8, and 7.19. While the identity of the recipient(s) of these letters remains in dispute, it has been argued that Neratius Priscus is the addressee of 2.13, 7.8, and 7.19.[10] Such an identification would reinforce Pliny's

---

Q. Corellius Rufus. Torelli cites Camodeca (*AE* 1976, 195) and Gaggiotti (1982b: 41) in support of this view, and Alföldy (1982: 356) concurs. Their motivation for this hypothesis is an understandable desire to identify the Neratius Corellius of the Ligures Baebiani with both the Neratiolus attested in an inscription from Xanthos and Corellius Pansa, consul of 122, but their conclusion seems forced and requires the assumption of two unsubstantiated parallel lines. Furthermore, their argument is unnecessarily complex, when a simpler explanation is at hand.

[8] See especially Iulius Frontinus and Attius Suburanus in Chapter 3.

[9] A stemma illustrating this thesis may be found in Appendix A, Figure 4.

[10] Radice 1969: vol. II, 574 ; Sherwin-White 1966: 756. A. Birley (2000: 74) has argued for Neratius Priscus as the recipient of 2.13, 6.8, and 7.8. All such conjectures are based on the likelihood of its recipient's interest or involvement in each letter's content – a difficult basis to secure.

continued relationship with Corellia Hispulla as beneficial to him, both for the maintenance of a long-standing political connection with its attendant obligations and for the ongoing cultivation of a contemporary one with her highly respected husband.

In 7.11, Pliny is quite forthright about his obligations to the husband and son of Corellius' sister. Corellia was married to Minicius Iustus, an early supporter of Vespasian. Of equestrian status, he had served as camp prefect for Galba in the conflicts of 69, but because he was considered too strict a commander for civil conflict, he was relieved of duty and sent to Vespasian (Tacitus, *Hist.* 3.7). The Minicii were a leading family in Laus Pompeia, the town from which Pliny's Corellii are thought to have originated. As Syme (1958: 66 n. 4) and Alföldy (1982: 355) point out, the *nomen* Corellius is exceedingly rare, appearing in northern Italy only at Ateste and Laus Pompeia. The connection between the families stems quite naturally from their proximity, and both families rise to consular status under Flavian rule. Both Stein and Syme believe that Minicius Iustus' name appears on the *Testamentum Dasumii*,[11] a document that is significant in defining a number of ties among prominent families of the late first and early second centuries.

The son of Corellia and Minicius Iustus, unidentified by Pliny, was probably L. Minicius Rufus, consul ordinarius of 88. According to the custom of his day, Minicius Rufus might well have taken his cognomen from his mother's side of the family, because her brother was prominent politically under the Flavians and of consular rank. While Pliny's connection to Corellius was certainly critical to his political development, a further bond with a man serving in the elevated role of consul ordinarius would have been a boon to Pliny as he was just beginning his *cursus* as quaestor and a brand new senator at this time.[12] Pliny speaks of Corellia's son in the past tense (he is presumably deceased) as someone with whom he had had the greatest bonds, *maxima iura* (7.11.4) – bonds so strong that, a few years after his term as consul, Minicius Rufus had presided over Pliny's games during the latter's term as praetor. If his identification as Minicius

---

[11] *CIL* vi 10229: ... *inicius Iustus*; Syme 1958: 177n.; Stein, *RE* XV, Minicius 16.
[12] Like most of the milestones in Pliny's career, the date of his service as quaestor is in dispute but undoubtedly falls between 86 and 89.

Rufus is accurate, Pliny's obligations through him to his mother are both personal and political.

The final member of Corellius Rufus' family to be considered is his wife, Hispulla. Little is known of her beyond the few words of mention she receives in *Epistulae* 1.12, as she sends for Pliny in the hope that he can dissuade Corellius from starving himself to death. Her name, however, offers the possibility of an important link between the Corellii and the Calpurnii, the family of Pliny's wife, Calpurnia, whose aunt is Calpurnia Hispulla. Like the name Corellius, Hispo and Hispulla are rare cognomina, and thus it is highly probable that Pliny is related to the Corellii through his marriage to Calpurnia.[13] The conclusion that the two families are connected by marriage is critical in any evaluation of Pliny's letters addressed to women, because the inclusion of Corellia and Corellia Hispulla within Pliny's extended family circle changes the nature of his correspondence with women. If we assume that Pliny's marriage to Calpurnia predates the publication of any of his letters and that the wives of Pliny and Corellius are kinswomen, then all of the female recipients of Pliny's correspondence had some family connection to him.

The Letters

Just as he gradually builds his image as the Stoics' avenger throughout the nine-book collection, Pliny will reveal the depth of his association with Corellius in a carefully arranged series of letters that appear in six books, beginning with Pliny lamenting his death and culminating with an act that marks Pliny as a mature politician, independent of Corellius for perhaps the first time. The sequence offers the reader both the impression of an evolving relationship between mentor and protégé and an intriguing temporal circularity or even reversal, as Corellius is as alive at his last appearance in the letters as he is dead in his first.

The importance of the women of the family is not immediately apparent in Pliny's initial introduction to the Corellii. In fact, they

---

[13] Alföldy (1982: 355) does acknowledge this possibility but suggests an alternative, that she may be related to the family of Terentius Hispo and Terentia Hispulla from Mediolanum.

seem incidental to Pliny's narrative, but it is here that the reader begins to understand the depth of Pliny's association with Corellius, which he will perpetuate through his affiliation with the Corelliae.

LETTER 1.12: HISPULLA, CORELLIA HISPULLA, CORELLIA. Critical to any understanding of the contribution that Corellius makes to Pliny's political image is the looming presence of Domitian in this first letter. In 1.12, the hatred that Pliny expressed for the despot in 1.5 is made personal through Pliny's identification with Corellius. The letter serves several other purposes: it is a character sketch of Corellius, an expression of Pliny's affection for him and grief at his demise, and a clear indication of Pliny's status within Corellius' household.

Pliny opens the letter with a statement of his loss, *iacturam gravissimam feci, si iactura dicenda est tanti viri amissio,* whereby he makes clear the severity and nature of his bereavement. His choice of *iactura* to describe the death of Corellius is particularly startling. The term occurs elsewhere in Pliny's letters just once, and there the word refers to a monetary loss.[14] There is no reason to believe that Pliny alludes to any financial matter in 1.12, but *iactura* has other, more common connotations. It may be used to indicate a deprivation, a sacrificial loss made for the preservation of something or someone else, or the loss of men in battle.[15] The word's most immediate effect here is to prepare the reader for the account of Corellius' demise that follows: death by deprivation – starvation. In addition, with its unique use in this letter, Pliny marks the loss of Corellius as an intense wound, different from other losses he would incur. Finally, Pliny's choice of *iactura* suggests that the death of Corellius is connected in some way to the health of the state, his suicide acting as recompense, a release from suffering that is finally allowed to him – after many years of pain – as a reward for outliving the tyrant Domitian.

As Stanley Hoffer (1999: 142) points out, Pliny's account of Corellius' determination to survive Domitian if only by a day (1.12.8) is surely contrived by Pliny, because Corellius was alive in 97 and well enough to serve Nerva. However, with the juxtaposition of the

---

[14] In 6.8, Pliny expresses his concern that Atilius Crescens would suffer severe financial difficulties were the sum of money that he had loaned to the now deceased Valerius Varus not returned to him in full.

[15] Caesar, *BG* 7.26.2; Livy, 10.45.10, 30.25.8, 40.40.12.

deaths of Domitian and Corellius, Pliny suggests bold opposition to the tyrant that he shares by association with Corellius. There is, in fact, no evidence that Corellius was openly defiant toward the *princeps* or that he suffered in any way during Domitian's final years, yet Pliny presents Corellius' determination to endure his suffering for as long as Domitian lived as a rebellious act, one that Pliny approves merely by having heard Corellius' plan and then recounting it.[16]

In a narrative seemingly focused strictly on the circumstances of Corellius' illness and death, Pliny subtly sets out the dimensions of his own importance within his friend's household. The key scene precedes Corellius' end by at least a few months, probably as much as a year, as Domitian still lives. Corellius has taken ill and is at his house outside of Rome. While Pliny does not say whether he was summoned by Hispulla on this occasion as he was later, it is safe to assume that he was specifically notified concerning Corellius' condition. Pliny's arrival provokes the withdrawal of everyone from the bedroom, including the slaves, because of his status as a highly trusted friend (7). Even Hispulla leaves, deferring to Pliny's relationship with her husband. Perhaps Corellius did not share political matters with his wife, although elsewhere in the letters faithful wives like Hispulla, including Arria (I), Fannia, and Pliny's own wife, Calpurnia, have detailed knowledge of their husbands' political activities (*Ep.* 3.16, 7.19, and 4.19) – and it is likely that Hispulla was well aware of her husband's intentions. Rather, Pliny here emphasizes his standing in the household (7) and signals the sensitive nature of Corellius' ensuing statement: "*cur*" inquit "*me putas hos tantos dolores tam diu sustinere? ut scilicet isti latroni vel uno die supersim*" (8) – just the sort of pronouncement that would surely have brought Domitian's condemnation had it been reported to him.

Relieved of his oath by the emperor's murder, Corellius feels free to die. His suicide is a classic Stoic death, one that is made entirely by choice rather than obligation, as Pliny has already made clear earlier in the letter when he characterized Corellius' decision to die as a reasoned rather than forced one (3).[17] However

---

[16] The very same idea is expressed by Tacitus in his treatment of Agricola's death as a release from Domitian's control (45).

[17] The death of Cato epitomizes the idea of a Stoic death as chosen rather than compelled. His suicide was assumed as a model not only by adherents of Stoicism but also by many of senatorial rank in the first century C.E.

much Pliny might understand intellectually Corellius' determination, he implies that he would certainly have done his best to prevent his friend's death if he had had the opportunity. It *is* Pliny whom Hispulla calls when she and Corellia Hispulla cannot dissuade Corellius from starving himself. Her desperate plea in these final moments seems contrived by Pliny, because death by starvation is hardly a precipitous event, but it may be that Corellius was in northern Italy and Pliny in Rome, a journey of several days, and Corellius had already refused to eat for four days when she sent for help (9). Hispulla's faith in Pliny's singular influence is evident in her urgent summons that he alone could change Corellius' intention to die (9). When Pliny had nearly reached them, he received a second message from Hispulla, warning him of Corellius' steely resolve (10), a message that seems sent more out of concern for Pliny than Corellius, a way to prepare Pliny for what he would find when he arrived. While the reader never hears of Hispulla again, her confidence in his presence and request for his assistance solidify Pliny's association with all of the Corellii.

Pliny does not offer a deathbed scene in this letter, and the reader is left to wonder whether Pliny was actually present when Corellius died. Instead, the letter continues with Pliny's attempts to console himself and his repeated declarations of sorrow at the loss of this great influence on his life, *doleo, doleo autem meo nomine* (12).[18] Pliny calls him "teacher, guide, and witness" – *vitae meae testem rectorem magistrum* – and expresses his profound anxiety that his life will be less safe without Corellius' oversight (12).

The reader would hear little more of Corellius after 1.12 were it not for the women of the family. Corellia Hispulla and her aunt Corellia make only brief appearances in 1.12, mentioned not by name but only according to their roles as child and sister in Pliny's lament. His relationship with these women, Pliny says, is one of the many reasons for Corellius to continue living (3), but it is insufficient. While they

---

[18] Pliny's grief is expressed with the word *doleo* and *dolor*; forms of these words are used in only a few of his obituary letters. Those receiving his sorrow include the poet Martial (3.21), the Helvidiae (4.21) and Fannia (7.19) (see Chapter 1), Iulius Avitus (6.6), Verginius Rufus (6.10), the son of Vestricius Spurinna (3.10), and Iunius Avitus (8.23). In addition, his wife's miscarriage (8.10) and his concern for the illness of some of his slaves receive his *dolor* (8.16 and 8.19).

could not prevent Corellius' death, their appearance in 1.12 and presence in later letters are crucial to Pliny's continued characterization of his mentor. Because even the earliest letters date to late 96 or early 97, the year in which Corellius' death seems to have occurred,[19] no opportunity existed for Pliny to publish letters in which he is writing directly to his mentor or even to report contemporary encounters with Corellius. Pliny can make reference to their relationship only in his accounts of past events, as he does in 5.1, 7.31, and 9.13, where Corellius appears only peripherally.

The Corelliae, however, offer an ideal channel through which Pliny may illuminate his Corellian connections. Because his association with the women is one compelled by a personal relationship rather than official obligation, he can focus quite naturally on his ties to Corellius as the motivating force for his continued involvement in the women's concerns, thereby avoiding the blatant artificiality that any extensive characterization of his mentor and their relationship might have if inserted into correspondence addressed to or focused on anyone outside of the family.

LETTER 3.3: CORELLIA HISPULLA. Pliny's ongoing association with the family after the death of Corellius is first evident in *Epistulae* 3.3 in which Pliny recommends Iulius Genitor as tutor for the son of Corellia Hispulla. Although Corellius' daughter is the letter's recipient, Pliny offers no indication, as he did in his letters to Mauricus regarding the children of Rusticus, that he is responding to her request for his opinion. Indeed, Pliny's recommendation seems unsolicited and imposed upon Corellia Hispulla. The supposed aim of the letter is not apparent until nearly halfway through, when Pliny finally states the need to find a teacher of Latin rhetoric for Corellia Hispulla's son and subsequently offers his choice of Genitor, praising the candidate's qualities.

Rather than opening with a statement of his topic, Pliny begins with an explanation of his interest in the future of Corellius' grandson and carefully lays out the need for the boy to grow up to resemble his well-respected forebears and then sets forth the means by which that goal may be attained.

---

[19] Sherwin-White (1966: 111) comments that Corellius died in 97 or 98, not much later and probably earlier than Nerva died.

1) *Cum patrem tuum gravissimum et sanctissimum virum suspexerim magis an amaverim dubitem, teque et in memoriam eius et in honorem tuum unice diligam, cupiam necesse est atque etiam quantum in me fuerit enitar, ut filius tuus avo similis exsistat; equidem malo materno, quamquam illi paternus etiam clarus spectatusque contigerit, pater quoque et patruus illustri laude conspicui.*

Because I hesitate as to whether I admired or loved your father, a most venerable and upright man, more, and I treasure you, both in his memory and out of respect for you, it is imperative that I desire and even strive as much as it is in me that your son be like his grandfather; truly I prefer that he resemble his maternal grandfather, although he has a paternal grandfather who is both renowned and esteemed and a father and uncle who are remarkable for their distinguished praise.

That Pliny's motivation for writing is his devotion to the memory of Corellius Rufus is immediately manifest in the opening words of the letter – *cum patrem tuum.* Pliny expresses his devotion to Corellia Hispulla and her father with a series of first-person subjunctive verbs – *suspexerim, amaverim, dubitem, diligam, cupiam, enitar* – whose collective effect serves to emphasize Pliny's personal stake in the boy's future and his sense of duty to the family of his mentor. He *should* (*necesse est*) see to it that Corellia Hispulla's son become like his grandfather, and so (as the reader will later find out) he has chosen to take on the responsibility for finding a tutor. Pliny's stated affection focuses on his great admiration and love for Corellia's father, whom he praises with the superlatives *gravissimum* and *sanctissimum.* Pliny then expresses his love for his addressee, *te… diligam,* but he limits his connection with Corellia Hispulla before he states it by qualifying his love for her as motivated by his remembrance of her father, *in memoriam eius* (1). Pliny does add that his fondness for Corellia is also based on his respect for her, *in honorem tuum,* but following his effusive declaration of love for her father, Pliny's apparent connection to Corellia Hispulla as indicated in these few words is almost an afterthought. It is his past association with Corellius that compels Pliny not only to desire that Corellia's son be like his grandfather but to strive to bring about that resemblance.

Pliny adds that the boy's paternal grandfather is *clarus spectatusque,* as well, and that his father and uncle are also praiseworthy (1). As discussed previously, Corellia's husband and in-laws were men of great importance, whose position might be beneficial to Pliny's own and with whom Pliny would surely have wished to cultivate a close

82   *Pliny: Model Protégé*

alliance. Pliny's stated preference for his own mentor as model for Corellia's son illustrates well the deference expected of a dutiful protégé, but Pliny's partiality, were it stated in an unqualified manner and excluding the boy's paternal connections, might well have been insulting or at least dismissive of the boy's living male relatives. Pliny takes care, therefore, not only to pay homage to Corellius by stating his understandable bias but also to praise Corellia's husband and in-laws by including them with Corellius as models for shaping the boy's character. Pliny wraps up his recitation of the young man's noble ancestry neatly by declaring his belief that Corellia's son will grow up to be like all of them, *quibus omnibus ita demum similis adolescet,* if he is steeped in *honestae artes* (2).

Having explained his motivation, Pliny then expounds upon the means by which Corellia Hispulla's son will be shaped to resemble his models. First, Pliny acknowledges that her son has been too young to leave her side until now. With a series of passive periphrastics, Pliny then stresses strongly the need for Corellius' grandson to move beyond home schooling (3). Thus, it is imperative to find a tutor, *circumspiciendus rhetor,* whose school is known for *severitas, pudor,* and *castitas* (3). Pliny concludes his justification for the ensuing recommendation of Iulius Genitor by emphasizing that "not only a teacher but a guardian and mentor for the boy must be sought," *non praeceptor modo sed custos etiam rectorque quaerendus est* (4). Pliny's use of three passive periphrastics in this section of the letter is quite exceptional. While the construction is not uncommon in the letters, Pliny rarely uses it to impose actions upon his addressees.[20] Rather, Pliny is frequently inclined to employ periphrastics in senatorial or court-room debates, in self-directives, and in aphoristic statements, all of which involve strong declarations of opinion, resolution, or truth.[21] In 3.3, with these powerful directives, Pliny lays out the paramount

[20] I have found that only 11, including the 3 cited here, of more than 180 uses of the passive periphrastic appear as directives to Pliny's recipients. Of the remaining 8, 7 either refer ultimately to Pliny or are expressions of Pliny's enthusiasm regarding some aspect of his addressee's future (1.10.2, 1.10.11, 2.4.1, 2.19.9, 3.6.5, 3.15.3, 8.13.2). Only one, advising Maximus as to how he should behave as a Roman official in Greece, has an imperative tone (8.24.9).

[21] The three categories, in formal debates, self-directives, and maxims, account for more than two-thirds of all passive periphrastic uses in the first nine books of Pliny's letters.

importance of finding a tutor and appears to have imposed the task on Corellia, as she must comply with Pliny's recommendation if her son is to reach the potential of his birthright.

In the final periphrastic clause, Pliny inserts himself into the process of raising Corellius' grandson properly. Before he asserts the need for a *custos ... rectorque*, Pliny praises the beauty and natural talent of *noster adulescens* (4). With his use of the first-person possessive, Pliny makes himself part of Corellia Hispulla's family, assuming a fraternal role, and Pliny's concern for "our boy" not only is as great as Corellius' would have been but is, in fact, prompted by Pliny's overwhelming love and admiration for his own mentor. More telling still is Pliny's use of the word *rector*, used elsewhere in the letters only to describe Corellius Rufus' relationship to Pliny and Pliny's role as mentor to Ummidius Quadratus and Fuscus Salinator.[22] Pliny is determined that the boy must receive the same guidance that Pliny had both enjoyed and provided, but Pliny does not offer himself for the position of *rector* for Corellia's son. Perhaps it is not a task to be undertaken by a family member, who might be hindered in severity by his affection for the boy. Yet it is Pliny's duty and desire – as he makes clear at the start of the letter – to do whatever he can to ensure the boy's resemblance to his grandfather by finding him a *rector* who will act as both Pliny and Corellius had in steering their protégés, offering advice and admonition, and serving as models to be emulated. Pliny's intention to play an active role in the boy's future is confirmed in the statement that follows his final directive: *quaerendus est. videor ergo demonstrare tibi posse Iulium Genitorem* (5). With his recommendation of Genitor and his abrupt shift from third-person periphrastics to the first-person verb, *videor*, the force of Pliny's directives shifts from Corellia to Pliny himself. Pliny has taken up the task that he had just outlined, that of seeing to the boy's future.

As Pliny offers praise for Genitor, he begins with his love of the tutor, *amatur a me* (5), and ends with *pro Genitore me sponsorem accipe* (6). By focusing on his personal relationship with Genitor and standing guarantor for his rectitude, Pliny takes full responsibility for the future of Corellia's son – a future that depends, as Pliny has just stated, upon the qualities of the tutor to whom the boy is assigned.

---

[22] Corellius as *rector*: *Ep*. 1.12.12 and 4.17.6; Pliny as *rector*: *Ep*. 6.11.2.

Given that the boy's politically prominent father and uncle can hardly be thought unable to attain a suitable candidate for the position, Pliny's action would seem presumptuous were it not for his intimate and ongoing relationship with the Corellii. As someone who has fashioned his life on his own *rector* just as a son would model himself on his father, Pliny, *in loco fratris*, binds himself not only to Corellia but also to the Neratii in sharing their commitment to the boy's welfare. Finally, when Pliny extols Genitor's commitment to ensure that the boy will live up to the standards of his forebears and the names he carries on, he links the tutor with himself and with Corellia: *nec minus saepe ab illo quam a te meque admonebitur, quibus imaginibus oneretur, quae nomina et quanta sustineat* (7). Explicit in *a te meque* is the bond that Pliny had suggested with *noster*; that is, Corellia and Pliny share the obligation to educate her son. Corellia's role is now relegated to that of *admonitor*, and the reader can certainly assume, even with her inclusion, that Pliny intends to serve as chief overseer.

Pliny tells us almost nothing about Corellia Hispulla in this letter. He remarks that the boy has been kept in Corellia's close company – *contubernium* (3), indicating that she has done her part in his upbringing by keeping him safely wrapped away from the rigors and temptations of the world outside her household. Her son has come safely to an age when her care is insufficient, and, Pliny says, he needs to proceed *extra limen* (3). Beyond her mere presence in his life, Corellia's future role in her son's upbringing is not apparent. In fact, Pliny makes clear that her task is over, although the existence of the letter certainly suggests that she will have a say in the choice of a tutor for him. Pliny brings to bear all of his powers of persuasion, with reminders of his long-standing and ongoing association with her family. The reader is meant to see Pliny as so closely tied to the Corellii that he can select a tutor and oversee the future of the family's one male heir. The preservation of Corellius in the person of his grandson and Pliny's active involvement in the boy's future will ensure the longevity of a relationship through which Pliny may maintain bonds not only with the Corellii but with the Neratii as well. Corellia certainly must have shared Pliny's concern for the boy's future, but she remains in the background of the letter, an obscure figure known only as daughter of Corellius and mother of his grandson. It is Pliny who will assure his mentor's legacy.

LETTER 4.17: CORELLIA HISPULLA. Corellia Hispulla herself, or at least her defense by Pliny, is the apparent subject of *Epistulae* 4.17, in which Pliny responds to a request from Clusinus Gallus (unknown outside of Pliny's letters) that he represent Corellia Hispulla in a case brought against her by the consul-elect, Gaius Caecilius. No details of the charges are offered in the letter. Indeed, Pliny says only that Gallus has called the action brought against Corellia "new" – perhaps, Pliny surmises, because the defendant is a woman, *(ut ais) nova lis fortasse ut feminae intenditur* (11). All the reader knows about Corellia is that she is *Corelli filia* (1). In fact, Pliny mentions her name in only the opening and closing sentences of the letter – referring to her elsewhere as *filia*; indeed, it is her role as daughter that is essential to Pliny, as it provides him with the opportunity to describe in detail his association and identification with Corellius and to characterize his ongoing obligations to the family.

Pliny begins by thanking Gallus for reminding him about the action against Corellia Hispulla and then complaining that Gallus had felt it necessary to ask him to defend her. Pliny echoes the letter's opening words, *et admones et rogas*, when he begins to explain why he is perturbed, *admoneri enim debeo ut sciam, rogari non debeo ut faciam, quod mihi non facere turpissimum est* (1);[23] that is, Pliny's reputation would be damaged were he not to undertake Corellia Hispulla's defense. Indeed, how could he hesitate, he remarks, for she is the daughter of Corellius (1)? Yet, following this rhetorical question, Pliny presents the very excuses he might have justifiably used for declining Gallus' request to defend her, including his *amicitia* with her accuser, C. Caecilius, his respect for the man's *dignitas*, or deference to his position as consul designate (3). But, Pliny concludes in this brief debate, all else is insignificant compared with the fact that she is Corellius' daughter – *sed mihi cogitanti adfuturum me Corelli filiae omnia ista frigida et inania videntur* (4). The reader is left in no doubt as to the depth of Pliny's commitment to Corellius' family. It supersedes, by far, a lesser *amicitia*, Pliny's admiration for Caecilius, and even his respect for the office of consul. These public obligations

---

[23] Zucker (1963: 41) calls this double-barreled opening a form of polite and cultured communication but here it seems an ideal setup by Pliny for the protest that follows.

become meaningless when they are weighed against Pliny's responsibility to the *filia Corelli.*

His brief deliberation and weighing of loyalties lead Pliny into a
reverie that actually constitutes the heart and true subject of 4.17,
praise of Corellius Rufus and, by reflection, of Pliny's own character.
Pliny conjures an image of Corellius in the present tense, *obversatur
oculis ille vir* (4), offering Corellius as a vivid model for comparison
with himself. Pliny calls Corellius *gravior, sanctior,* and *subtilior* than
any of his contemporaries (4). In the context of this praise Pliny
reports that as his relationship with Corellius deepened, he admired
him all the more, *magis admiratus sum postquam penitus inspexi* (4). To
confirm that he had ample opportunity to know Corellius' most private behavior, Pliny repeats *inspexi enim penitus* (5) and proceeds to
describe in greater detail the closeness he enjoyed with his mentor.
Pliny remarks that there was nothing that Corellius kept hidden from
him, treating him not as a younger man but as he would an equal (6).
Acknowledging that it is rather daring to put himself on a par with
the elder statesman, Pliny is careful to present their equivalence as
Corellius' judgment rather than his own.

The reader learns next that Corellius had acted as his *suffragator, tes-
tis, deductor, comes, consiliator,* and *rector* as Pliny fulfilled his *cursus hono-
rum* (6) – that is to say, that Corellius was Pliny's supporter and guide
in every way possible. Although Corellius was undoubtedly in failing
health and getting old while Pliny was running for and holding various
offices, Pliny reports that Corellius appeared young and vigorous – *quasi
iuvenis et validus conspiciebatur* (6). Pliny implies that Corellius was an
avid campaigner for him, giving him enthusiastic support. The image
of Corellius as energetic is surely meant to suggest that he remained
involved in political matters throughout his life and was committed
to grooming Pliny for the same long career he himself had enjoyed.
Indeed, his service to Nerva near the very end of his life supports an
image of him as politically vibrant even in his declining years.

Pliny expands upon Corellius' devotion to his future, reporting
that Corellius promoted Pliny's public and personal reputation even
in the presence of the emperor. Pliny builds his reader's anticipation
as he recalls remarks that Corellius had made to Nerva and other
men of rank. In a discussion about promising young men, several
people were praising Pliny, while Corellius kept that silence that Pliny

says gave his next statement *plurimum auctoritatis* (8). As Corellius had withheld his words, so Pliny delays his quotation of them. Finally, Pliny sets forth the words with which Corellius praised him to the emperor Nerva by equating Pliny's actions with his own: *"necesse est,"* inquit, *"parcius laudem Secundum, quia nihil nisi ex consilio meo facit"* (8).[24] Pliny accepts the tribute paid him and recasts it in more openly flattering terms: *nihil me facere non sapientissime, cum omnia ex consilio sapientissimi viri facerem* (9). Pliny's actions are *sapientissima* as advised by a man of equal wisdom. By his use of the same superlative to describe his actions and Corellius' character, Pliny becomes a perfect reflection of his most intimate friend and mentor.

In addition to the ties he has just delineated, Pliny goes on to quote Corellius' dying words of assurance to Corellia Hispulla ("as she was accustomed to recount them," *ipsa solet praedicare*): *multos quidem amicos tibi ut longiore vita paravi, praecipuos tamen Secundum et Cornutum* (9). With this statement, apparently often repeated by her, Corellius conferred upon his daughter his friendship with Pliny along with its attendant expectations of service and loyalty. Pliny is obliged to support Corellia both because of her father's words and because she regularly recounts them, keeping alive through their retelling Pliny's *amicitia* with her father.

Pliny seems acutely aware of his continuing duty to Corellius and declares that it is incumbent upon him not to fail Corellius' trust in him – *fiduciam providentissimi viri* (10) – and so he will appear on Corellia Hispulla's behalf, even if it means giving offense to the prosecution by doing so. In fact, Pliny makes clear that he expects to win not only praise but pardon for undertaking Corellia's defense, as he intends to speak at greater length at the trial than he is able to in the course of a letter concerning his obligations to the family of Corellius Rufus (11). It is reasonable to assume that Pliny often invoked his relationship with Corellius as a source of affirmation and support in court. The letter suggests that it was even more critical for him to do so in the context of his representation of Corellia so as to mitigate the offense he might cause to his opponent. Yet, in light of the depth and

---

[24] It is most likely that shortly before his death Nerva appointed Pliny as prefect of the Treasury of Saturn, an office that generally led to the position of consul. Corellius' service on the emperor's land commission gave him ready access to Nerva and undoubtedly contributed to Pliny's rise to the consulship.

longevity of Pliny's relationship with Corellius, it is hard to imagine that anyone would have questioned his decision to speak for Corellia. Pliny's weighing of arguments for and against representing her serves not so much to persuade the reader of the rightness of his decision as to demonstrate his sense of propriety and fidelity to the man responsible for molding his character. While Pliny has every expectation that his explanation will receive approval, his letter is a more permanent account of his reasoning and one that will reach a much wider audience than those present in court.

For all his praise of Corellius, Pliny offers no opinion or assessment of his daughter's character or any inkling of the outcome of the case against her. Rather the occasion allows Pliny to delineate his deep connections to the family and particularly to explain how his bonds to Corellius now obligate him to those left behind after his death.

LETTER 7.11: CORELLIA. That an *amicitia* with Pliny was bequeathed from Corellius to his daughter is clear from the examination of *Epistulae* 4.17; but in fact Corellius' sister, too, was the beneficiary of his long association with Pliny. The extent and nature of Pliny's obligations to Corellia may be seen in a close reading of *Epistulae* 7.11, in which Pliny explains to his wife's grandfather Calpurnius Fabatus why he has sold property to the sister of Corellius Rufus at less than its market value.

The letter opens with *miraris*, one of a group of words that Federico Gamberini (1983: 136–145) has noted as marking the letters he believes reflect Pliny's "real" correspondence.[25] It is, in fact, not unreasonable to assume that Calpurnius Fabatus, concerned with his granddaughter's financial security, might have questioned both Pliny's disposal at below market value of property that he had inherited and the authority of Pliny's freedman Hermes to agree to such a transaction on his master's behalf.[26] For the purpose of this evaluation,

---

[25] I believe that a "real" letter would not need a full recitation of Fabatus' objections to the sale of Pliny's land, although some scholars have argued that the insertion of specific information unnecessary in a letter that was actually sent indicates Pliny's efforts at clarification in his revision of the letters before publication.

[26] The identity of the testator from whom Pliny inherited the property is not indicated in the letter. It might have been a member of his wife's family, and thus Fabatus would be especially concerned. But a particular connection to Cornelia's grandfather need not be assumed, as the property Pliny sold to Corellia was located on Lake Como and thus near Fabatus, and in several other letters Pliny discusses with

however, whether Pliny ever received such an inquiry from Fabatus is irrelevant. Pliny uses *miraris* to set the scene for the defense of his actions that constitutes the focus of the letter. Pliny explains the purpose of his letter as his desire for Fabatus' approval and the pardon of his *coheredes* (2), and he offers, as introduction to his explanation for selling his portion of their inheritance separately from them, the fact that a greater duty commanded him (2). Pliny expounds upon his obligations (3–5), then returns to the *hereditas* and his *coheredes*, and concludes the letter with a *sententia* that encapsulates his viewpoint on the disposition of his material goods, juxtaposing the *utilitas* of his fellow heirs with his own commitment to *amicitia* (8).

Pliny himself stresses that this letter provides no ordinary accounting of the facts, but rather an *exemplum* (8), though one that his *coheredes* are not compelled to follow. Indeed, by peppering the letter throughout with first-person pronouns and possessive adjectives, Pliny makes clear that it was his decision alone to sell his portion of the inherited property contrary to customary practice. In this way, Pliny makes himself, rather than the property transaction or the action of his freedman, the focus of the letter. No other letter of any length has as many of these first-person possessive adjectives as 7.11, nor does any have a greater density of first-person pronouns.[27] With this powerful focus on his own thinking and actions, Pliny opens himself to an assessment of his sense of propriety, his ability to order his life, and his behavior in accordance with the expectations of his friends and family. In much the same way that 4.17 treated Pliny's deliberate weighing of his obligations to Corellius' daughter against those he had to the consul-designate Caecilius, in this letter Pliny contrasts his duty to his fellow heirs with his bonds to Corellius' sister.

At the heart of 7.11 (3–4) is Pliny's explanation of his many ties to Corellia:

Fabatus the disposition of property near his hometown. As to the appropriateness of Hermes acting on Pliny's behalf, Sherwin-White (1966: 416) notes that the authority of an agent to bind his master was only loosely defined at this time and had yet to be widely accepted.

[27] Statistical analysis of the distribution of these pronouns and adjectives (see Appendix C) shows a marked propensity for Pliny's use of them in the letters that focus on women as compared with those whose subject is men. The use of first-person forms is natural to epistolography but is entirely absent or nearly so in a surprising number of Pliny's letters.

(3) *Corelliam cum summa reverentia diligo, primum ut sororem Corelli Rufi, cuius mihi memoria sacrosancta est, deinde ut matri meae familiarissimam.* (4) *Sunt mihi et cum marito eius Minicio Iusto, optimo viro, vetera iura; fuerunt et cum filio maxima, adeo quidem ut praetore me ludis meis praesederit.*

I cherish Corellia with the greatest respect, first as the sister of Corellius Rufus, whose memory is sacred to me, then as a very dear friend of my mother. I have also long-standing ties with her husband Minicius Iustus; and I had the greatest of bonds with her son, indeed to such an extent that he presided over my games when I was praetor.

Pliny emphasizes his *summa reverentia* (3) for Corellia. Taken out of context, this line would suggest that Corellia and Pliny had a close friendship, but Pliny carefully expounds the reasons for his esteem in terms that limit it almost entirely to one based on her familial relationships rather than any personal interaction that Pliny may have had with her. Corellia's connections to her brother, her husband, her son, and Pliny's mother are what define her association with Pliny, and these are no ordinary bonds, as Pliny's use of such forceful adjectives as *sacrosancta* and *maxima* makes clear. It is important to note that Pliny uses the plural *iura* only seven times in the entire corpus of the letters: three instances are clear references to laws (5.9.6, 8.14.10, 8.24.4), one indicates the obligations Pliny has to the Baetici based on their hospitality to him (3.4.5), and the remaining three are references to personal ties that Pliny has with the family of Corellius (7.11.4, 7.11.8) and with members of the Stoic opposition (9.13.3). Though Pliny frequently chooses the singular *ius* or *iure* to refer to specific laws or rights, nowhere else does he connect himself to individuals through *iura*. These special and formidable bonds likely exceeded the obligations of *amicitia*. Therefore, when Corellia expressed a desire to purchase land on Lake Como and thereby drew on his many obligations to her, Pliny responded by offering her any of his properties (*quod vellet*) at her price (*quanti vellet*), except the lands that he had inherited from his mother and father. Those he could not surrender even to Corellia (5).

The reader is left in no doubt that Pliny values highly his *maius officium* to the female relatives of men to whom he was obliged both socially and politically, and it is his *amicitia* with these men that he honors through his treatment of Corellia. Sure of the correctness of his actions, Pliny offers no apology to Fabatus, but he does stress by his refusal to part with his parents' property that his attachment to family ranks above his connection to the Corellii. In fact, the ordering of Pliny's loyalties is clear – to his family, patron, friends, political allies, female relations of his patron. Fabatus' understanding and approval are assumed by Pliny's use of the present indicative, *vides quam ratum habere debeam* (6), and thus we may assume that Pliny has presented an argument that suits the mores of his social milieu.

The rhetorical nature of 7.11 is affirmed by its instructive function. Having justified his behavior by laying out his various obligations to his fellow heirs and to Corellia and her family, Pliny summarizes his reasoning in several closing statements. Here, Pliny's tone becomes less explanatory and more didactic. First, he recalls the need for *coheredes* to accept his actions (7). There is no regret or contrition on Pliny's part, nor is he requesting their consent. Instead, by omitting the first-person possessive that he had previously used to refer to his fellow heirs (2), Pliny broadens his instruction to apply to anyone sharing an inheritance. All *coheredes* should understand his decision to sell his share separately. Pliny has merely done what was appropriate. That Pliny intends to offer himself as model is confirmed by his next statement in which he calls his treatment of Corellia an *exemplum*, although he also states that *coheredes* are under no obligation to do as he had done. While he appears with this statement to abrogate the necessity of his fellow heirs to follow his example because they do not have *eadem iura*, his concluding words strongly advise them to do so. Pliny declares: *possunt ergo intueri utilitatem suam, pro qua mihi fuit amicitia* (8). By juxtaposing *utilitas* and *amicitia* and privileging the latter by its position as the final word of the letter, Pliny is clearly recalling the two traditional subjects of deliberative oratory, and he firmly establishes himself as a champion of honor over expediency, a choice believed by its proponents, according to Cicero, to be attended by glory and immortal fame (*De or.* 2.82). Pliny's *coheredes* were surely expected not only to understand his actions but also, despite his denial that they were so compelled, to emulate his behavior in accordance with their own *iura* should they wish to attain the same outstanding reputation that Pliny seeks to fashion for himself.

Although Corellia's brother can no longer provide Pliny political connections and advice, through Corellia Pliny may remain true to his commitments. Pliny's devotion to Corellius' memory and the bonds with the Minicii that he expounds in 7.11 are so deep that he virtually begs Corellia in a subsequent letter addressed to her (7.14) to endure his generosity.

LETTER 7.14: CORELLIA. At first glance 7.14 may seem simply a polite refusal of Corellia's offer to pay the full assessed value of Pliny's property, but upon closer examination the letter is revealed to be carefully crafted by Pliny. It is a model of balanced words and phrases that by its very structure epitomizes the equality and reciprocity that Pliny has described between himself and the Corellii.

C. PLINIUS CORELLIAE SUAE S.

(1) *Tu quidem honestissime, quod tam impense et rogas et exigis, ut accipi iubeam a te pretium agrorum non e septingentis milibus, quanti illos a liberto meo, sed ex non-gentis, quanti a publicanis partem vicensimam emisti.* (2) *Invicem ego et rogo et exigo, ut non solum quid te verum etiam quid me deceat aspicias, patiarisque me in hoc uno tibi eodem animo repugnare, quo in omnibus obsequi soleo. Vale.*

Indeed, you are most honorable in that you ask and even demand so generously that I order to be accepted from you a price for my land not of 700,000 sesterces, the amount agreed upon by my freedman, but of 900,000, the amount on which you paid your five percent in taxes. I, in turn, ask and even demand that you consider not only what befits you but also what befits me, and that you permit me to resist you in this one matter in the same spirit with which I usually comply in all matters. Farewell.

Pliny opens this letter addressed to Corellia with an emphatic *tu*, used on only three other occasions to begin a letter: *Epistulae* 2.16, 4.14, and 6.12. In each instance, Pliny seems to remonstrate with his addressee for former statements or comments that each has made. In 2.16 (*Tu quidem*), Annius Severus is reprimanded for reminding Pliny regarding the legal status of his inheritance from Acilianus. Pliny plays bait and switch with Plinius Paternus in 4.14 (*Tu fortasse*), sending him hendecasyllables rather than the speech that Paternus expected. Finally, it is his wife's grandfather Calpurnius Fabatus whom Pliny addresses in 6.12 (*Tu vero*), encouraging the older man to speak frankly and to treat Pliny as he did his son, even reproving him if necessary; the reader immediately assumes that Pliny had previously received some communication from Fabatus apologizing for earlier harsh words. By opening these letters with *tu*, Pliny offers pointed counterinstructions to previous correspondence with his addressees. It is particularly enlightening to note that 7.14 opens with *tu quidem*, the same forceful beginning as the somewhat testy 2.16, in which Pliny sarcastically reports that he is aware of the law to which Annius refers: *quod ius ne mihi quidem ignotum est cum sit iis etiam notum qui nihil aliud sciunt* (2). Thereafter, Pliny proceeds to instruct Annius as to the finer points of inheritance law. There is little doubt that *tu quidem* is meant to signal Pliny's determination and opposition to previous communication in both 2.16 and 7.14.

Pliny notes Corellia's generosity in insisting, *et rogas et exigis* (1), that she pay him the full market price for his land, and then he reiterates the figures already given in 7.11. The letter's double-barreled opening is quite unusual. As both Sherwin-White (1966: 6–11) and Guillemin (1929: 145) have remarked, it is formulaic for a number of Pliny's letters to begin with a second-person-singular verb – *rogas, petis, quaeris, miraris* – but there are only two letters with an opening sentence that contains two second-person verbs, 7.14 and 4.17. Both letters are somewhat adversarial, and both are highly rhetorical. That both pertain to Pliny's relationship to the Corellii indicates, if nothing else, Pliny's attentive concern for the proper presentation of his relationship with Corellius Rufus. In each of the two letters, Pliny rebuts his addressee's entreaties. Pliny responds to Gallus' advice and request (*admones et rogas*) in 4.17 by employing the same verbs – *admoneri enim debeo . . . rogari non debeo*. Pliny is indignant at Gallus' assumption that he needs to be told the right course of action, and his use of Gallus' words serves to strengthen his protest. In 7.14, Pliny responds similarly to Corellia's entreaty (*et rogas et exigis*), repeating the verbs used to describe Corellia's demands – *ego et rogo et exigo* (2). Here, Pliny does not express any particular dismay but rather, in answer to Corellia, makes demands of his own. The echo in 7.14 is considerably more powerful than the one in 4.17 as Pliny begins his retort with the emphatic *ego* and then repeats Corellia's words in exact order, changing the verb forms only to reflect the first person. Pliny has not just responded to Corellia's demands; he has appropriated her words to reinforce his objections to her proposal.

The same marked use of personal pronouns and possessives that is apparent in 7.11 characterizes 7.14 also. Here the use of both the first- and second-person pronouns is striking, with three of the former and four of the latter, as well as one appearance of a first-person possessive adjective. Pliny reserves such frequent use of personal pronouns and possessives for letters in which he seeks the appearance of great intimacy with his addressee. For example, in both 1.4 and 6.28, letters that rank among the top five in repeated use of first- and second-person pronouns and possessives,[28] Pliny writes concerning his visits to estates owned by Pompeia Celerina and Pontus Allifanus, respectively. In each letter, he assumes a rather proprietary air, making clear that his host's house is like his own. The same familiarity expressed by the pervasive use of first- and second-person pronouns is evident in his brief letter to Sentius Augurinus in which Pliny praises highly the quality of his addressee's writing, the subject of which happens to be Pliny himself.[29]

Pliny divides 7.14 into two parts, marked chiastically by *tu quidem* and *invicem ego*: Corellia's protest and his own even stronger response. Pliny compares her price of 900,000 sesterces – *a te ... ex nongentis* – with the verbally weightier 700,000 sesterces he has already received from her – *e septingentis milibus*. Pliny offers an explanation of the two amounts, the lower from Pliny's freedman – *quanti illos a liberto meo* – and the greater based on the land's assessed value – *quanti a publicanis partem vicensimam*. Pliny's use of *quanti ... quanti* suggests a balance between the two amounts, and his explanation for the 900,000 sesterces figure is sufficiently heavy to balance Corellia's larger offer with the *septingentis milibus* Pliny wishes her to pay. Pliny's generosity and Corellia's sense of fairness are both marked by the verbal gravity of the explication for the larger value.

Pliny's balancing act continues in the second half of the letter. As noted previously, in the first half of the letter Pliny assigns to Corellia *rogas* and *exigis*, but the verbs are separated from the emphatic *tu* that begins the letter. As Pliny uses her words to overturn her entreaty to him, his first-person pronoun gives greater force to his requests – *ego et rogo et exigo* – that she consider what is fitting and that she allow him to ignore her request, *aspicias patiarisque*. He binds Corellia to him by stating that she should consider his needs equally with hers, *non solum quid te ... verum etiam quid me deceat*. Finally, with the phrase *me in hoc*

---

[28] *Ep.* 1.4 contains twelve uses of the first person and six of the second person in just 108 words, while 6.28 has eight first-person and five second-person uses in 87 words.

[29] *Ep.* 9.8 includes three first-person and four second-person pronouns and possessives in fifty-four words.

uno tibi, the subject Pliny overpowers Corellia, the object of *repugnare*, in this one matter. The scales have fallen just slightly on Pliny's side.

In his rebuttal Pliny refers obliquely to some compelling reason for his generosity, *quid me deceat* (2), but he provides no details of the nature of his obligations. In fact, the placement of his letter to Corellia just three away from 7.11 makes it unnecessary for Pliny to justify his action because he had already done so to Calpurnius Fabatus. Surely, 7.14 reflects at least Pliny's editorial hand, perhaps even extensive reworking of the letter, because in "real" correspondence, Pliny would be quite likely to present the full range of his arguments in an effort to convince Corellia to accept his magnanimity. Instead, having made the obscure remark that she should consider what was fitting for him to do, he asks for her compliance and ends the letter with a statement of his own customary obeisance. While highlighting his own honorable behavior, Pliny manages to depict himself as a willing follower of Corellia's wishes.

This analysis of the structure of 7.14 not only speaks to the importance to Pliny of cultivating his ties to the sister of Corellius and her other male relatives but also suggests the importance of maintaining equilibrium and control in his relationships. Corellia gets the land she desires at a good price, and Pliny is thus permitted to honor his *iura*. In this zero-sum game, the benefits appear to be mutual; however, Pliny's inclusion of two letters on the subject of the sale of his property below its taxable value compels further consideration. Pliny's insistence on the bargain price to which his freedman had agreed strongly suggests his intent to ensure that Corellia remains tied to him through his munificence, just as her powerful objections indicate that she would just as soon avoid such a condition. Pliny's inclusion of 7.11 and 7.14 in his collection assures us that, in this matter, he got his way. Thus, several benefits accrue to Pliny's account: he reaffirms the connections he has with Corellia and her relatives; he assumes the position of benefactor to his mentor's sister; he affirms his own commitment to *amicitia*; and he proves his *constantia* in adhering to his own decision and in supporting the actions of his agent – all now enshrined in a publicly circulated collection.

LETTER 9.13: CORELLIUS. Pliny makes a brief mention of Corellius' service on Nerva's land commission in 7.31.5, but it is the last appearance of Pliny's mentor in 9.13 that serves as a testament to

Pliny's political maturity. The setting of the letter, as discussed in Chapter 1, is the Roman senate in the year 97 as Pliny is about to give his speech in vindication of Helvidius (II). At this prelude to the pinnacle of Pliny's rhetorical success, Corellius is present, but Pliny has pushed him to the periphery of the action. Here, we do not see the *rector* of Pliny's career. Indeed, Pliny pointedly mentions his deliberate decision not to consult Corellius regarding his determination to take action against Certus (6).

Pliny notes that he always consulted Corellius as the *providentissimu[s] aetatis nostrae sapientissimu[s]que*, yet in this case he chooses to keep his own counsel, lest, he says, Corellius would stop him from acting (6). Pliny then offers the only comment in the letters that could be considered a criticism of Corellius or at least less than flattering, that he was a rather cautious and hesitant man, the very characteristics that would have preserved his life under Domitian but which were no longer required with Nerva as emperor. Pliny does go on to stress that his intended actions were potentially dangerous (10–11), but he also makes clear that he had considered all of the possible repercussions and was prepared for whatever consequences he might suffer (12).

While Pliny informs Corellius of what he is about to do, his failure to consult Corellius before taking so drastic an action as to bring an accusation against a fellow senator is a clear statement of his political separation from his mentor. Pliny has used his own wisdom and foresight to make a difficult decision, without the wariness of Corellius' political demeanor. Pliny has seen the future and, in his independent action, declares himself to be the part of the next political generation, with Corellius as an honored remnant of the past.

Conclusion

Among the many letters that delineate Pliny's political identity, none are more crucial than those concerning Corellius, whose presence in Pliny's life was fundamental to shaping his character and demeanor. But like a son coming to maturity and acting without his father's oversight, Pliny must also separate himself from Corellius, whose career was so closely connected with the past under Domitian. Corellius' political caution is hardly suited to the image of the bold avenger, risking his very life for those he supports, that Pliny wishes to culti-vate. The political pedigree that he works hard to claim through his Corellian relationships can, in fact, become a serious liability to his self-representation, unless it is fitted carefully into his own conception of his role in the administration of a Trajanic empire. And so Pliny's association with the Corellii is painstakingly drawn and interspersed with his construction of his relationship with the Stoics, in which he claims to be an enduring friend and a forceful opponent.

Pliny's expressed desire to attack the opposition's *delatores* in 1.5 introduces him as a man willing to risk himself, yet held back from doing so by the need for the approval of an elder statesman, not Corellius, but Mauricus. Pliny seems not to have the internal forti-tude to carry out what his heart would will. Just a few letters later, the death that he so laments in 1.12 will, in fact, provide the means for him to stand apart from Corellius, after which he is able to look back on their relationship, to explain all that Pliny had learned from him, to highlight his affection, and to make clear his ongoing obligations and service to the surviving family.

The hesitant Corellius, whose greatest accomplishment seems to have been outliving Domitian, is a problematic model for someone who wishes to be remembered for his boldness. Corellius' wisdom and sterling reputation were certainly assets, but Pliny needs to sup-plement them with other qualities, even while trying to strengthen his connection to Corellius. Thus, in the arrangement of the let-ters we can see the intertwining of those mentioning Corellius with those concerning the Stoics: 3.3, expressing Pliny's great affection for Corellius, is followed at 3.11 by Pliny's dangerous visit to the ban-ished philosopher Artemidorus; in 4.21 Pliny reminds the reader of his speeches in defense of the executed Helvidius (II) just four letters after 4.17, where Pliny explains the benefits he had received from Corellius and their deep mutual affection; and Pliny's letters to Corellia regarding the sale of his land, 7.11 and 7.14, are followed closely by his characterization of Fannia in 7.19. Thus, every men-tion of Pliny's relationship with Corellius is countered by a letter that recalls his less than cautious association with the Stoics; even the brief notice of Pliny's request for Corellius' support at a trial in 5.1.5 is followed just a few sentences later by the mention of Gratilla and Rusticus (5.1.8).

Finally the Stoics and Corellius come together in 9.13, in which the reader is transported back to a time contemporary with 1.5, where the dialogue between them had begun, not long before the death of Corellius, both in reality and in Pliny's collection. But, despite the presence of a living Corellius, the Pliny of 9.13 requires no man's approval before he undertakes his dangerous vengeance. He is an independent and mature actor on the political stage, still obliged to Corellius but no longer dependent upon him. Pliny's self-reliance is highlighted by his remark that a man should not ask for advice from people whose advice ought to be followed, if he has no intention of changing his mind to follow it (9.13.6).

That there seems no contradiction between the evolution of Pliny's political identity and the contemporaneity of letters 1.5 and 9.13 is a testament to the care with which Pliny has written and arranged the letters about the Stoics and Corellius. It is, in fact, particularly fitting that Corellius should have lived to see his protégé's most triumphant moment in the senate but not long enough to hear Pliny's *gratiarum actio* in obeisance to his emperor Trajan.

Corellius had no son to either confirm or deny Pliny's representation of his relationship with the elder statesman, but that denial could certainly have come from his daughter, his sister, or either of their spouses, so it is safe to conclude that Corellius did have a profound and enduring influence on Pliny's life, perpetuated through Pliny's association with the women that Corellius left behind. Indeed, the relationship that the Corelliae share with Pliny is marked by their receipt of letters from him. How close their association was, however, is open to question because it seems to be derived exclusively from his admiration for and attachment to their male relatives, primarily Corellius, but also their husbands and sons. Of course, Pliny's purpose in their inclusion is not the illumination of his interactions with female friends but rather the expansion of his self-portrait as Corellius' protégé and successor. Without Corellia and Corellia Hispulla, Pliny's political self-portrait would be limited to courtroom and senate scenes where he can hardly call himself *sapiens*. The topics of letters addressed to women remain, as expected, removed from the political sphere, providing Pliny with a venue for the display of his virtues beyond the lawcourts and the senate. As a result, in his interaction with women, Pliny's righteous behavior not only reinforces the integrity he demonstrates in the performance of his official duties but also assures the reader that his qualities are consistent and innate, not simply conjured up for public fora.

Pliny's close and ongoing association with the Corelliae also leaves us with a few lasting impressions of the power these women must have exercised over both family and financial matters. After all, it is Corellia Hispulla whom Pliny contacts about a tutor for her son. She clearly will have a say in the selection of the man who will profoundly affect her son's future, if only to pass along Pliny's recommendation to her husband. In the case of Corellia, there is little doubt that the substantial sum of money she is using to purchase Pliny's land is her own. Her marriage brought her powerful political connections in which Pliny may have shared through his *amicitia* with her, but she seems formidable in her own right as well. What we cannot know from these letters is whether the *iura* that Pliny has with the family extend to its women only because they have been forged with its men. Were such social bonds gender blind, creating connections between men and women as easily as among men? Would Pliny have spoken to the wife or sister or daughter of a mere acquaintance as he does to the Corelliae? I suspect that he would not have done so, indeed, that it would have been frowned upon for Pliny to suggest any such intimacy with a woman not connected to him through bonds he had forged with their male relatives. Yet those bonds clearly extended beyond the men who initially created them to women of the household, who could and did continue to cultivate them to the advantage of themselves, their *amici*, and ultimately to the benefit and even the survival of Roman elite society.

3

Pliny

Champion of the Vulnerable

Neque enim sum tam sapiens ut nihil mea intersit, an iis quae honeste fecisse me credo testificatio quaedam et quasi praemium accedat.

Pliny, *Epistulae* 5.1.13

For I am not so philosophical that it is of no importance to me whether certain affirmation and reward, as it were, accrue to those things that I believe I have done with integrity.

In Pliny's time, in marked contrast to the days of the republic, exchanging a life lived under the intense scrutiny of the emperor for one enjoyed as a country gentleman was becoming not only more acceptable but even desirable. *Secessio* was a safer path, and one that might bring significantly more cachet for elites through their local benefactions than the honorary offices available in Rome. But this newly defined elite identity by no means enticed all of Rome's upper class. Many Romans still firmly adhered to the ancestral call to *pietas*, in which all men were required to balance their lives between service to the state, proper cultivation of the gods, and care and support of family members.

His political career and interaction with Trajan, as illuminated by both the *Epistulae* and the *Panegyricus*, attest to Pliny's devotion to the state. In addition, the gods receive attention in his letters, albeit only on the margins of his self-portrait, in such considerations as the Corinthian bronze he hopes will be set up in the Temple of Jupiter (3.6.4) and the Temple to Ceres he wishes to rebuild and expand on his property at Tifernum Tiberinum (9.39.1).[1] Yet personal religious devotion was never of great importance to the reputation of individual Romans; instead elevated rank required care of the gods – illustrated well by letters to and from Trajan in book 10 in which Pliny requests the emperor's consent to move and to rebuild the Temple to the Magna Mater in Nicomedia (10.49, 50) – as a means to ensure divine support in maintaining the empire. It is the final of the three obligations, the one that required proper concern for one's family, that poses some difficulty for Pliny's self-representation.

While it is possible to imagine that Pliny undertook the role of paterfamilias upon the death of his uncle Pliny the Elder, he may, in reality, still have been under the legal protection of his tutor Verginius Rufus in 79 C.E., because he was just seventeen years old; he was, nevertheless, effectively the male head of his household, as his guardian's authority would have been exercised in legal and financial matters, not in the day-to-day functions of the *familia*. After the death of his mother, without siblings or children, Pliny's household was small indeed. How then can he display proper *pietas* in this final category?

Pliny's awareness that a man's familial relationships are crucial to a full assessment of his character is made clear in the *Panegyricus*, in which Pliny emphasizes the calm moderation and modesty with which Trajan runs his house as well as his remarkable hospitality (47–49).[2] His readers must, then, be drawn to look closely at Pliny's interactions with those over whom he has some personal authority away from the public eye – that is, his family; in Pliny's case, following the loss of his mother and with no surviving male kin, all are women related to him only through marriage.

Pliny's personal interaction with female relatives is illuminated most often in the *Epistulae* in the presentation of his concerns about

---

[1] We can, of course, say nothing of Pliny's beliefs. Other letters mention Diana, Jupiter, Minerva, Mars, Fortuna, and other gods (1.6, 1.7, 3.21, 4.11, 6.16, 7.9, 9.10), but in each case the deity's presence could be interpreted as a literary convention. The closest Pliny comes to a statement of conviction is in *Ep.* 8.8.5, in which he cites the oracles of Clitumnus, the river god, as proof of the god's divinity.

[2] As we might expect, Trajan's traits are all compared with the despicable behavior of Domitian, who, according to Pliny, locked himself behind the closed doors of the Domus Flavia to lap up the blood of his kinsmen and plan the destruction of his most outstanding citizens (*Pan.* 47.3).

the maintenance or distribution of property or money that he has
some access to or control over, undoubtedly because these are tangible assets whose proper management can readily illustrate his integrity and loyalty without deference to the testimony of his beneficiaries.
Pliny thus can establish himself as a proper provider and caretaker
of the women under his tutelage, but his excellence in this regard
is not restricted to family members alone. Letters having to do with
wills and legacies provide a number of examples of Pliny's determination to follow the wishes of the deceased, although the law does not
require him to do so, even when it is to his personal disadvantage.

The Roman obsession with having a proper will has been treated
at length by Edward Champlin (1991: 31), who argues convincingly
that the elder Cato, who bemoaned the fact that he had passed a
single day without a valid will (Plutarch 9.9), is a fitting representative of his segment of Roman society. There is little doubt that
Pliny agreed with the old republican, expressing his deep distress
that the historian Gaius Fannius had died with an old will, one
that failed to leave appropriate legacies to his newer friends and
still included former friends who had become hostile to him before
his death (5.5.2). It is perhaps unfair to Pliny to wonder whether
he might have fallen into the former category and felt the need
to explain the slight he endured when the will was made public
and his name was not included. Testamentary acknowledgment of
one's friends was a conspicuous requirement for the Roman elite,
and failure to include a friend was an insult. Leaving more to one
man than another made clear the esteem in which the deceased
held each man as well as the depth of his friendship with each.
Thus, Pliny is quite pleased to report that he and Tacitus generally receive similar legacies from the same testators, being held,
thereby, as social equals (7.20.6).[3]

Given the power of the Roman will to damage or enhance status
and, of course, to enrich its beneficiaries, it is not surprising that
testamentary matters were often contested, or that, in Pliny's day
when many judicial matters were under the control of the emperor,

---

[3] Both Radice (1969: vol. II, 530 n. 2), and Sherwin-White (1966: 428) cite the
Testamentum Dasumii (*CIL* vi, 10229) as proof of this claim. There is difficulty,
though, in their assumption that generalizations can be drawn from a document
that is, in many ways, quite extraordinary.

disputed wills seem to have consumed much of Pliny's time in court. No fewer than nineteen letters mention wills, with Pliny named as either heir or the recipient of a legacy in six.[4] Pliny even permits his slaves to make wills of a sort, despite the fact that they are not legally permitted to do so, and enforces their wishes, provided that the beneficiaries are members of his household, which he calls his slaves' *civitas* (8.16.1–2). There is little doubt that the ability to create a will was for Pliny not just a privilege but also the mark of a civilized society in which both life and death solidified relationships among its members. Furthermore, the proper execution of the wishes of the deceased is a process for which he appears to have great respect.

Pliny notes forcefully in the first letter in his collection concerning his receipt of a legacy that he is aware of the legal requirements regarding wills but has laid down for himself a personal law by which he treats the wishes of the deceased as though they were legally binding, even if the testament does not comply with the law (2.16.1–2). Subsequent letters focus on the plight of various women both as testators and heirs, and each contributes both to our understanding of the Roman obsession with wills and to Pliny's intention to extend his reader's perception of the integrity he displays in his relationships with family members to include vulnerable women throughout upper-class Roman society.

The Women of Pliny's Family

By far the most important of the five women in the letters who can be assigned without question to Pliny's family is his wife, Calpurnia, followed closely by her aunt, Calpurnia Hispulla, and Pompeia Celerina, the mother of Pliny's unidentified first (or second) wife. It may seem odd to the reader that his mother, Plinia, remains virtually anonymous, but there is little doubt that her death precedes the publication and even the original composition of any of Pliny's letters, and so Pliny relegates mention of her to indirect reference or memories of the past. A final minor character, Calvina, whose

---

[4] Pliny receives a legacy or is named heir in *Ep.* 2.16, 3.6, 4.10, 5.1, 5.7, 7.20.

relationship to Pliny is defined only as *adfinis*, completes the handful of family members.

Sixteen of Pliny's letters mention these women. Four that concern only Calpurnia are considered in the following chapter on ideal wives (6.4, 6.7, 7.5, and 8.10); the remaining twelve are as follows:

Letter	Women
1.4	Pompeia Celerina (mother-in-law) – *recipient*
1.18	(Pompeia Celerina)* (mother-in-law)
2.4	Calvina (adfinis) – *recipient*
2.15	(Plinia) (mother)
3.19	(Pompeia Celerina) (mother-in-law)
4.1	(Calpurnia) (wife)
	(Calpurnia Hispulla) (wife's aunt)
4.19	Calpurnia Hispulla (wife's aunt)– *recipient*
6.3	Pliny's nurse**
6.10	(Pompeia Celerina) (mother-in-law)
6.16	(Plinia) (mother)
6.20	(Plinia) (mother)
8.11	Calpurnia Hispulla (wife's aunt) – *recipient*
	Calpurnia (wife)

 * A name in parentheses indicates that the woman is identifiable although unnamed by Pliny.
** Pliny's nurse is not included among the five family members as she is unnamed and unidentifiable.

As the chart reflects, in the first three books (before his introduction of Calpurnia in 4.1) Pompeia Celerina is Pliny's most important female relation, indeed the first member of his family the reader encounters in book 1 and his first female addressee. Celerina is likely the mother of Pliny's first wife. The number of Pliny's marriages is still debated, with Sherwin-White (1966: 71, 264, 559–560), among others, insisting on two brief early marriages – in both of which Pliny was widowed – before his later marriage to Calpurnia. His argument is based on the second letter of book 10, in which Pliny thanks Trajan for granting him the privilege of *ius trium liberorum*. Because there is little doubt that Pliny received this benefit early in the emperor's reign, Sherwin-White assumes that Pliny had not yet married

Calpurnia, a young woman with whom he might yet have children, and that Pliny's reference in the letter to his two childless marriages thus excludes his union with her. In reality, there was no need for Trajan to withhold the grant of the *ius trium liberorum* simply because Pliny might still become a biological father. By Pliny's time, the privilege had become a political reward, bestowed upon supporters of the *princeps*. In addition, there is no other indication in Pliny's letters of a third marriage, or of individuals with whom he might have become associated through such an alliance – for example, the parents or siblings of another wife. Such an argument *in vacuo* is strengthened significantly by Pliny's overwhelming tendency to cite his connections with even the most insignificant and obscure acquaintances. While there is no proof that Pliny was married to Calpurnia when he wrote 10.2, there is equally a dearth of evidence for a third marriage.

Pompeia Celerina is the recipient of *Epistulae* 1.4, in which Pliny praises the slaves of her estates in Umbria and Etruria because they have consistently welcomed him as though he were their master rather than she. Pliny names four cities in which Celerina has houses, and he will in subsequent letters refer not only to her vast resources but also to his own access to them as a source of capital (3.19). She was clearly a woman of substantial means, likely the daughter of L. Pompeius Vopiscus C. Arruntius Catellius Celer, who held the suffect consulship in or before 77.[5]

Celerina's first husband cannot be securely identified, nor does Pliny give his readers the name of his first wife, or offspring of that union, by whose nomenclature any hypothesis might be verified. Raepsaet-Charlier cites epigraphical evidence that Celerina's husband may have been L. Venuleius Montanus Apronianus, married, according to the inscription, to a (Pompeia?) Celerina (*CIL* xi 1735). Venuleius held the suffect consulship in 92. Raepsaet-Charlier further proposes that L. Venuleius Apronianus Octavius Priscus was their son, an identification suggested by his origins in Etruria where some of Celerina's property was located. He was chosen to serve as consul ordinarius in 123 and later was proconsul of Asia (*CIL* xi 1525). In

---

[5] Raepsaet-Charlier 1987: Pompeia Celerina 626 and 627. Sherwin-White (1966: 92) grants that she was probably related to Celer but does not attempt to define that relationship. Celer also served as governor of Lusitania and, perhaps, nearer Spain.

this reconstruction of Celerina's first marriage, Pliny's deceased wife would have been called Venuleia, and Pliny's ongoing relationship with Pompeia Celerina would have offered him both the economic benefits that he refers to and political connections to Celerina's son, although he makes no reference to such a relationship in the letters.

The identification of Celerina's second husband is more secure. Q. Fulvius Gillo Bittius Proculus is named by Pliny as the stepfather of the wife whom he had lost (9.13.13). Bittius served as prefect of the Treasury of Saturn with Publicius Certus and then as consul suffectus in 98 without him, following the removal of Certus from office after Pliny's vindication of Helvidius (9.13.23 – see Chapter 1).[6] Pliny had an ongoing political and personal relationship with Bittius and Celerina, consistently referring to her as his mother-in-law throughout his life.[7] Indeed, immediately after his first two letters addressed to Calpurnia, Pliny places a letter to Lucceius Albinus in which he states that he has been visiting his mother-in-law at Alsium, where one of Celerina's estates was located (6.10.1).

Pliny could continue to refer to Pompeia Celerina as his *socrus* because his wife, Calpurnia, was orphaned. There is no mention in Pliny's letters of her mother, and Pliny calls her father *amissus* (4.19.1). In their stead are her paternal grandfather, L. Calpurnius Fabatus, and her aunt Calpurnia Hispulla. Fabatus, a prominent figure in Pliny's letters, is the recipient of nine letters and is mentioned in two others.[8] All of the correspondence concerns family or property matters, especially the management and disposition of estates owned either by Pliny or by Fabatus. Because Fabatus' life was centered on the town of Comum, Pliny's letters quite naturally address local matters, focused on his hometown.[9] Fabatus had enjoyed a

[6] In 98 (the year of Bittius' consulship), Pliny and his close friend Cornutus Tertullus served as treasury prefects, likely succeeding Bittius and Certus.
[7] See especially 10.51, in which Pliny thanks Trajan for transferring her relative Caelius Clemens to his province, undoubtedly written in the last year or two of Pliny's life.
[8] Fabatus receives 4.1, 5.11, 6.12, 6.30, 7.11, 7.16, 7.23, 7.32, and 8.10. He is mentioned in 5.14 and one of the letters to Trajan – 10.120.
[9] The letters to Fabatus are certainly an important means for Pliny to emphasize his ongoing connections to his hometown. But even more crucial to his self-representation is his relationship with Fabatus, one through which he can demonstrate his respect and deference for an older male family member – the only one he has, in fact.

full equestrian military career, including a minor governor's post in Africa Proconsularis. He was apparently charged with complicity in accusations of black magic and incest brought during Nero's reign (in 65) against both Iunia Lepida, the wife of C. Cassius Longinus, and Iunia's brother's son Lucius Silanus. Tacitus says that Fabatus was among those who appealed to the emperor and that he was saved by his lack of importance (*Ann.* 16.8).

Sherwin-White (1966: 264–265) suggests that these accusations cut short Fabatus' career, but C. P. Jones (1968: 116) argues convincingly that the inscription (*ILS* 2721) listing the posts held by Fabatus dates those offices to the period after 65. It may well be that, like many of his peers who were content to define their success through local honors, Fabatus was satisfied with attaining standing in his hometown or that he was simply not politically useful enough to be adlected to senatorial rank by the emperor. He seems to have suffered no calculated exclusion. In the letters, Pliny treats him with the careful respect required both by his age and by his role as grandfather of Calpurnia. He also provides Pliny with a consistent link to Comum, as he praises Fabatus' accomplishments on the local political scene in his hometown.

Details of the life of Calpurnia Hispulla are sketchy at best. No husband is mentioned in Pliny's letters, and she seems to have lived with her father until his death, as evidenced by Pliny's final letter to Trajan, in which he states that his wife is traveling back to Italy from Bithynia to be with her aunt after Fabatus' death (10.120.1). There can be no doubt that Calpurnia Hispulla raised her niece, as Pliny credits her with filling the place of Calpurnia's unnamed father (4.19.1). Pliny offers ample evidence that his family had been acquainted with this branch of the Calpurnii for some time. In his praise of Calpurnia Hispulla, he recalls the respect she had for his mother, and he remarks that he had received encouragement from her since his boyhood (4.19.7). Perhaps the friendship between the Plinii and Calpurnii had also made possible Pliny's long-standing relationship with Q. Corellius Rufus through the family connections of the latter's wife, Hispulla (see Chapter 2).

Pliny's mother, never named in the letters but presumably called Plinia, remains a marginal figure in his letters. Beyond her mention in connection with Calpurnia Hispulla, she appears only in the letters regarding the eruption of Vesuvius and the death of her brother Pliny the Elder (6.16, 6.20). In addition, she is referred to obliquely through Pliny's mention of the land she had left to him. References of this sort appear in his letter to Corellia regarding his sale of land to her (7.11) and his mention of the affection he has for his mother's property because he had inherited it from her (2.15). While she is only a shadowy presence in the letters, Pliny stresses his reverence for her memory.

Pliny addresses one last female relative, but her identity is so obscure as to remain beyond even hypothesis. Her name was Calvina, and Pliny attests that he and she are *adfines* (2.4). *Adfinitas* generally indicates a relationship forged through marriage. The term itself does not require a cognate connection, and so Calvina, like Pompeia Celerina and Calpurnia Hispulla, might be related to Pliny through one of his wives. Because of their formal relationship and its inherent obligations, Pliny takes it upon himself to make good on her late father's debts. Pliny offers no further details of her life.

Women are what remain of Pliny's family, and none of them seems to have any connection with his father or his father's family. He does consult Calpurnius Fabatus for advice as he might his own father or grandfather, and thus the older man assumes a kind of paternal role, but while Pliny shows respect for Fabatus, filial affection is not apparent. Except in one fleeting reference to paternal property he had inherited (7.11), Pliny never at all mentions his father, who must have died when Pliny was quite young. Like Fabatus, Pliny's father had probably enjoyed a successful career at the local level, serving perhaps as a senior magistrate in Comum, but even that possibility is purely speculation (Sherwin-White 1966: 69–70).

Although he discusses his uncle Pliny the Elder's literary works and his courage during the eruption of Mount Vesuvius, Pliny's interaction with him in the letters is virtually nonexistent – limited only to the distant past while Pliny was a promising but unremarkable youth. Pliny does identify the elder Pliny as his *pater per adoptionem (Ep.* 5.8), but not until after his uncle's death. While Pliny the Elder may have been his nephew's guardian, his public duties and extended absences serving as procurator in various provinces surely precluded any close relationship. Pliny does offer a biographical sketch of his uncle and a bibliography of his works in 3.5, but the tone of the letter is detached,

with no reference to interaction between the two Plinys. In 6.16 and
6.20, the Elder Pliny, like his sister Plinia, becomes a character in
Pliny's historical accounts of the eruption of Vesuvius. There is no
question that through these letters Pliny offers his uncle's life and
death as a model for selfless courage in the face of disaster, yet Pliny is
surprisingly disconnected from the narrative of an event at which he
was present, if only peripherally. The elder Pliny is certainly immortalized by his nephew, becoming a hero of the past; however, while
6.16. and 6.20 do much to enhance the image of the Elder Pliny – a
man to whom the gods had given the opportunity *facere scribenda aut
scribere legenda* (6.16.3) – they offer almost no information about the
relationship between the two Plinys.

Because of their untimely deaths, his close family members cannot
serve as witnesses to Pliny's adult demeanor. Their loss leaves Pliny
dependent on the women of his marriage alliances to portray his
private life; likewise, he must rely upon his affiliation with role models to detail how he might have interacted with his father.[10]

Women and Legacies

Eight of Pliny's letters focus on the issue of the appropriate distribution of estates and the proper behavior of testators and heirs. In
six of these women are prominent, whereas Pliny is the sole focus
of the other two.[11] Sabina and Pomponia Galla both leave part of
their estates to Pliny; Attia Viriola – assuredly well known to Pliny's
contemporaries – is represented by him in a dispute over her father's
will; Verania Gemina and Domitia Lucilla, prominent women associated with the principate, are used by Pliny as exempla in anecdotes to
illustrate the proper and improper behavior of legatees; and Calvina,

[10] The reader can also deduce from Pliny's critique of the behavior of others' parents
what he felt the ideal father-son relationship to be, but he tends to focus on the
parental role rather than that of the son. For Pliny's assessment of proper paternal
behavior, see 4.13, 5.19, and 9.12, in which, respectively, Pliny highlights the important role of parental oversight in a boy's education, explains the ways in which a
paterfamilias may be gentle, and criticizes those who treat their sons too harshly.

[11] Pliny inherits from women: 4.10, 5.1; Pliny advocates: 2.4, 6.3; Pliny offers exempla:
2.20, 8.18; Pliny inherits from men: 2.16, 5.7. In both 2.16 and 5.7, Pliny is the sole
heir of male testators in accordance with whose wishes Pliny disburses what he has
inherited.

Pliny's *adfinis*, is relieved of her burdensome inheritance. Calvina (2.4) has been discussed with the women of Pliny's family. The five other women to be considered in this category are as follows:

Letter	Women
2.20	Verania Gemina
	Aurelia (unknown)
4.10	Sabina
5.1	Pomponia Galla
6.33	Attia Viriola
8.18	Domitia Lucilla

Verania Gemina, the wife of L. Calpurnius Piso Frugi Licinianus, is the focus of *Epistulae* 2.20, one of a series of letters in which Pliny damns the disgraceful behavior of M. Aquilius Regulus. Pliny presents first and at length the most shocking negative example of Regulus' legacy hunting, his manipulation of Verania. The other two victims are the consular Vellius Blaesus and an *ornata femina* Aurelia,[12] both of whom are otherwise unknown, as Pliny offers no details about them. Pliny does, however, pointedly identify Verania, calling her *Verania Pisonis*, Piso's Verania, adding, lest there be any doubt as to whom he means, that he is talking about the Piso who was in line for the principate – "the one whom Galba adopted" – *huius dico Pisonis quem Galba adoptavi* (2.20.2).

Verania's husband, Piso, was the son of M. Licinius Crassus Frugi – consul in 27 and descendant of the triumvir M. Licinius Crassus – and Scribonia, the great-great-granddaughter of Pompeius Magnus. Piso had no record of service to the empire, either in civil office or in the military. Because of his familial connections, he had suffered exile for some years before his recall and adoption by Galba, but his absence from Rome can offer only partial explanation of his failure to hold any magistracy. Perhaps, deterred by the unfortunate fates of his brothers and father – all of whom were condemned to die by either Claudius or Nero – Piso was loath to seek office.[13] There is no

---

[12] She may be a relative of the Aurelii Fulvi or Prisci, both prominent in the late first century, but her precise affiliation cannot be determined.

[13] Piso's eldest brother, Pompeius Magnus, named for his famous ancestor, was married to the emperor Claudius' daughter Antonia. Both Piso's father and brother

question that his prominent ancestry would have made him most susceptible to public scrutiny, particularly by a suspicious and insecure emperor. Ironically, Piso's lack of a political career made him an attractive candidate for adoption by Galba, who, by choosing a successor without political experience, avoided any accusation of elevating one of his colleagues over the others or of choosing someone to succeed him who might threaten his own tenure in the principate. Tacitus speaks admiringly of Piso's character, likening it to one shared by men of former, more-principled times, but he adds that Piso had many critics for whom his *severitas* was threatening (*Hist.* 1.14–18). Neither Piso's character nor his inexperience in public office protected him when Otho seized the principate by force. Piso was brutally murdered, and his severed head paraded through the city (*Hist.* 1.43–44).

Verania Gemina was an aristocrat in her own right, the daughter of Q. Veranius, a new man who after his adlection in 48 served as consul ordinarius of 49. Most famous for his service as governor of Britain, Veranius was a member of Germanicus' staff who was rewarded by Tiberius for his avid prosecution of Germanicus' accused murderer, Gnaeus Calpurnius Piso (unrelated to Verania's husband Piso).[14]

Verania's character and the respect in which she was held are evident in literary references to her actions following her husband's assassination. Both Plutarch and Tacitus report that she pleaded with Piso's attackers for permission to ransom his head, in order to perform the proper funeral rites and to cremate him.[15] Perhaps it was

---

had accompanied Claudius to Britain, with *ornamenta triumphalia* awarded to Crassus Frugi twice, but the emperor executed both, along with Scribonia, in 46 or early 47 (Seneca, *Apocol.* 11.2–5). Another brother, M. Crassus, consul in 64, was forced by Nero to commit suicide.

[14] Tacitus reports that as members of Germanicus' staff Veranius and P. Vitellius had actively pursued the prosecution of Gn. Calpurnius Piso for the murder of Germanicus. Following the *senatus consultum* regarding Piso's condemnation, Tiberius rewarded Veranius by recommending to the senate his admittance to the pontifical order (*Ann.* 3.10, 13, 17, 19). More than a decade ago, Werner Eck, Antonio Caballos, and Fernando Fernández (1996) published the text of the decree condemning Piso as found in Spain, inscribed on bronze. The discovery of the inscription offers scholars a unique opportunity to compare Tacitus' account and the inscribed decree. Some of the latest work was published in 1999 as an issue of the *American Journal of Philology* 120.1, edited by Cynthia Damon and Sarolta Takács.

[15] Plutarch, *Galb.* 28; Tacitus, *Hist.* 1.47. Plutarch also mentions that Galba's body was seized and desecrated before it was recovered by the elder Helvidius Priscus and turned over for burial.

her boldness that prevented her demise. In any case, Verania lived for almost thirty years after her husband's death at the hands of Otho's emissaries. Her devotion to Piso may be assumed by her failure to remarry and, despite the decades between their deaths, their shared resting place in the same funeral urn.[16] Verania's connection to two highly regarded men makes her a sympathetic victim in Pliny's condemnation of Regulus' crass behavior, especially because her own conduct was no less exemplary than that of her father and husband.

Both Sabina (4.10) and Pomponia Galla (5.1) name Pliny as one of their heirs. Pliny addresses *Epistulae* 4.10 to Statius Sabinus, his *coheres*, regarding the proper disposition of Sabina's wishes. The concurrence of their names can hardly be accidental, but no specific relationship between the two can be divined. Sabinus receives several other letters from Pliny from which we learn that he was a military man from Firmum who was a patron of that city (*Ep.* 6.18).[17]

There is difficulty, too, in identifying Pomponia Galla who, according to *Epistulae* 5.1, had disinherited her son Asudius Curianus and had made Pliny and Sertorius Severus her heirs, along with several *equites*. Pomponia's agnate connections are suggested only by nomenclature that implies she belonged to the family of C. Pomponius Gallus Didius Rufus, who served as proconsul of Crete and Cyrene in the late 80s. Sherwin-White (1966: 312) proposes that she is his daughter, but it seems more reasonable to identify her as his sister because Pliny's letter – detailing her will and the objections of her grown son – appears to date to the late 90s. Her death probably occurred before 95.[18] C. P. Jones (1968: 127) rightly cautions against ready acceptance of these proposed familial connections of

---

[16] *ILS* 955, 956. The urn was found at Villa Buonaparte near the Via Salaria with that of Piso's father and eldest brother. See especially Chilver 1979: 106.

[17] Such details are confirmed by inscription evidence – *CIL* ix 5370 and 5406. Although two other letters, 9.2 and 9.18, are addressed to someone named Sabinus, and Sherwin-White (1966: 482, 501, and 758) assigns these to Pliny's friend from Firmum, subsequent research and Pliny's reference to the hardships of military life (9.2.4) have led Birley (2000: 65) to conclude, quite rightly, that these letters should be assigned to Julius Sabinus, the garrison commander of Dacia.

[18] Raepsaet-Charlier 1987: Pomponia Galla 638. Pomponia may also have been connected with A. Didius Gallus Fabricius Veiento, who was exiled in 62 for libeling senators and influencing Nero in the sale of offices. He later served as consul suffectus three times under the Flavians, assuming the role, according to Juvenal (4.113–129), of one of Domitian's advisers.

Pomponia Galla because both of her names are common ones. In fact, because it was not unusual in the first century c.e. to give a female child names deriving from both her mother's and father's families, there is no certainty that Pomponia Galla is the sister or daughter of a Pomponius Gallus rather than the child of some couple whose names were Pomponius and Galla.[19] Nor does Pliny's naming of her son, Asudius Curianus, offer any help, as he is unknown elsewhere. Her association with Pomponius Gallus must remain tentative.

More secure is the identification of Attia Viriola, whose cause Pliny undertook to regain the patrimony denied to her. There is no mention of her late father's name, but Pliny's description of her as *splendide nata* indicates her equestrian rank, as Ségolène Demougin (1975: 177) has shown. Pliny reports his speech on her behalf and mentions that not only was her stepmother defeated but her kinsman Suburanus also lost his bid to claim Attia's inheritance. The names and rank suggest that Attia was closely related to Sextus Attius Suburanus Aemilianus, who served as praetorian prefect under Trajan, after which he was elevated to senatorial rank and served as consul suffectus in 101 and consul ordinarius in 104.[20] If Attia was Suburanus' sister, as seems most likely, it is possible that their father had disinherited her brother along with her.[21] Thus, Pliny's defense of her bears on his relationship with Trajan, and its setting in the Centumviral Court adds luster to a speech that Pliny refers to as a Demosthenian masterpiece (6.33.11).

The final woman considered here is Domitia Lucilla whose complicated history of adoption and inheritance serves as a vehicle for Pliny

---

[19] One could expand the possibilities for a child to receive such a name to include any alliance between the Galli and Pomponii, even several generations removed from anyone bearing such names.

[20] Suburanus had also served as *adiutor* to Iulius Ursus in both Rome and Egypt. Ursus receives two of Pliny's letters, 3.17 and 6.26, and is the one through whose intercession Pliny receives the *ius trium liberorum*.

[21] Raepsaet-Charlier (1987: Attia Viriola 126) is careful to point out that Attia may have been the cousin or niece of Suburanus rather than his sister. Mommsen had suggested that she was the daughter of Suburanus. Sherwin-White (1966: 399) argues that, if this were so, Pliny would not have referred to him in "such a colorless way." More to the point is the age of Attia's father, described by Pliny as an octogenarian at his death. Even if the letter, and therefore the case, is dated to just before Pliny's departure for Bithynia, Suburanus would have to have been well over seventy before serving his first consulship in 101.

to describe the proper disposition of an estate.[22] Domitia Lucilla's story is one of familial devotion and future imperial success. In *Epistulae* 8.18, Pliny offers in detail an account of the family's somewhat contorted history. Domitia was the natural child of Cn. Domitius Lucanus, whose father-in-law, Curtilius Mancia, disliked him so intensely that he made Domitia his heir on the condition of her emancipation from her father's control. To circumvent Mancia's intention while meeting his stipulation, Lucanus' brother Cn. Domitius Tullus adopted his niece Domitia. Further confusion is added by the fact that the brothers were themselves adopted by the Gallic orator Domitius Afer[23] and were thereafter known as Cn. Domitius Afer Titius Marcellus Curvius "Tullus" and "Lucanus." Adding to the difficulty of separating the lives of the two brothers is their pursuit of similar careers, including adlection *inter patricios* just before their service in suffect consulships in the early 70s, possibly even in consecutive years. Each serves as prefect of auxiliary forces in addition to other military posts, and as proconsul of Africa, with Lucanus in the role of legate to Tullus during the latter's term as proconsul. Tullus was alone in serving a second time as consul suffectus in 98, after the death of his brother.

As a result of all of the family's machinations, Domitia Lucilla inherited estates from her grandfather (Curtilius Mancia), her fathers, both natural and adoptive (Lucanus and Tullus Domitius Afer), and their adoptive father (Domitius Afer), becoming thereby an extremely wealthy woman. Domitia's first husband is unknown, but by 108 she was already a mother and grandmother, having married P. Calvisius Tullus Ruso, to whom she bore a daughter, also called Domitia Lucilla. Ruso, who served as consul ordinarius in 109, was the son of P. Calvisius Ruso Iulius Frontinus, adlected at about the same time as Lucanus and Tullus. Pertinent to Pliny's life and letters is Syme's explanation of nomenclature that might otherwise be accounted for by adoption. Syme (1985b: 46–47) proposes that P. Calvisius Ruso Iulius Frontinus took his last two names from his mother's family[24] and that she was a sister of Sextus Iulius Frontinus, whom Pliny calls, together with Q. Corellius Rufus, one of the two most distinguished men of his day.[25] Frontinus was clearly one of Pliny's models, and Pliny is pleased to tell his reader that Frontinus had repeatedly nominated him for the augurate with the intention that Pliny be his successor in that office (4.8.3).

Domitia Lucilla's imperial connection comes through her daughter, who inherited her fortune, married M. Annius Verus, and bore to him the future emperor Marcus Aurelius. Though the emperor was not born until 121, about a decade after Pliny's death, there is no doubt about the influence and notoriety of these wealthy women in Pliny's lifetime. Furthermore, if Syme's hypothesis regarding the connection between the Iulii Frontinii and the family of Domitia Lucilla is correct, Pliny might well have been acquainted with the nephew of his mentor Iulius Frontinus and his granddaughter, the younger Domitia Lucilla. While Pliny had not personally participated in the proceedings that he reports in 8.18, he cannot resist recounting such a tantalizing tale of family intrigue and the redemptive conduct with which all prove themselves meritorious.

The anonymity of Sabina and Pomponia Galla, from whom Pliny receives inheritances, should be viewed in sharp contrast to the prominence of the women who appear as exempla in Pliny's letters regarding proper and improper legacies. Pliny undoubtedly cites the circumstances of well-known women like Verania Gemina, Attia Viriola, and Domitia Lucilla to add weight and validity to the models that he offers. Pliny is relying on his reader's familiarity with these prominent women, even if only through knowledge of their reputations, to ensure their success as exempla. Yet, the obscurity of the other women from whom Pliny inherits in no way detracts from the primary purpose of the inclusion of letters regarding Pliny's role in the disbursal of their estates: the presentation of his personal principles regarding inheritance and the integrity he displays in the subjugation of his own interests to the wishes of the deceased.

---

[25] *Ep.* 5.1. Sextus Iulius Frontinus was consul suffectus in the early 70s and again in 98 and consul ordinarius in 100. The last two consulships were served with the emperor Trajan. He is best known to us as the author of works on aqueducts and military strategy.

The Letters

LETTERS 6.16 AND 6.20: PLINIA. It is only fitting that an examination of the role of women in the portrayal of Pliny's generosity and integrity toward his dependents and clients begins with the first woman in his life, his mother. Direct reference to Pliny's mother occurs only in his two letters to Tacitus regarding the eruption of Mount Vesuvius, 6.16 and 6.20. The former, which focuses on the actions of Pliny's uncle, offers only a brief mention of her presence with Pliny at Misenum during the catastrophe, while the latter provides an account of their experiences during the eruption. Plinia remains a shadowy figure even amid the details of 6.20, hurrying to rouse Pliny just as he prepared to wake her (4) and waiting with him for word of her brother's fate (20). The only extended passage in which she appears describes events as she and Pliny are fleeing Misenum, when she instructs him to go on without her lest they both perish. Pliny declares that he will not be saved except together with her. Taking charge, he speeds her along and out of immediate danger (12). Pliny's self-portrait is thus enhanced by his devotion to his mother, both alive and dead, and her overwhelming concern for his safety, but there is little opportunity in these historical accounts to give details of his relationship with her. The depth of their connection can only be suggested indirectly.

Because Plinia is dead long before the publication of the letters, Pliny chooses to express his feelings for her through his respect and handling of places or people with whom she was associated. In this vein, Pliny complains to Julius Valerianus in 2.15 that he is unhappy with the productivity of his maternal estates but that he loves them anyway because he has them from his mother (2). While she is gone, the land he has inherited from her continues to connect him to her; thus, Pliny loves her property as he had loved her, even though the land is not providing the income that might be expected from it. The importance of inherited property as symbolic of the favor and regard of the testator for his or her heir is discussed at length by Edward Champlin (1991: 11–21). In light of the enormous value that Romans placed on the receipt of appropriate legacies, it is no wonder that Pliny holds onto his parents' land so firmly and expresses his affection for it so vehemently. His possession of their property is evidence that he has successfully fulfilled his filial duties. The subject of land inherited from Plinia arises again when Pliny recalls that he had promised to sell any of his holdings on Lake Como to Corellia except land inherited from his mother and father, *exceptis maternis paternisque* (7.11.5) (see Chapter 2). Pliny's unwillingness to part with his patrimony again reflects his ongoing respect and affection for his parents. While both maternal and paternal lands are included among those Pliny will keep, he privileges his mother's property by naming it first. In addition, Pliny had already remarked earlier in 7.11 that his affection for Corellia was based, to some degree, on her friendship with his mother, as he calls her *matri meae familiarissimam* (3). Finally, in his praise for Calpurnia Hispulla, he ties her closely to Plinia by noting that she respected his mother as she would have her parent (4.19.7). Plinia's land and her friends embody the means through which Pliny may paint himself as a dutiful and affectionate son whose devotion to his mother reaches far beyond her death.

The close connection that Pliny draws between Plinia and Calpurnia Hispulla also allows him to cast the latter as a surrogate mother. There is no question that he and she have a close relationship. She is, in fact, the only woman besides Pliny's wife to receive more than one letter from him. While the two letters (4.19 and 8.11) concern her niece Calpurnia, Pliny's wife, both provide Pliny with an opportunity to praise Calpurnia Hispulla and to display the sensitivity and kindness that the reader might assume would be evident in correspondence with his mother if it existed.

LETTERS 4.19: CALPURNIA HISPULLA. It is hard to imagine a more complimentary description of Calpurnia Hispulla than the opening sentence of 4.19. Not only is she a model of devotion, *pietatis exemplum*, who shared deep affection with her deceased brother,[26] but she has taken on his role, *ut ... affectum verum etiam patris amissi repraesentes*, in the upbringing of his daughter, Calpurnia, whom she loves as her own (1). Pliny's declaration that Calpurnia's aunt has

---

[26] Sherwin-White (1966: 296) inexplicably assumes that the death of Calpurnia Hispulla's brother was probably recent. It is equally plausible that he had been dead for most of his daughter's life, and so Pliny may genuinely praise Calpurnia Hispulla for her proper guidance of Calpurnia in her brother's stead as well as for her assumption of a maternal role.

filled not only the role of loving aunt and surrogate mother but also that of father is astonishing, especially in view of the presence of Calpurnia's grandfather, Calpurnius Fabatus, who clearly remains a prominent part of Calpurnia's life until his death during Pliny's tenure in Bithynia. Pliny concludes his introduction to 4.19 with the statement that his wife has turned out to be "worthy of her father, aunt, and grandfather," *dignam patre dignam te dignam avo*. Pliny's inclusion of Calpurnia Hispulla with Calpurnia's father and grand-father confirms her intimate involvement in Calpurnia's upbring-ing. While she appears as the central figure in the tricolon and is thus subordinate to the men of whom Calpurnia is so deserving, she remains the only woman in any of his letters to whom Pliny connects a protégé as worthy.

Pliny reiterates Calpurnia Hispulla's motherly concern for Calpurnia in 8.11, in which Pliny reports his wife's miscarriage. There he calls her affection for Calpurnia *materna indulgentia molliorem* (1). In reality, Calpurnia Hispulla's critical role in Calpurnia's upbringing undoubtedly echoed the role that Plinia assumed in her son's young life following the death of his father. Both women appar-ently relied on the guidance of an older male relative, but neither Fabatus nor Pliny the Elder seems to have been closely involved in his young charge's life. Lest the parallel between Calpurnia Hispulla and Plinia go unnoticed Pliny firmly establishes Calpurnia Hispulla as a strong force in his own formative years.[27] Not only does he remark that she shaped him with her praise (7), but he even credits her with recommending that Calpurnia learn to love him, *quae denique amare me ex tua praedicatione consueverit* (6). Finally, Pliny offers thanks to Calpurnia Hispulla for giving Calpurnia and him to one another (8)

---

[27] In his consideration of the roles of paternal and maternal aunts in Roman society, Bettini (1991: 104–105) finds little evidence for a child's interaction with the *amita* (paternal aunt), but what testimony there is indicates that she would have the same strict, even fearsome approach to her niece expected of her brother or his father. Calpurnia Hispulla is part of Bettini's consideration, but her position is compli-cated by her need to act both as substitute mother and father. Thus, she bears both authority and affection for Calpurnia. Although Bettini does not include consider-ation of Calpurnia Hispulla's relationship with Pliny, the emphasis that Pliny places on her close friendship with his mother, her deep affection for him, and her role in arranging his marriage seems to cast her in the role of his *matertera* (maternal aunt) as Bettini explicates it (67–99).

as if she had arranged their marriage.[28] With his final statement, Pliny has made Calpurnia Hispulla's surrogacy complete. She assumes duties that might have been performed by his deceased parents, profoundly influencing his young life and even finding him a wife. Calpurnia Hispulla thus fulfills the same roles for Pliny that she had for her niece, and the deference with which Pliny treats her is that which he would have owed to Plinia.

LETTER 1.4: POMPEIA CELERINA. Another maternal figure in the letters is Pompeia Celerina, through whom Pliny establishes himself as a trustworthy son in the guise of a son-in-law. Pliny's letter to her is remarkable for the intimate relationship that it suggests between them. While its subject is, at least superficially, the excellent treatment that Pliny receives from her slaves when he stays at one of her estates and the laxity of his own slaves at home, Pliny uses so many first- and second-person pronouns and adjectives that he effectively creates a strong sense of affiliation between himself and Pompeia, a connection so profound that he has complete access to and use of her property, as he would that of his own mother. Although her daughter has died, Pompeia remains part of Pliny's family, and he has no need to stand on ceremony with her.

Pliny begins the letter with an exclamation regarding the copious amenities of Pompeia's estates and quickly establishes both the long tenure and closeness of his relationship with Pompeia. He declares that notification from her to the caretakers of her estate is unnecessary, as his letter is sufficient to prepare the household for his arrival: *ex epistulis meis, nam iam tuis opus non est: una illa brevis et vetus sufficit* (1). Pliny privileges his own letter by citing it first, but at the same time he secures the permanence of his place in Pompeia's family by referring to the sufficiency of a brief note that she must have sent to her estates some time before. The reader readily assumes that in it she had directed each of her various households to receive him at any time as if he were its master and to provide unlimited access to the comforts of the estate. Yet with those very words, Pliny begins his verbal appropriation of Pompeia's property as his letter abrogates any

[28] Pliny was at least in his mid-thirties at the time of his marriage to Calpurnia and had, undoubtedly, undertaken for himself to consult with Calpurnius Fabatus to contract it.

need for a letter from her, *epistulis meis ... tuis* (1). In fact, Pliny goes on to say directly that Pompeia's estates are more his than his own are: *non mehercule tam mea sunt quae mea sunt, quam quae tua* (2). The repetition of *mea sunt* (2) reinforces the concept that Pliny holds sway in her various households. Further evidence of his position in her *familia* is the fact that he is treated better by her household than by his own, *sollicitius et intentius tui me quam mei excipiunt* (2). Again with *tui me quam mei*, he has linked Pompeia's property with his own, and the repetition of the first person suggests that Pliny is in control.

That there is more going on in 1.4 than a polite interchange between social equals is well illustrated by another letter regarding Pliny's experience as a visitor. In 6.28 Pliny reports to Pontius Allifanus that he has received exceptional treatment at Allifanus' Campanian estate. Pliny's use of eight first-person and five second-person pronoun and adjective forms in this brief note produces the same intimate tone found in the note to Pompeia, but without any sense that Pliny intends any appropriation of his host's property. While Pliny mentions that Allifanus wants Pliny to have full use of his possessions, Pliny is quite careful to assign the offer strictly to Allifanus and to limit his own willingness to make use of his friend's property: *dices oportere me tuis rebus ut meis uti. etiam: sed perinde illis ac meis parco* (3). Pliny may enjoy Allifanus' hospitality, but he is careful to avoid taking advantage of it. No such constraint is even hinted at in Pliny's letter to Pompeia.

Pliny's control of Pompeia's property in 1.4 is further indicated by a statement that he makes regarding her property in another letter. In 3.19, Pliny seeks the advice of Calvisius Rufus regarding the possible purchase of land adjacent to Pliny's estate in Comum. Pliny pointedly refers to Pompeia's money as a source of capital readily available for his use, as if it were his own: *accipiam a socru, cuius arca non secus ac mea utor* (3.19.8). Here, just as he had in 1.4, Pliny makes no distinction between his own and Pompeia's resources. Furthermore, Pliny's ready promise of Pompeia's capital suggests almost tutelary control of her funds rather than the balanced reciprocity expected of a relationship predicated on *amicitia*.[29]

---

[29] In his analysis of Pliny and Pompeia's friendship, Hoffer (1999: 51) cites Pliny's use of *mea* in 3.19 only parenthetically in support of his interpretation of *mea* and *tua* in 1.4

Pliny continues by expressing his expectation that should Pompeia visit his estates she would be treated well by his households. He hopes not only that she would enjoy his possessions as he had hers but also that her arrival would shake his slaves from their neglectful treatment of him. Her presence, Pliny implies, was a formidable one. Pliny concludes with an aphorism regarding the tendency of slaves to lose their fear of a considerate master but to have the potential to be stirred to win his favor when company is present by serving his guests well (3). Pliny's comments seem at first to be a *topos* on the tendency of slaves to respond better to someone other than their masters, an interpretation apparently reinforced by the concluding *sententia*. Certainly, the topic provides Pliny with a perfect means through which to extend an expression of his own hospitality; Pompeia, however, will not just enjoy the comforts of Pliny's households. Pliny expects that she will motivate his slaves to be more attentive to him as any guest might, but there is never a hint that her own slaves are at all lax in their treatment of her. Pompeia's slaves obey her in order to please her, while his take advantage of him because he is considerate. It is hard to imagine that Pliny would allow himself to appear so weak in controlling his own household unless he had a specific purpose in doing so. Rather Pliny has a greater need to present Pompeia Celerina as a woman in firm command of her own resources than he does to portray himself as an effective master. Indeed, Pompeia's strength is crucial to her role in Pliny's self-presentation, as it specifically modifies the reader's view of Pliny's continuing access to her property. She has willingly granted Pliny full use of her estates because of their close association, rather than because he has been able to take advantage of her vulnerability.

as an indication of the equal sharing of resources, but such an analysis is made without consideration of the vastly different nature of the two letters and their recipients and without an in-depth analysis of their rhetorical structure. The anxiety that Hoffer identifies in 1.4 is centered on the potential dangers of slaveholding, and he concludes that Pliny writes his idyllic portrayal of their shared property and their interaction with their slaves to Pompeia, because slaves were less threatened by female owners than male ones. Hoffer claims that Pliny thus can present a sharp contrast between his and Pompeia's treatment by their slaves, because slaves worked harder for women than men. Hoffer may be right in his reading of Pliny's concern with relationships between slaves and masters or mistresses, but in focusing only on the issue of slavery, he ignores entirely the intimacy and presumption with which Pliny treats his mother-in-law's property, hardly the way any Roman would treat an equal.

Although a number of scholars have seen Pliny's letter to Pompeia as an indication of the improved social status of women, in no way do Pliny's words imply that he and Pompeia are equals.[30] Such an interpretation of 1.4 necessitates some idealized parity between Pliny and Pompeia, for which there is no supporting evidence. The letter presents two clear and distinct motivations originating in Pliny's determined self-representation. First, Pliny wishes to portray himself as a gentle master and willing host, aware of the need to reciprocate Pompeia's hospitality and hopeful that his household will be as welcoming as hers is to him – desires that are apparent in his wish that she will "enjoy my possessions as I do yours," *primum ut perinde nostris rebus ac nos tuis perfruaris* (3). More important to Pliny's image is the demonstration, early in the corpus of his letters, of his affiliation with and continued devotion to his mother-in-law. Although the date of 1.4 cannot be fixed with any assurance, it is virtually certain that it postdates the death of Pliny's first wife. Despite the fact that his wife's death has ended any formal ties he had to her mother, despite the fact that she is married, despite the fact that he has no legal access to her money without her consent, Pliny has not only maintained his relationship with Pompeia but – as 1.4 makes clear – continues to cultivate it, even visiting her at her estate in Alsium long after his marriage to Calpurnia (6.10). That Pliny would presume to call her possessions his own and to use her substantial financial resources for his personal business indicates with certainty the depth of their association. Thus, Pliny is established as a faithful son-in-law, so trusted that he enjoys free access to the possessions of a strong woman to whom he is no longer formally tied. This close relationship and his ready access to Pompeia's resources even after the bond of kinship between them has been dissolved make Pliny seem even more trustworthy than if their relationship were legally compelled.

---

[30] Hoffer (1999: 50) has concluded that Pliny's purpose for such a statement is to present to his reader the image of a Golden Age society in which he and Pompeia share property and power, and their slaves serve them with pleasure rather than fear. Vidén (1993: 93–94) has also taken the view that Pliny treated women with whom he associated as his equals. While piecemeal or decontextualized snippets of text from Pliny's letters may seem to point at some measure of equality between men and women, neither scholar's viewpoint can be supported by a comprehensive reading of Pliny's corpus.

Whether Pompeia ever took Pliny up on his reciprocal offer of hospitality is not stated in the letters. The reader is left with the sense that despite his honorable intentions, Pliny was more the beneficiary of Pompeia's generosity than she was of his, a circumstance not inappropriate to his assumed role as surrogate son.

LETTER 2.4: CALVINA. As comfortable as Pliny seems in his role as son/son-in-law, he is equally at ease with assuming the responsibilities of a father. As discussed in the preceding chapters, he takes on such duties in the recommendation of tutors and husbands. Even more illustrative of his willingness to assume a paternal role is his treatment of his *adfinis* Calvina, whom he addresses in 2.4.

Calvina's father died leaving her an estate apparently deeply in debt. Pliny begins his letter to her with a somewhat sympathetic statement that she might have hesitated to accept her inheritance were her father in debt to anyone other than Pliny. The circumstances are so serious that even a man would find the estate a burden (1). Pliny then shifts to the purpose of the letter, to inform Calvina of what he has done, *adfinitatis officio* (2), to relieve her difficult situation. Pliny offers detailed treatment of his financial contributions to Calvina and her father that is astonishingly direct, even blunt. He has paid off her father's other debts, leaving himself as sole creditor. He reminds her that he had provided her entire dowry, giving 100,000 sesterces directly and lending her father the balance. While purportedly offering these details as assurance to Calvina of his *facilitas*, his willingness to be of service to her, Pliny seems to reveal a stronger motivation in the words that follow: *debes famam defuncti pudoremque suscipere* (2). Her father's reputation would be threatened by the many debts he had left behind, and it is up to Calvina to prevent such disgrace.

Pliny has crafted well the image of the deceased as a spendthrift, unable to provide for his daughter in life or death, but also as a man whose memory Pliny seeks to rehabilitate by relieving all his debts. Taken as "real" correspondence, the letter suggests that the failure of Calvina's father to manage his affairs properly might somehow reflect badly on his kinsman Pliny. Yet it is impossible to believe that Pliny has acted on Calvina's behalf in order to preserve her father's reputation, as he has directed her to do. Certainly, the saddling of his daughter with oppressive debt would sully her father's image, but if he was burdened with excessive financial obligations before his demise, his reputation had already been tainted. In fact, were it Pliny's intent to safeguard the *fama* of Calvina's father, he would not have included 2.4 in a collection for publication, for in doing so he assured wider knowledge of the man's imprudent behavior. Furthermore, while it is clear that Pliny includes the letter as a means of highlighting his magnanimity in freeing his relative Calvina from oppressive debt, he might have made a simpler statement of his actions on her behalf as he does elsewhere in the collection without the recitation of his own financial circumstances that concludes the letter.[31]

Once Pliny has assured Calvina that he is not just offering words to assist her but that he has assumed and paid all of her father's debts and will seek no repayment – thus clearing Calvina of any liability – he offers a lengthy explanation of his ability to be so generous. The following sentence is key to Pliny's autobiographical intent in 2.4: *nec est quod verearis ne sit mihi onerosa ista donatio* (3). Lest Calvina be concerned that what he had done to relieve her burden had caused him any financial hardship, Pliny proceeds to offer an explanation of his own financial conduct. His resources depend upon income generated by the farming of his property, the rewards of which are often *minor an incertior* (3), but Pliny's *frugalitas* serves as a spring that allows his *liberalitas* in canceling her debts.[32] He is, therefore, characterized by seemingly contradictory virtues – parsimony and generosity – with the former enabling judicious use of the latter. Pliny is quick to point out that he still must exercise control over his giving, *tamen ita temperanda est* (4), but in this case only for others, not for Calvina.

It is no surprise that Calvina's father is unnamed. Pliny's concern for his *fama* might lead his reader to imagine that Pliny is protecting the spendthrift; yet by failing to name him, Pliny effectively

---

[31] See particularly 1.9, 4.13, and 6.32 in which Pliny discusses his generosity.

[32] In the final decades of the republic, *liberalitas* was not a trait one necessarily wished to be known for. It almost always described the kind of generosity shown by a superior to an inferior or employed during an electoral campaign to procure votes, and it almost always smacked of high-handed behavior. But in Pliny's time, more than a century after the inception of the principate, *liberalitas* was an imperial virtue, one that Pliny admires greatly and repeatedly in that best of emperors, Trajan (*Pan.* 3, 25, 27, 28, 33. 34, 38, 43, 51, 86). The shift in meaning of the term, provoked chiefly by the changed political climate of the principate, is discussed in detail by Manning (1985).

obliterates his memory and positions himself to assume a paternal role in Calvina's life, continuing to do what her irresponsible parent could not – provide for her fiscal well-being. Pliny will not stand by while his *adfinis* suffers from her father's long-standing poor judgment. In fact, Pliny's earlier investment in Calvina's future through his provision of her dowry would surely have prompted his continued interest in her fiscal well-being. There was little honor to be gained by Pliny for having financially supported a young woman who would become destitute later, and so his second gift has the additional benefit of preserving the value of his first one.

Pliny has carefully emphasized his beneficence to Calvina and his fidelity to her and to her father's *fama*. This type of generosity is also highlighted in a number of other letters that focus on Pliny's *donationes*. But what his account of the relief of Calvina's debt offers Pliny in addition is the means to present his own fiscal behavior as a contrast to that of Calvina's father. Relying on old-fashioned values of moderation and thriftiness, Pliny not only avoids being a debtor but also acts to relieve the debts of others. Pliny's painstaking description of how he handles his financial affairs, offered as reassurance to Calvina that he will not find his generosity overly burdensome, serves as a subtle but clear indication to the reader of Pliny's virtue. Pliny's self-portrait now includes his commitment to proper stewardship of his resources, and thus he offers himself as a model of proper restraint and appropriate liberality.

LETTER 6.3: PLINY'S NURSE. Pliny's continuing concern for the status of his donations is evident also in 6.3 in which Pliny thanks Verus for undertaking the management of the small farm that Pliny had given to his nurse. The property has since depreciated, evidently because of poor oversight. Pliny is quick to point out that he is entrusting Verus not only with the physical property but also with his gift: *tu modo memineris commendari tibi a me non arbores et terram, quamquam haec quoque, sed munusculum meum* (2). Perhaps Pliny is anxious to rectify his error in having chosen poorly the initial administrator of the farm. It is certain that his gift would seem rather miserable if after some years his nurse were found to be living on an unkempt and ramshackle property. Pliny is, therefore, as eager as its owner for the farm to prosper: *quod esse quam fructuosissimum non illius magis interest quae accepit, quam mea qui dedi* (2). This is not to say that Pliny has no genuine regard for the welfare of his nurse or that of Calvina. His gifts offer proof of his willingness to provide them appropriate support. But his actions are equally influenced by his need to preserve and magnify the social capital that he has gained by his *donationes* and to present himself as a seasoned steward of fiscal and human resources, carrying out his *officia* as protector of the defenseless.

Pliny's generosity and sense of justice as they are reflected in his personal conduct are not restricted to family members alone. The legacy letters provide a number of examples of Pliny's determination to follow the wishes of the deceased when the law does not require him to do so, even when it is to his personal disadvantage. The letters considered in the following sections focus on the plight of women both as testators and heirs, and each contributes to the reader's perception of Pliny as a man of integrity not only within his most intimate circle but in all of his social interactions.

LETTER 2.20: VERANIA GEMINA. Verania Gemina is the first female testator to appear in Pliny's letters. She has died, but before her demise, Pliny's nemesis M. Aquilius Regulus had coerced a legacy from this distinguished lady. The upper crust of Roman society was, of course, the only stratum that possessed estates sufficient to require the writing of a will, and large sums of money were often at stake in its disposition. The acknowledgment of family and friends was the testator's final act in the give and take of Roman social relations, one whose reward was an appropriate funeral, memorial, and *fama*, assuring the deceased of at least one form of immortality. The Roman fixation on wills led to fear of their falsification or manipulation and to the practice of legacy hunting. Consequently, the manner in which legacies were granted to and treated by their recipients was one means that propertied Romans employed to separate the righteous man from the scoundrel. Regulus, cast in the role of the villain, preys upon Verania in 2.20 and serves thereafter as an example of everything Pliny opposes.

The efficacy of legacy hunting is manifest in Pliny's presentation of Regulus, who Pliny says rose from poverty to great riches by compelling others to name him in their wills (2.20.13). Pliny's hatred for Regulus surely colors his depiction of his adversary's character, but the behavior he describes must have been a regular feature of upper-crust

Roman society.[33] According to Pliny, Regulus took shameless advantage of Verania. As she lay dying, Regulus barged into her sick room and made a display of astrological calculation and soothsaying in order to elicit mention in her will (2.20.2–5). Verania felt that she was in danger and quickly wrote a codicil to her will and, as she lay dying, shouted aloud the wickedness of her new legatee. Undaunted, Regulus sought other victims. He was unsuccessful in procuring a legacy from the second victim Pliny names, Blaesus, whom Regulus had just begun to cultivate (*quia nuper captare eum coeperat*, 2.20.7). Finally, Pliny recalls the case of a woman named Aurelia, whom Regulus, when he was witnessing the signing of her will, had compelled to leave to him her best clothing, the very garments that she had worn for the occasion (2.20.11). We may assume that the two women were more vulnerable to coercion than Blaesus, perhaps because he had more experience in dealing with the likes of Regulus or simply because women were easier prey. In either circumstance, Pliny is deeply offended by a man who accepts legacies that he did not deserve – those born of coercion rather than proper social conduct (2.20.11).

Pliny's apparent reluctance to accuse Regulus of misconduct in the prosecution of Rusticus (1.5) (see Chapter 1) certainly did not prevent him from maligning his enemy's character throughout the letters. In 2.20, Pliny does embellish his presentation of the consistently despicable conduct of Regulus, but the episodes he reports have a greater value than the simple condemnation of his enemy. In a corpus whose wont is to present positive models for its readers, in Regulus Pliny offers his only negative exemplum, one against which the reader may compare Pliny's own mores. Regulus fills this role in other letters whose topics include oratory and unseemly public displays of emotion, but nowhere does Regulus serve more pointedly as an anti-Pliny whose baseness highlights Pliny's nobility than in the legacy letters.

In sharp contrast to Regulus the despicable legacy hunter, Pliny – the deserving heir who carefully abides by his self-directive to honor

---

[33] The power of accusations of captation in the defamation of a man's character is readily apparent in the invective of Juvenal (e.g., 1.37–41, 5.137–140, or 10.201–202) and Martial (e.g., 2.26, 12.10). Champlin (1991: 201–202) provides a comprehensive list of the many ancient references to *captatio* and other methods of preying on testators.

the wishes of the deceased – appears in two letters that concern estates left to him by women. In each case, Pliny must deal with fellow heirs who may disagree with the testator's intent, and thus each provides a forum in which Pliny can contrast his own values with those of his *coheredes*.

LETTER 4.10: SABINA. In 4.10, a letter directed to Sabinus, we learn that he and Pliny have been named as Sabina's heirs, while her slave Modestus has been left a legacy with the words *Modesto quem liberum esse iussi* (1). Because Sabina had not specifically directed her heirs to free Modestus, Pliny and Sabinus are not required by law to emancipate him. Furthermore, if he remains a slave, he cannot receive a legacy. Pliny remarks that he has consulted legal experts who have informed him that there is no requirement for them either to free Modestus or to give him his legacy. It is clearly to Pliny's financial advantage to retain both the slave and the money bequeathed to him, but Pliny's sense of honor forbids him to do so. The fact that Pliny undertakes to write to Sabinus regarding their obligation to consider Sabina's intent suggests Sabinus' reluctance to do what Pliny believes is proper. Of course, Sabinus may not have been opposed to freeing Modestus and granting the legacy, and Pliny may simply have been seizing an opportunity to highlight his own unwavering integrity. Yet when Pliny expresses his certainty that Sabinus will agree, *confido accessurum te sententiae meae* (3), assuming and thus compelling his addressee's compliance, he causes the reader to wonder why Sabinus had questioned what was appropriate to begin with. When Pliny says that his fellow heir is assiduous in carrying out the wishes of the deceased, *religiosissime soleas custodire defunctorum voluntatem, quam bonis heredibus intellexisse pro iure est* (3), we are assured that it is Pliny who guards Sabinus' conscience. Pliny, the *bonus heres*, understands that he is bound, *pro iure*, to attend to Sabina's intentions. The law that binds Pliny is of his own devising, yet it has the same force as if it were universal. Thus, Modestus will enjoy his freedom and a legacy as if Sabina had taken care of the matter explicitly in her will. When he might have ignored her wishes to his own benefit, Pliny will repair Sabina's failure to make the proper arrangements for her slave by taking the actions she had meant to stipulate.

Their inexperience or unfamiliarity with the law must often have hindered Roman women in the correct disposition of their estates, sometimes with dire consequences for those, like Modestus, they wished to benefit from their wills. It was thus crucial for a woman to align herself with men of integrity who would guard her testamentary intentions despite any legal flaws in the document itself. Perhaps Sabina could have asked Pliny to verify the legality of the will, but Roman wills were subject to frequent changes, and it was surely more practical to name him as an heir with the expectation that he would attend to her wishes more closely than the law required. Indeed, despite her lack of care in producing a defective will, Pliny concludes the letter with the statement that Sabina had in fact been *diligentissima* where it counted the most – in choosing as her heirs men like Pliny whose honor compels them to behavior that is above reproach.

LETTER 5.1: POMPONIA GALLA. In the complex case of Pomponia Galla's will (5.1), Pliny again puts on display his good character. The letter is remarkable not only for the unusual circumstances that Pliny recounts but for the insight that it provides into Pliny's skill in backroom dealing and for the baldness with which he expresses his delight in the advantages he gains behind the scenes because of his reputation for and exercise of integrity.

Pliny addresses the letter to Annius Severus, unknown to us except for his residence in Comum, who receives two other letters concerning inheritance, one in which Pliny reports that he has bought a small Corinthian bronze statue with a legacy he had received (3.6) and an earlier letter, 2.16, the first in the collection to discuss Pliny's approach to any testamentary funds he receives: *propriam quondam legem mihi dixit, ut defunctorum voluntates, etiamsi iure deficerentur, quasi perfectas tuerer* (2.16.2) – to follow the wishes of the deceased whether or not the law requires it. Annius is thus a particularly appropriate recipient of a letter that offers a detailed look at Pliny's personal rule in action.

Pliny begins the letter with good news. He has just received a legacy from Asudius Curianus, whose mother Pomponia Galla had disinherited him some years earlier, choosing instead to divide her estate among Pliny, Sertorius Severus, and several men of equestrian rank. In the dispute over Pomponia's estate that followed her death, Pliny assumed the role of her protector, diligently safeguarding her intentions and even representing her in court, as there was apparently no male relative besides the son whom she had disinherited to do so.

After Pomponia's death, Pliny reports that Curianus had approached him privately in order to make a deal in which he would receive Pliny's share of her estate, an amount that he would eventually return to Pliny (5.1.2). Pliny responded with a statement that encapsulates his reasons for including letters that seem intensely personal: he is determined to reveal his character as immutable, regardless of the circumstances in which he is called upon to act. Pliny states that it was not his habit to act differently in private than in public (3); that is, he did not make back-room deals in contravention of his public demeanor.[34] Furthermore, Pliny told Curianus that he did not consider it appropriate to give money to a rich and childless man (3); however, Pliny agreed to waive his claim to the inheritance should Curianus show that his mother had disinherited him unfairly, warning him that he would not hesitate to find in favor of Pomponia if he judged it proper (4). Pliny's determination, *constantia*, to be fair in his treatment of Curianus is assured by his choice of two outstanding citizens, Corellius and Frontinus, *duos quos tunc civitas nostra spectatissimos habuit* (5), to weigh the arguments with him. Yet, Pliny's diligence on behalf of Pomponia's wishes is also confirmed through his rebuttal of the case presented by Curianus, which Pliny chose to offer in defense of her decision to disinherit her son, as no one else was present to defend the honor of the deceased (6). The panel of three found in favor of the disinheritance. Pliny had successfully protected Pomponia Galla's testament and intentions.

If Pliny had concluded his report of Curianus' attempts to abrogate his mother's intentions with his own triumphant defense of Pomponia's will, his actions might be perceived as entirely self-serving, a means of preserving his personal stake in her estate through the exclusion of Curianus as heir. But Pliny avoids any possibility that such a charge might be leveled at his conduct in this case, as he continues with an account of his actions some months later when Curianus had called Pomponia's remaining heirs before the Centumviral Court to contest their claim on his mother's estate. Because of their friendship with Arulenus Rusticus and Verulana Gratilla, Pliny's fellow heirs were anxious to settle, some fearing that they too might be subjected

---

[34] Proving the consistency of his behavior *palam et secreto* is, of course, one of the primary aims of Pliny's publication of "private" documents. Pliny's declaration to Curianus, then, is a direct statement of that element of his self-portrait.

to some criminal charge in the dangerous last years of Domitian's reign (8). Pliny reports that he intervened, brokering a deal between the heirs and Curianus, as a result of which Curianus obtained more than a fourth of Pomponia's estate, the amount to which a legal heir was entitled under the *Lex Falcidia* (Champlin 1991: 118). Pliny had agreed, in fact, to ensure that in addition to money from the other heirs, Curianus would receive an amount equivalent to Pliny's share. A double benefit thus accrues to Pliny's reputation, first for success-fully upholding the wishes of the testator and later for protecting his fellow heirs by forfeiting his own inheritance, even though he was under no legal obligation to do so.

Pliny returns to the matter of the recently received legacy with which he opened the letter, emphasizing that Curianus had marked Pliny's conduct *notabile honore* (11). Pliny himself believes his deed to have been in accord with the custom of former times, the good old days he so admires (11). He describes his reward as twofold, affecting both his reputation and his conscience, *tuli fructum non conscientiae modo verum etiam famae* (10). Pliny ends the letter with a telling state-ment of his own desire for recognition: *neque enim sum tam sapiens ut nihil mea intersit, an iis quae honeste fecisse me credo, testificatio quaedam et quasi praemium accedat* (13). Pliny's forthright admission that he seeks a return for his virtuous behavior seems a startlingly unguarded moment in a collection of letters that offer an overwhelmingly pos-itive view of their author. But it must be remembered that in Pliny's milieu, reciprocity was crucial to strong social alliances. Magnanimity without return was a poor investment. Pliny's statement is neither dis-ingenuous nor shocking, but merely a reflection of the zeitgeist of Roman society. Pliny's account of his reward, received in the form of a legacy from Curianus, is instructive for his reader – proper behavior receives its just reward, even when none is anticipated. Righteousness may thus be enhanced by financial remuneration.

In his negotiations to arrange a settlement between Curianus and his co-heirs outside of court, Pliny may seem to have forgotten his obligation to carry out Pomponia Galla's intentions. Yet, Pliny's previ-ous judgment of Curianus' testamentary rights, concluding as it did that Pomponia Galla had been justified in disinheriting her son and had left a valid and righteous will, was likely sufficient defense of her wishes for Pliny to claim that he had done his duty. Pliny had proved the justice of her actions in a public forum, airing, we must presume, Curianus' failure as her son. The more pressing needs of the living, his fellow heirs, superseded any further responsibility to the deceased.

In describing his own behavior in the disposition of legacies, Pliny leaves no doubt as to the appropriate role of the inheritor: he must set aside his own interests to carry out the will of the deceased. Pliny allows Sabina and Pomponia Galla, whose lineage may have been apparent to those who knew Pliny well but whose connections are hard to discern otherwise, to remain virtually anonymous, offering few or no clues as to their rank or distinguished relations. Thus, the focus of each letter falls on Pliny and his actions, not on the roles of the testators who are relegated to the background.

The efficacy of the relative anonymity of Pliny's benefactors in his self-representation is balanced well by the prominence of the women in the remaining legacy letters, which serve to offer *exempla*, both positive and negative, for the proper formulation of testaments.

LETTER 6.33: ATTIA VIRIOLA. *Epistulae* 6.33 is addressed to Voconius Romanus, to whom Pliny is sending a copy of a speech he made on behalf of Attia Viriola. As noted in the discussion of 1.5 in Chapter 1, Romanus was one of a number of young men whom Pliny sought to promote and with whom he corresponded. In fact, Romanus receives eight letters from Pliny – a number that makes him Pliny's favorite correspondent among the beneficiaries of his guidance. It is to Romanus that Pliny sends his *Panegyricus* with a request for his reactions and comments (3.13), as well as 6.15, a cautionary tale about the need to carefully choose one's audience. It is no surprise, then, that he should also receive a letter that focuses not only on the tenor of a speech that Pliny calls his *De Corona* (6.33.1) but also on the setting in which it was delivered, with the expectation, no doubt, that Romanus would see both as exemplary.

Pliny opens with a quote from Vergil (*Aen.* 8.439) and a command to his reader to put aside any writing or reading in favor of his *oratio*, which Pliny calls *divina* (6.33.1). Having admitted the arrogance of such a remark, *num superbius potui*, Pliny then modifies his self-praise by comparing the speech only with his others, *inter meas pulchram* (6.33.1). While the speech, of course, does not survive, an extensive description of its features is presented in the second half of the letter, and Pliny concludes with another statement of its quality. The remainder of the letter provides context for Pliny's defense of Attia. Pliny claims (6.33.7) to offer this background in order to entice Romanus to read this masterpiece and to provide for his addressee the ambience of the trial.

Pliny drops the name of his client, *est haec pro Attia Viriola* (2), at the start of his scene setting. There seems every reason to expect that Romanus would recognize her name, as Pliny offers only a few biographical details that would identify her to the letter's recipient. He proceeds to describe a trial scene packed with 180 judges and a corona many rows deep. Attia's status, *dignitate personae*, is only one of Pliny's explanations for the significance of the trial. He cites in addition the unusual nature of the case, *exempli raritate*, and the large number of judges. Attia is of high birth and is married to a praetorian senator, and she has been disinherited by her father only a few days after the latter remarried (2). Her father's new wife is called only *noverca*, stepmother, a word that almost always carried sinister overtones for the Romans. Stepmothers were consistently suspected of doing just what Attia's had apparently done, of abrogating the innate rights of children to their patrimony.[35] Pliny reinforces the standard negative appraisal the *noverca* would receive, using the words *amore captus* to describe Attia's father (2). Thus, her stepmother is also unequivocally labeled as a legacy hunter, *captator*, the likes of whom Pliny has already expressed his disdain for in his treatment of Regulus in 2.20.

Although the vote was divided, Attia's stepmother lost her sixth share of the estate (6). Pliny adds a rather curious note at this point regarding the defeat of another petitioner who was attempting to gain a share of the old man's estate. Suburanus, Pliny says, had been disinherited by his own father, yet had sought no restitution of his own patrimony but instead had chosen to go after a piece of Attia's father's estate. Pliny chides him for his *singularis impudentia* (6) in

---

[35] See especially Gray-Fow's 1988 study of the *noverca* in Roman literature and history, in which he reviews evidence for the idea of stepmothers as dangerous not only to their stepchildren's inheritance but even their lives. Pliny does not consistently play on the theme in his letters and, in fact, presents Fannia as the devoted *noverca*, but we can be assured in a case involving legacies that his readers would have reacted according to long-held prejudices against stepmothers.

seeking someone else's inheritance when he himself had been disinherited and thus did not dare to seek his own. Perhaps Pliny includes
this tidbit of information to amuse his addressee or to give Romanus
a sense of the complex atmosphere of a *iudicium quadruplex* in which
it is likely that multiple parties brought suits bearing on the same
issue or estate. But it may well be that Pliny's purpose is to secure the
identification of Attia Viriola with Sextus Attius Suburanus, Trajan's
praetorian prefect. The Suburanus named in Pliny's letter is, at best,
a nephew or cousin of Attia Viriola. Although Pliny has no part in his
defense and, in fact, expresses open disdain for Suburanus' claim
on the estate, his inclusion in Pliny's account associates Attia Viriola
with the name Suburanus. Thus, Pliny establishes a firm but unspoken connection to Attius Suburanus through his defense of Attia. If
Attia and Suburanus, Trajan's prefect, are brother and sister, Pliny's
defense of her inheritance rights and his attack on the *noverca* are
equally valuable to the protection of her brother's patrimony.

Pliny returns to a description of the speech that he delivered, noting
its variety of style and abundant material and anecdotes (8). He speaks,
too, of his passionate delivery, *dedimus vela indignationi, dedimus irae, dedimus dolori* (10), and calls the case *amplissima* (10). The reader can imagine the full force of Pliny's wrath in his attack on Attia's stepmother for
her captation and on her beguiled father for his gullibility and his unjust
behavior in disinheriting this fine, innocent noblewoman. Attia's cause
gives Pliny the perfect venue to showcase his indignation at the improper
treatment of heirs through a masterful display of his rhetorical skill.

Opportunities for great oratory in settings that attracted large audi-
ences were rare in Pliny's time, when fiery political speeches had no
place. Pliny clearly relishes the opportunity provided by his speech for
Attia Virola – the defense of a politically prominent woman in a four-
fold court setting, whose unusual arrangement must have attracted
substantial interest and audience.[36] While 6.33 purports to provide
background for the reading of Pliny's speech, the letter's publication
was, in reality, a subtle mechanism for ensuring broader knowledge
of his highly praised rhetorical skill and Pliny's affiliation with and
service to prominent individuals close to the heart of Roman power.

---

[36] Sherwin-White (1966: 399) comments that Pliny's letter 6.33 is, in fact, the main
evidence for the nature of this multiple procedure.

LETTER 8.18: DOMITIA LUCILLA AND HER *NOVERCA* (WIFE OF DOMITIUS TULLUS). Whereas Attia's father had allowed himself to be manipulated by his new wife, Domitia Lucilla's father had been careful to treat his daughter justly. In 8.18, Pliny reports the passing of Domitius Tullus, whose adopted daughter, Domitia Lucilla, was the heiress of his enormous fortune. Pliny recounts in detail the disinheritance, adoptions, and estates that contributed to Tullus' vast fortune and praises Tullus' wife for her devotion to the old man in caring for him throughout his physical decline. He makes it plain that, when she agreed to marry a wealthy man who was chronically ill, Tullus' wife had been an object of serious criticism because of her rank and previously upright conduct, *natalibus clara, moribus proba* (8.18.8). Despite the widely held initial judgment of her actions as that of a *captatrix*, she had redeemed herself in Pliny's view by her devoted care of the old man. In this letter, the *noverca* defies the standard negative definition. For, although Tullus leaves his wife a legacy of his country estates and money, his child Domitia Lucilla was his sole heir. His will is proof of both the strength of his determination and the sincere devotion of his wife. Because of his estate's great size and the powerful connections Domitia enjoyed, Tullus' action is the ideal exemplum for Pliny to offer regarding the appropriate distribution of an estate whose primary beneficiaries should rightly be the descendants of the deceased.

It is now generally believed that the *Testamentum Dasumii*, a lengthy inscription dating to the early second century that gives the details of the disposition of a vast estate, is the will of Domitius Tullus. The inscription provides the names of those who are to receive legacies, among whom are listed a certain Secundus and Cornelius, presumably Pliny and Tacitus, both of whom were members of the senate and must, if their identification is correct, have been *amici* of the testator.[37] Pliny may indeed then have been privy to the intimate details of Tullus' life through direct association with the family, although he never mentions that there is any relationship between himself and Tullus or that he has benefited from the will in any way. Pliny himself admits that he has reported *omnes fabulas urbis* (8.18.11), the city

---

[37] *CIL* vi 10229, line 17. For discussion of the inscription and its connection to Domitius Tullus, see particularly Eck 1978 and Syme 1985b.

gossip, but the extent of his knowledge suggests that the stories he has heard have their origins in the intimate circle of those who were closely affiliated with the family. Pliny has, moreover, presented his reader with a model testament, as Tullus leaves legacies to members of his family rather than the hangers-on who, Pliny reports, displayed their apparently unfulfilled "shameless expectations," *improbas spes* (8.18.3), of obtaining some of his estate by their vilification of the deceased. Pliny's approval of Tullus' actions serves to blacken even further the actions of legacy hunters like Regulus.

Pliny ends his letter about Domitius Tullus with a *sententia* that reveals the nature not only of 8.18 but of all of Pliny's letters regarding legacies as exempla by which he structures his own behavior and on which he would have others model theirs: *ad rationem vitae exemplis erudimur* (8.18.12). Above all, Pliny presents his own conduct in direct contrast with that of Regulus. Not only does Pliny despise legacy seeking, but, in consideration of the wishes of the deceased, he is even willing to forfeit inheritances properly assigned to him in order to fulfill the wishes of the deceased or to protect his fellow heirs. In the legacy letters, Pliny is clearly guided by principle and honor, an advocate for those unable to defend themselves.

Conclusion

The advantage that Pliny gains by the inclusion of letters that show his life away from the public eye is clear – his internal life is shown to be as spotless as his external one. His lack of living relatives does compel him to find surrogate figures through whom to reveal his familial character, and he must rely on his wives' families for women with whom to interact, yet this seems no great hindrance to the efficacy of his self-representation as a loyal, reliable, and trusted family member. The legacy letters then serve to extend Pliny's integrity in his interactions with women all the way to the imperial court.

The reader cannot help but notice just how remarkable these women are, even those who require Pliny's assistance. Verania, Aurelia, Sabina, and Pomponia are women of means, perhaps substantial resources but certainly enough to prompt them to make wills, and they seem to have done so independently, with no male relatives in sight, except perhaps those they have disowned. Yet the women's seeming independence is quickly brought into question by the issues surrounding their legal position. While Sabina wanted to free her slave and leave him some money, she failed to make a proper will whose stipulations would assure that her wishes were followed. Without someone to defend her intention to disinherit her son, Pomponia's desire to do so would undoubtedly have been overturned on her son's appeal to the courts. Verania and Aurelia fall prey to the despicable captator Regulus and leave legacies to him that were not what they had intended. All are without male support, and all are in danger of having their lasting reputation, secured in the Roman world by a well-wrought will, marred because of their own inability to counter the treachery or faithlessness of men around them. Verania and Aurelia are beyond Pliny's help, but their plight serves well as a foil to the positive examples of his intervention on behalf of Sabina and Pomponia, whose final wishes are realized because of his determined efforts, despite the obstacles thrown in his way by men less honorable than he.

At the other end of the process and just as in need of a champion are women whose inheritances are imperiled or perilous. The courageous Calvina, so beleaguered by her father's impropriety, is willing to shoulder the financial burdens imposed upon her by his testament. Despite her desire to do what is demanded of her, Calvina will clearly be crushed by her father's debts without Pliny's intercession. Attia will be cheated out of her rightful portion of her father's estate without Pliny's impassioned speech on her behalf. Pliny thus realigns wills gone astray to the benefit of both female testators and heirs. Only Domitia Lucilla, whose father took care of his own immortal fame by the proper disposition of his estate and the care with which he chose his wife, will receive what is rightly hers without hardship. Pliny makes abundantly clear that the well-being of women, despite their apparent fiscal independence, can only be assured if they are protected by men whose integrity is unquestionable.

His reader never hears what Pliny does in writing his own will, but there is no doubt that it will be legally sound, socially acceptable, and a fitting contribution to his own immortality. It will serve whatever family members he has, honoring them and caring for them; it will recognize his friends; and, as always, it will encourage others to follow his example.

4

Pliny

Creator of the Ideal Wife

gloria dignus, qui ... uxorem quam virginem accepit,
tam doctam politamque reddiderit.

Pliny, Epistulae 1.16.6

He is deserving of glory who took a wife as a maiden and rendered
her so learned and polished.

Pliny knew well that no woman was more central to his image than
his wife. Indeed, many letters stress that the presence of a good and
loving wife is an indication of a life well lived. But Pliny makes equally
clear that a good wife does not simply arrive at a man's doorstep on
the day she is led into marriage with him. Praiseworthy wives must be
carefully selected and cultivated by their husbands, trained by each
man to behave in ways that accord with his character and ambitions.
Pliny does offer his readers a model for the ideal wife, as scholars
have noted for many years; however, the model is not the simple one
so often assembled from his many references to the qualities of wives.
Instead, we should see in the letters guidelines through which Pliny's
readers may fashion their wives, beginning with the selection of a
good candidate (the bride) for instruction, proceeding through the
early phases of her training, and culminating in the final product,
a seasoned matron whose chief concern will be the enhancement
of her husband's reputation. Pliny is acutely aware that the success
of his instruction and thus his ability to manage his household will
be judged according his wife's behavior. The glory or disgrace that

women might reflect upon the men in their lives was in fact a long-standing theme of Roman oratory and history.

Pliny's Predecessors and His *Panegyricus*

Just as a Roman woman's proper comportment might bring acclaim to her husband, her misbehavior was likely to bring him condemnation, particularly within the imperial house and senatorial ranks. Indeed, in Pliny's time, writers were much more likely to focus on the negative behavior of women than on their virtues. The damage that a man might suffer from his wife's dishonor is nowhere more apparent than in Tacitus' use of the scandalous behavior of Messalina and the power-hungry machinations of Agrippina to defame the emperor Claudius in *Annales* 11–13.[1] Tacitus offers his readers negative exempla of wives that contrast perfectly with Pliny's positive ones. But, of course, both men inherit a long-standing literary and rhetorical tradition that tied the conduct of women to the characters of the men with whom they were associated. Such a connection was not limited to wives and husbands. Cicero's vicious attack on the profligate behavior of Clodia, the chief accuser against Marcus Caelius for whom he speaks in the *Pro Caelio*, provides him not only a means to protect his client but also an arena to condemn Clodia's brother Clodius, Cicero's archenemy. Further evidence is offered by Sallust, who in the *Bellum Catilinae* uses his association with Sempronia to blacken the character of Catiline.

Sallust and Cicero were themselves employing traditional invective that defamed men with the poor conduct of their women, as illustrated by Livy's account of Cato's speech in opposition to the repeal of the *Lex Oppia* in 195 B.C.E.[2] At the height of the Second Punic War, the law was passed prohibiting women from the public display of substantial wealth – wearing more than a *semuncia* of gold or dyed garments and riding in carriages within one mile of Rome.[3] Livy's

[1] See particularly Joshel (1995).

[2] In purely chronological terms, of course, Livy's work follows that of Cicero and Sallust. Further obfuscation ensues as Livy undoubtedly draws on late republican material in composing Cato's speech. We may reasonably assume that the nature of Cato's speech was generally known, and it is what Cato says rather than precisely how he says it that pertains to my argument.

[3] See Livy 34.1–8; Tacitus *Ann.* 3.33–34; Valerius Maximus 9.1.3; Aulus Gellius 10.23 and 17.6. The Oppian Law, itself, seems to have been directed not so much at

Cato begins with a condemnation of husbands for not exercising proper control over their wives within their own households, for – he says – the freedom women have been given at home has emboldened them to seek political power en masse in the forum (34.2.1–3). Thus, according to Cato, the failure of men to control their wives has profound repercussions for the stability of the state. Cato fears the erosion of male authority, and so he directs his audience to consider that women are hard to contain even with all the laws that make them subject to men. If laws are repealed one at a time, he argues, eventually women will become not equal but superior to men (34.3.1–4). Finally, Cato invokes the *maiores*, whose example all honorable Romans were expected to follow, as he tries to shame his audience of men for failing to restrain their women.[4]

Whether Livy is citing a copy of Cato's speech or creating the kind of speech Cato was supposed to have given, these words surely reflect the traditional views that the elder Cato was famous for espousing, emphasizing particularly the firm hand a *paterfamilias* was expected to impose upon all members of his household, including his wife. The *familia*, in Cato's view, is a microcosm of the state, in which the failure of authority to restrain improper behavior in its members imperiled the survival of the enterprise as a whole.

The moral legislation enacted by Augustus gives further testimony to the continued importance of women's personal behavior to the welfare of the state in Livy's day. The focus, furthermore, of the *Lex Iulia de Adulteriis* was on the containment of adulterous women, whose comportment a husband was compelled by the law to monitor and punish. A husband who tolerated his wife's errant behavior

---

restraining women, but at restraining the display of excess wealth, through which the growing inequality of assets among the elite of Rome would become entirely too obvious for the continuing pretense of shared political power. The dominance of certain powerful and prosperous *gentes* in attaining high political office during the time of the law's propagation and repeal is well illustrated by the Cornelii Scipiones, whose members held one of the consulships in seven of the thirty-two years between 222 and 190 B.C.E.

[4] Although Cato notes the presence of women during the delivery of his speech, he consistently refers to them in the third person, while addressing the men directly in the second person. The women thus become objects of concern, rather than actors in the political drama, despite the fact that the cause of Cato's concern is their actions.

was himself subject to prosecution, and charges of this type were still being brought in Pliny's day.[5]

Augustan legislation proved to be no panacea for anxious husbands in the empire. A century after Livy wrote his annals, Tacitus presents a speech in which M. Valerius Messalla Messallinus cites the Oppian Laws as he argues in favor of women accompanying their husbands to the provinces. Valerius' view is that the *Lex Oppia* may have suited the times in which it was passed and then repealed, but the ultimate responsibility for a woman's behavior falls on her husband.

placuisse quondam Oppias leges sic temporibus rei publicae postulantibus: remissum aliquid postea et mitigatum, quia expedierit. frustra nostram ignaviam alia ad vocabula transferri: nam viri in eo culpam si femina modum excedit. (Ann. 3.36)

At one time, when circumstances in the republic demanded, the Oppian Laws were pleasing: afterwards they were relaxed and weakened, because it was expedient. In vain is our laziness rendered in other terms: for if a wife exceeds her bounds, her husband is to blame for it.

Law, then, was no substitute for vigilance or remedy for *ignavia* on a husband's part.

While Cato the Elder might not have supported the repeal of the *Lex Oppia*, the words that Livy has him speak in opposition to such an act suggest that he would certainly have understood and supported Valerius' declaration of male culpability. It is not surprising to learn from Cicero that Cato, like Cicero himself, was indebted to the *Oeconomicus* of Xenophon (*Sen.* 59), a work that provides not only a manual for the management of a profitable household but also guidelines for the proper cultivation of a wife. Cicero says elsewhere that as a young man he had translated the *Oeconomicus* into Latin (*Off.* 2.87). Sarah Pomeroy (1994: 69–71) has concluded that Cicero's translation was quite well known, with citations of it appearing in later works by Varro, Columella, Pliny, and Quintilian. Pliny's familiarity with Xenophon's work is reflected well by the traits that Pliny admires in model wives. In fact, Xenophon's rather egalitarian view of a woman's potential for complete control of the household, matching or even superseding the authority of her husband within the domestic sphere, seems more suited to the Roman household than the Greek one.

[5] See Chapter 5 regarding the adultery of Gallitta.

In the dialogue that Xenophon presents in the *Oeconomicus*, Ischomachus notes first that his wife was only fifteen when she came to him and that she had spent her previous years under careful supervision so that she would see, hear, and speak as little as possible (7.4). He then expounds upon the knowledge a bride should have when she comes to her husband's household – how to weave, how to assign wool-working tasks to slaves, and how to control her appetites (7.4) – and then carefully explains the process of instructing her in techniques of proper management. If her husband trains her well, by training the slaves in turn she will increase their productivity and their value and so enrich the household (7.35–36, 41). Earlier in the dialogue, Socrates makes clear that it would be remarkable if a young wife, still a child at marriage, had any knowledge of what she should do as a married woman (3.13). Thus, when Ischomachus' wife is distressed that she cannot find an item he requires, he insists that the blame is his because he did not instruct her as to the proper organization of their possessions (8.2). Good wives are made, not born, although the process requires that they come to their husbands with certain basic qualifications – particularly wool-working experience, a source of household wealth but presumably something that their husbands would have had little or no knowledge of.[6]

Roman funerary inscriptions, generally dedicated by bereaved husbands and sons, clearly reflect a similar emphasis. Here the traits a good wife possesses include modesty, devotion, and skill with wool. Other qualities may be added to these, but few inscriptions appear without them. The *Laudatio Turiae*, dating to the first century B.C.E., offers insight into the virtues a husband might find most valuable. In the midst of his long commemoration of Turia's many acts of faithfulness to her father, to her sister, and to himself, the author inserts a list of her domestic virtues:

domestica bona pudicitiae, obsequi, comitatis, facilitatis, lanificii studi, religionis sine superstitione, ornatus non conspiciendi, cultus modici cur memorem? (*ILS* 8393: 30)

---

[6] Pomeroy's (1994: 61–65) discussion of the value of textile production to the Greek household would also apply to Roman ones. She notes particularly that soft goods were not only used by the members of the household but might also be a source of ready cash.

Why should I recall your domestic qualities – modesty, obedience, affability, courteousness, wool working, religious scruple without superstition, splendid dress without ostentation, modest appearance?

Turia's husband, having given the customary nod to these traditional virtues, is actually more concerned with his wife's efforts to preserve his life and her enduring devotion to him. The latter is so great that she proposed a divorce when she was unable to conceive in order that he might have children with some other wife (31). His refusal and the commitment it suggests, as well as her determined *constantia*, reflect *gloria* on both partners.

In Pliny's day, then, the elements of an ordered marriage suitable for a man of rank were the selection of a suitable wife, who had certain basic skills but little exposure to the world; the education of the young wife to become a full partner in the household; and the ultimate reward of being supported and honored by her devotion.

The same elements of a prosperous marriage are evident in Pliny's praise of Trajan's relationship with his wife Plotina. In the *Panegyricus*, Pliny takes great pains to contrast the demeanor of the *optimus princeps* with that of his predecessors, and in so doing he chooses to include a discussion of the women in the emperor's inner circle. Pliny begins his consideration of Trajan's personal life by noting that such an examination would be entirely in accordance with the emperor's *gloria – nihil accommodatius fuerit ad gloriam quam penitus inspici* (83.1) – because his behavior at home was as outstanding as his conduct as emperor (83.2). Pliny then notes that even great men had suffered disgrace for their failure to choose or control their wives: *multis inlustribus dedecori fuit aut inconsultius uxor adsumpta aut retenta patientius.* Their *domestica infamia*, Pliny adds, prevented these men from being considered *maximi* (83.4). Pliny must surely refer here to the notorious wives of the preceding century, condemned by Tacitus and mocked by Juvenal, and so he begins his characterization of Trajan's excellent wife with a profound but simple statement of Plotina's value to the emperor: *tibi uxor in decus et gloriam cedit* (83.4).

Trajan's *gloria* is quite naturally a focus of Pliny's *Panegyricus*, but elsewhere in the speech Trajan alone is responsible for his own *gloria*, as he repairs the relationship between the emperor and the senate and restores opportunities for glory to those who rank below him.[7] It is Trajan's interaction with and treatment of men of Pliny's rank in public view that merits *gloria*. Unlike some of his predecessors, he does not try to fabricate *gloria* or steal it from others (16, 81). Instead of riding in a litter, he walks with everyone else (23) as an ordinary citizen, even appearing in person as a candidate for the consulship and swearing his oath standing while the current consul remains seated (63–64). Finally, Pliny calls it a source of *gloria* that Trajan carries out the duties of friendship neglected by emperors past, obligations necessary to the maintenance of his position (85). Trajan's glory, like that defined by Cicero 150 years earlier, hinges upon the praise of leading men and the witness of the multitude.[8]

Gloria follows Trajan's actions in the forum, but the true proof of his excellence is the careful inspection of his *intimi secessus* (83.1). Thus, Plotina has a responsibility to Trajan's *gloria*, to benefit his reputation by her comportment. As the only person besides Trajan mentioned by Pliny in connection with the emperor's *gloria*, she is intimately tied to the *bona fama* he requires to maintain his position. While he has ultimate responsibility for his *gloria* when he is outside the *domus*, she alone can assure Trajan's *gloria* within the *domus*.

Pliny then offers an explanation of Plotina's excellence. She is *sancta* and *antiqua*, so virtuous that she could be chosen as wife by the pontifex maximus (83.5).[9] Plotina is an exceptional wife, devoted to her husband rather than his power, as she demonstrates by traveling modestly as if she were an ordinary citizen, but the credit for her character redounds directly to the emperor – *mariti hoc opus qui ita imbuit ita instituit* (83.7). Trajan has instructed her properly, and so her character and actions are a direct reflection of his own. The *gloria* that results from her comportment is Trajan's rather than Plotina's, while *her gloria* will come from her willing subordination to the emperor, *nam uxori sufficit obsequi gloria* (83.7).

---

[7] In fact, Pliny presents Trajan as a man who avoids seeking *gloria* (*Pan.* 3, 20).
[8] Cicero offers considerations of *gloria* in several works (*Sest.* 139, *Tusc.* III.2, 3 and, of course, the lost treatise *De Gloria*), the most pertinent of which to this discussion is *Phil.* I, 29: *est autem gloria laus recte factorum magnorumque in rem publicam fama meritorum quae cum optimi cuiusque, tum etiam multitudinis testimonio comprobatur.* It remains to be seen how great were such deeds as Trajan *not* demanding to be left a legacy in everyone's will (*Pan.* 43).
[9] Trajan, like his predecessors in the principate, *was* pontifex maximus. Pliny is merely emphasizing that he had selected a bride of exceptional purity.

Pliny concludes his characterization of Plotina by emphasizing that her husband is her model, *maritum ... imitetur,* and his self-control demands hers – *modestia viri ... debet verecundiam uxor marito* (83.8). Trajan has succeeded in choosing and cultivating an outstanding wife. While the descriptors Pliny uses in praising her character are substantially more elevated than those in the *Laudatio Turiae* (he is, after all, describing the empress), Plotina shares with Turia the *bona domestica* of self-control, modesty, and submission to her husband. Pliny's presentation of Plotina as an "old-fashioned girl" (*antiqua*) fits well the new order–old values theme of the *Panegyricus,* as her portrait contrasts sharply with those of her predecessors Domitia, Agrippina, and Messalina.

Trajan's influence at home extends also to his sister (in the same way that Augustus' had extended to Octavia), as Pliny notes that in her character may be seen his *simplicitas, veritas,* and *candor* (84.1). But Trajan's sister, Ulpia Marciana, has the good fortune to have been particularly well born; her qualities, like his, are innate. Pliny comments that when she is compared with Plotina, one would have to question whether training or birth was more conducive to proper living (84.1). Trajan has, of course, not trained his sister – a task that would have fallen to her parents and her husband. But he comes from the same stock and serves as a model for her behavior as well as that of Plotina – *te enim imitari, te subsequi student* (84.4). The women are united in support of the emperor, refusing honors offered to them and choosing instead to be honored by their identification with him (84.7), for each of them reflects his character, Ulpia Marciana by nature and Plotina by the emperor's careful instruction.

Trajan's ability to conduct his private affairs and to oversee the behavior of the women within his household provides evidence for Pliny that the emperor's excellence is complete, permeating every aspect of his life. Although Cato would never have approved of any emperor, Trajan has demonstrated his qualifications to command and secure an empire, by restoring domestic order in the house of the *princeps.*

Trajan, the best of emperors, was the ultimate model for elite Roman men of his era to emulate. Pliny, therefore, undertakes in his letters to offer guidance for Roman men to follow with their *uxores* and to place the comportment of his own wife within a long tradition of ideal wives.

Pliny's Trifold Model of the Ideal Wife

Previous scholarship on Pliny's letters has endeavored to draw a single, unified image of the ideal wife, generally by reinforcing and expanding Pliny's portrait of Calpurnia with his remarks about other wives.[10] In fact, many wives in Pliny's letters are virtually anonymous, identified simply as *uxor.* They often appear only to fulfill their designated positions in support of their husbands, especially during times of trial or illness.[11] Pliny goes so far as to call Vestricius Spurinna's wife an *uxor singularis exempli* (3.1.5), without any elucidation of the qualities that warranted such high praise and without the mention of her name. Even Pliny's portrait of the elder Arria, in which he quotes her extensively (as discussed in Chapter 1), is one-dimensional, concentrating entirely on her actions in matters concerning her husband. Pliny's knowledge of Arria, moreover, is gained secondhand from Fannia. Yet, Pliny does offer more in-depth portraits of several women besides his wife, and it is these women to whom we must look for a full understanding of Pliny's ideal wife.

The type of detailed characterization that Pliny employs with numerous male exempla – that is, portraits that assign virtues and include descriptive adjectives that speak to individuality – is provided for only four women; Minicia Marcella; Pliny's wife, Calpurnia; her aunt Calpurnia Hispulla; and Clodia Fannia.[12] While Calpurnia

---

[10] Through a careful examination of the vocabulary with which Pliny praises his wife, Calpurnia, and describes their affection for one another, Maniet (1966) attempts, with mixed success, to define both the depth of their relationship and the authenticity of Pliny's presentation of it. His analysis of the letters is particularly useful in its efforts to understand the significance of sociologically complex descriptors like *castitas,* but Maniet does not explore the importance of Calpurnia's character and the success of their marriage to Pliny's image. So convinced is Maniet of Pliny's sincerity that he never questions why the ideal wife is a prominent theme in the letters. More recently, Jo-Ann Shelton (1990) has reexamined Pliny's presentation of his ideal wife, with particular regard to the benefits that might accrue to Pliny. Her analysis forcefully overturns the conclusion of previous studies that Pliny and Calpurnia enjoyed an equal partnership. Shelton, like Maniet, considers the language Pliny uses and concludes that Pliny's wife is defined as excellent because she conforms to her husband's expectations. But ultimately both Shelton and Maniet are focused on the accuracy of Calpurnia's portrait. Neither has considered the extent to which Pliny's own competence is defined by the choice and education of his wife or the ways in which his *aeternitas* might depend upon her devotion to him.

[11] *Ep.* 1.12, 1.22, 4.15, 5.18, 8.23.

[12] Pliny's many letters of condolence and recommendation are replete with lists of virtues in both noun and adjective form such as *gravitas/gravis* and *sanctitas/*

Hispulla assumes the role of parent to her niece (Pliny's wife) and surrogate mother to Pliny, the three remaining women present Pliny with the opportunity to set forth models for the ideal wife in three phases of her lifetime. The following chart lists the letters in which the four women appear.

Letter	Women
3.16	Clodia Fannia
	Arria the Elder
4.19	Calpurnia
	Calpurnia Hispulla – *recipient*
5.16	Minicia Marcella
6.4	Calpurnia – *recipient*
6.7	Calpurnia – *recipient*
7.5	Calpurnia – *recipient*
7.19	Clodia Fannia
8.10	Calpurnia
8.11	Calpurnia
	Calpurnia Hispulla – *recipient*

Minicia Marcella is a maiden on the threshold of marriage. Indeed, not only is she betrothed, but the wedding date has been set. Her premature death, the subject of 5.16, fixes her image in time as the ideal bride. Calpurnia is Pliny's ideal young wife, married to him for long enough, perhaps two or three years, to have developed the avid interest in his writings and work as an advocate that he describes in 4.19. In 4.19, Pliny presents her as beginning to grow into her role as wife and highlights their mutual affection, her love of his *gloria,* and his great hopes for their shared future, on which he expands in several other letters to or about her. Clodia Fannia completes the cycle of female portraits as she provides an exemplum of a mature woman, fully devoted to her husband during his life and still committed to

sanctus. Although some of the qualities assigned appear almost formulaic (e.g., an older, influential man should have *gravitas*), no two individuals share exactly the same traits. Few men are described only by a list of virtues, except when they serve as evidence for the strong family background of younger men whom Pliny praises – for example, Publius Acilius, the uncle of Minicius Acilianus (1.14.6). In his major characterizations, Pliny includes anecdotes and often evidence of his personal knowledge of the demeanor of the man he praises.

perpetuating his *fama* long after his death. In his treatment of Fannia,
Pliny provides his most detailed characterization of a woman, assigning to her a number of powerful attributes and offering her as an
exemplum not just for wives but also for men (7.19.7). Fannia, near
the end of her life, represents the ideal matron whom Pliny hopes
Calpurnia will come to resemble.

These three women are bound together by the qualities that they
have in common; each shares some of the virtues of the other two,
among which are *suavitas, castitas, gravitas,* and *sanctitas.* Yet each
woman has traits that make her unique or befit her stage in life. In
addition, each is closely connected to the men in her life – father,
grandfather, husband – and is praised by Pliny as worthy of those
relatives. Taken together with supporting evidence from the many
wives whom Pliny mentions in other letters, the characters of Minicia,
Calpurnia, and Fannia provide Pliny's readers with a comprehensive
portrait of the ideal wife throughout her life and a deep understanding of her value to her husband. Thus, Pliny creates a model for men
to follow in choosing and fashioning their wives to reflect well on
them – in the same way that Pliny has molded and continues to mold
Calpurnia – and offers an example of the reward that both he and
they can anticipate.

The Ideal Betrothed (Letter 5.16)

Minicia Marcella, daughter of C. Minicius Fundanus, is the only
woman in the letters whose death prompts an encomium from Pliny.
Other letters that concern the passing of a woman focus heavily on
the men to whom the deceased is related with little or no characterization of the woman herself.[13] Although 5.16, too, has much to do with
Fundanus, its central theme is his remarkable child. Pliny expresses his
distress at Minicia's death, describes the young woman's outstanding
qualities, highlights her affection for all of those around her, praises
her patient endurance of her final illness, bewails the dreadful timing
of her death just before her marriage, and stresses her close resemblance to her father and his subsequent sorrow at her loss.

---

[13] See especially the discussion of 4.21 regarding the deaths of the Helvidiae in
Chapter 1.

While Pliny's letter about Minicia has many of the elements of a *consolatio*, it is addressed not to the bereaved but to the otherwise unknown Aefulanus Marcellinus, who also receives Pliny's lament for the untimely death of Iunius Avitus (8.23).[14] Avitus had died just as he was about to assume the office of aedile, leaving behind a young widow and an infant daughter. Pliny extols his virtues, particularly his affability – calling him *iucundus et gratus* (8.23.5) – and grieves the loss of someone with such great potential. Like Minicia Marcella who was about to enter her adult life, Avitus dies on the threshold of what Pliny suggests would have been an outstanding career.[15] Thus, it is fitting to see this pair of letters, sent to the same addressee, as presenting models of excellent youth.

Both 5.16 and 8.23 are highly ornamented letters, with numerous examples of alliteration, anaphora, dicola, and tricola. The opening sentence of 8.23 illustrates Pliny's elevated style with a startling combination of the three literary devices: *omnia mihi studia, omnes curas, omnia avocamenta exemit excussit eripuit dolor, quem ex morte Iuni Aviti gravissimum cepi*. The two letters are filled with such devices: *qua illa temperantia, qua patientia, qua etiam constantia novissimam valetudinem tulit* (5.16.3); *statim sapiunt, statim sciunt omnia, neminem verentur, neminem imitantur* (8.23.3); *iam destinata erat egregio iuveni, iam electus nuptiarum dies, iam nos vocati* (5.16.6); *qua industria, qua modestia quaestor* (8.23.5); *ut facilius admittat, multum faciet medii temporis spatium* (5.16.10). Many more instances might be cited. Together, these ornaments transform Pliny's considerations of the character and loss of Minicia and Avitus from mere correspondence to exempla that enshrine the deceased. The two letters combine to offer their reader a comprehensive portrait of the tragedy of premature death and unfulfilled promise.

[14] Sherwin-White (1966: 346) suggests that the recipient of 5.16, Aefulanus Marcellinus, might have been connected to Fundanus' wife, Statoria Marcella, but this seems unlikely, as Pliny gives no indication that there is any familial connection between Marcellinus and the bereaved father. Pliny does refer to Fundanus as *noster*, which suggests that his recipient is acquainted with Minicia's family, but there is no suggestion that Aefulanus has suffered a personal loss with the death of the young woman. Statoria Marcella's name is found on the same funerary monument (*ILS* 1030) on which her daughter's name is inscribed.

[15] Because he had already served in the office of quaestor, the minimum age for which was twenty-five, it is tempting to set Avitus' age as twenty-eight. Avitus would then be about to enter the fifth hebdomad of his life, leaving behind his youth and entering male adulthood. But Pliny does not give his age, only the impression that Avitus is at a transitional moment in his life when he dies.

While 5.16 and 8.23 share many stylistic qualities, Pliny's treatment of Minicia Marcella's passing has a formality that 8.23 lacks. In the latter, Pliny makes clear that he had a close personal relationship with Iunius Avitus by stating twice in the letter that Avitus had assumed the *latus clavus* in Pliny's house (8.23.2, 6). His recollection of his protégé reads like a eulogy, filled with personal remembrance and admiration. It begins with a statement of Pliny's distress and an explanation of his relationship with Avitus, proceeds with praise of the young man and a rather rambling account of his accomplishments, and ends with an expression of Pliny's sympathy for the bereaved family and a final statement of his own grief. By contrast, in his consideration of Minicia's death, Pliny seems more removed from the loss, as he crafts an elegant and highly structured lament.

The letter can be divided neatly into two distinct halves; the first contains the elements of a traditional dirge, while the second begins with a detailed, dramatic description of the process undertaken by Minicia's father to change his arrangements for a wedding into those for a funeral and continues with a description of Fundanus' character and Minicia's close resemblance to him.

Pliny opens 5.16 with a brief statement of his sadness and its cause – *tristissimus haec tibi scribo, Fundani nostri filia minore defuncta* (1). The mention of Minicia's bereaved father so early in the letter signals his importance in Pliny's narrative as the one most affected by the loss of his remarkable child. Grieving relatives, moreover, are a critical part of traditional laments. Pliny continues with an extended treatment of Minicia's charm and her love for her father, his friends, and those who attended her. Her sweetness and affection for all around her, expressed through her embrace and clinging to her father's neck (2) are strongly reminiscent of Catullus' description of Lesbia's *mellitus passer*, sitting in her lap or hopping about (*Carm.* 3.8–9). Indeed, the form of Catullus 3 has long been recognized as that of the dirge, albeit turned love poem and as such being rather tongue in cheek.[16] Just as in his poem Catullus shares the sorrow of his lover and views the loss of the deceased through the bereaved, so Pliny views the loss of Minicia through her relationship with and likeness to her father.

---

[16] See especially Quinn 1973: 96.

Pliny begins his character sketch of Minicia by saying that he has seen nothing more *festivius* (cheery) and *amabilius* (lovable) than she (1). Both adjectives are unusual in his letters. Minicia is the only person to be called *festiva*, a word that Pliny uses elsewhere to describe his villa or a bronze statue that he has purchased.[17] As Pliny speaks of few children and even fewer female children, it is difficult to assess whether the adjective is particularly appropriate to Minicia's age, in which case its use may be intended to underscore Minicia's youth. Indeed, the term is also used sparingly to describe individuals in Latin literature that predates Pliny. The fact that Cicero employs it to describe a slave, a dissolute young man, and a cheerful old Greek man suggests that the term may indeed have been one suitable for charming children but not dignified adult males.[18] There is somewhat less concern with Pliny's use of *amabilius*. Although it, too, is rare in the letters, Pliny describes both Minicia and Fannia as *amabilis*, a quality assigned to no one else and one that seems desirable in female acquaintances. In other authors, however, it appears more often to describe the affection provoked in their elders by children, especially male ones. The son of Cicero and the nephew of both Cicero and Atticus are described as lovable; Horace notes that his father considers Antilochus *amabilis*; and Suetonius employs the term to describe Augustus' affection for young boys.[19] It is not a word connected particularly with women but rather seems to define a relationship characterized by profound affection, like that of Catullus for his brother, whom he calls *vita amabilior* (65.10). That Pliny describes Minicia and Fannia as *amabilis* would seem to elevate their status to that of male child and *amicus* respectively. Though such a conclusion may seem startling, it is firmly supported by Minicia's close resemblance to her

---

[17] *Ep.* 2.17.4; 3.6.1. The adjective also appears in 9.17.2, where Pliny denies that he finds coarse entertainment amusing.

[18] Cicero laments the death of his *festivus* reader Sosthenes (*Att.* 1.12.4); uses the term to describe Falcidius, a spendthrift who has dispersed all the funds entrusted to him and lied about it (*Flac.* 89); and employs *festivus* to characterize Cephalus whom Socrates visited (*Att.* 4.16.3). Another Greek, Lysiadesis, is also termed *festivus* by Cicero (*Phil.* 5.13), but no free Roman man is so called. Cicero does comment that Papirius Paetus is the *imago antiquae et vernaculae festivitatis* (*Fam.* 9.15.2), but charm that is characterized as common or home grown and brings to mind the *vernae* of a Roman household is hardly suitable praise for Roman men of rank.

[19] Cicero, *Fam.* 12.16.1; *Att.* 5.19.2; Horace *Carm.* 2.9.13; Suetonius, *Aug.* 83.

father, explicated by Pliny later in the letter, and Fannia's reflection
of the spirits of her husband and father as discussed in Chapter 1.
Pliny adds to his glowing evaluation that no one is "worthier of a
longer life" or even "immortality" – *nihil ... nec modo longiore vita sed
prope immortalitate dignius vidi* (1) – high praise indeed for a young
woman who was only on the verge of entering her adult life.

Minicia's tender age is confirmed, as Pliny tells his reader that she
had not yet completed fourteen years (2). In reality, the inscription
on her tomb survives, and it sets her age as just short of her thirteenth
birthday, but Pliny clearly means to emphasize that she is about to
enter the next stage of her life through marriage, the traditional time
for which would have been at the end of the second hebdomad of
life – fourteen years of age.[20] Despite her youth, Minicia had already
exhibited qualities associated with older women. Pliny cites her *anilis
prudentia* and *matronalis gravitas*, old woman's wisdom and matronly
dignity. While it is common for Pliny to offer a list of characteristics
in his biographical sketches, he rarely uses descriptive adjectives to
qualify those virtues. He clearly wants to distinguish Minicia from her
more ordinary peers as an exceptionally self-possessed and mature
young woman. Pliny's use of *anilis* is particularly pointed, as *prudentia* elsewhere in the letters is cited almost exclusively in praise of
older men.[21] The word itself means wisdom born of practical understanding or proficiency and thus is naturally associated with age and
experience. *Gravitas*, too, is often associated with maturity, but Pliny
employs it liberally in praising the comportment of both young and
old. Its meaning for men varies between serious demeanor in those
still young and authoritative distinction in older men. A similar range
might be expected in its assignment to women on the basis of the
exercise of their position within the household, but Pliny's use of
the word with women is severely limited. In fact, only Minicia and the
matron Fannia possess *gravitas*. The possession by one as young as
Minicia of qualities that are so closely associated with age and experience – confirmed by the modifiers *anilis* and *matronalis* – may be
explained again by her likeness to her father.

---

[20] Bodel (1995) has argued persuasively that Pliny's account is accurate in that it does
not state her age directly but suggests it indirectly.
[21] *Ep.* 1.14.6, 3.1.10, 3.2.2, 5.7.5, 8.23.3.

Minicia's mature characteristics would seem entirely inappropriate in a bride-to-be were they not modified by two other qualities that
Pliny adds, girlish charm and a maiden's modesty, *suavitas puellaris*
and *virginalis verecundia* (2). Cicero was fond of describing the company of his friends as *suavitas*, and, as he mourns the loss of Tullia, he
mentions the comfort he felt when visiting her because of her *sermo et
suavitas*.[22] Pliny too uses the term elsewhere in the letters to describe
the pleasurable social atmosphere of Trajan's company and to praise
the writing and speaking of several individuals, including the letters
he receives from his wife Calpurnia (6.7.3),[23] but Minicia is the only
person whom it describes. While it is tempting to see Cicero's grief
reflected in Fundanus' sorrow, we cannot know how familiar Pliny
was with Cicero's references to Tullia;[24] however, his assignment of
suavitas to Minicia certainly assures the reader of the pleasure her
presence brought, and his use of *puellaris* associates the quality with
her role as daughter.

Pliny's assignment of *verecundia* to Minicia is also unusual in the
letters. The word itself appears with some frequency, but generally it
is applied to one's sense of restraint in accepting praise or reward.
It is clearly a powerful quality, as Cicero calls it the guardian of all
virtues.[25] Pliny ascribes the trait, along with *frugalitas*, to his native
region of Italy, Cisalpine Gaul (1.14.6). The *verecundia* that Minicia
possesses aligns her behavior with that with which Pliny is familiar,
behavior that he admires as proper for the women in his hometown.
Minicia is his kind of girl. There is little doubt here that Pliny means

[22] *Fam.* 4.6.2. *Suavitas* is particularly present in Cicero's intercourse with Atticus and
his brother Quintus (e.g., *Att.* 4.1, 12.1.2; *Ad Q.* 1.3.3, 2.4.3), but many others also
receive the distinction.
[23] *Ep.* 1.16.4, 2.13.6, 3.1.7, 4.3.2, 5.8.10, 6.8.7, 6.31.14.
[24] Nicolson's (1998: 91–93) study of the afterlife of Cicero's letters rightly calls into
question the depth of Pliny's acquaintance with Cicero's correspondence, as (he
notes) few specific allusions to Cicero's letters can be found in Pliny. There are
many thematic similarities between Pliny's letter 5.16 and the famous *consolatio* of
Sulpicius Rufus sent to Cicero following Tullia's death (*Fam.* 14.5). These include
the writer's sorrow, acknowledgment of the bereaved father's grief, and praise
of the lost daughter. Pliny may well have been familiar with Sulpicius' letter, but
because it is also likely that such themes were standard elements in letters of consolation, there is no way to prove that he was.
[25] *Part. or.* 23.79: *custos virtutum omnium, dedecus fugiens laudemque maxime consequens,
verecundia est.*

the word to suggest chastity, that is, the modesty appropriate to a betrothed young woman, a supposition that is affirmed by the modifier *virginalis*. With the guardian of her qualities firmly in place, her self-control assured, Minicia was ready to enter the next phase of her life. The final position of *virginalis verecundia* in Pliny's remarkable list of her qualities marks not only its importance but also the stage to which Minicia's life had progressed, the threshold of marriage.

Pliny's use of age-determinate adjectives broadens the relevance of the qualities of *prudentia, gravitas, suavitas,* and *verecundia* to describe not only Minicia's traits but also the potential of every woman's life. Minicia becomes thus the embodiment of the foremost virtues of the ideal girl, maiden, wife, and old woman. While Pliny has made clear that Minicia is only part way through the cycle, by giving her qualities appropriate to each age he makes her a representative of female virtue at every stage of life and elevates her as a model for others to follow.

Having established that Minicia was extraordinary and wise beyond her years, Pliny places her at her proper age as he expands upon his description of Minicia as *amabilis*. She was an affectionate young woman who clung to her father's neck, lovingly and modestly embraced his friends, and loved her various attendants (3). But Pliny quickly makes clear that these childlike qualities did not indicate that Minicia was frivolous or her interests superficial, for she was much more interested in reading than playing – *quam studiose quam intellegenter lectitabat; ut parce custoditeque ludebat* (3). Her studious nature and apparent intellectual maturity were undoubtedly attractive to Pliny, who calls his uncle, his protégés, and himself *studiosus*. Readers, naturally, are frequently mentioned in the letters, but those who read persistently (*lectito*) are not. Besides himself, Pliny uses the verb with only four other people: Minicia Marcella; his wife, Calpurnia; Baebius Macer; and Pomponius Bassus.[26] With Minicia, Pliny's focus falls not on what she reads but the manner in which she does so – that is, she is fully engaged in her studies. We may assume she would thus have been a wife in whom a man engaged in literary pursuits might find support and companionship.

Pliny completes his presentation of Minicia's character by detailing her behavior during her final illness, in the course of which she

[26] *Ep.* 3.4.1, 4.19.2, 4.23.1, 6.7.2.

displayed restraint, endurance, and resolution: *temperantia, patientia,* and *constantia* (3). All three terms are closely linked with forbearance during illness. Pliny refers to his own *temperantia* and that of Corellius Rufus in trying to deal with illness (1.12.9; 7.17). Titius Aristo, whom Pliny praises highly, displays *patientia* during his illness, and Pliny advises Geminus to endure his ill health *patienter* (1.22.7; 7.1.1). Finally, it is the loss of *constantia* in the face of illness that propels both Corellius Rufus and Silius Italicus to commit suicide by starvation (1.12.9; 3.7.2). Of the three critically ill acquaintances for whom Pliny employs the term *constantia,* only Minicia retained her determination throughout her illness, and Pliny assigns to her alone all three qualities. Her fortitude is further extolled by Pliny as he recalls her interactions with her doctors and family members throughout her long illness, obeying the former and encouraging the latter, while never losing her *vigor animi,* even in the face of death (5.16.4–5). In death, as in life, Minicia's qualities not only far surpassed those to be expected in an outstanding young person but even exceeded those of men whom Pliny praises highly. Her character thus is exemplary, and her loss is profoundly tragic.

Pliny completes his discussion of Minicia's qualities with an exclamation of the bitterness of her passing, *o triste plane acerbumque funus* (5.16.6), both reminding the reader of Catullus' *o factum male, o miselle passer* (*Carm.* 3.16) and setting the stage for Pliny's treatment of her wedding turned funeral.

Pliny commences the second half of the letter with another statement of his own distress, focused not on Minicia's death but on the sorrowful sight of her father Fundanus preparing her funeral (5.16.7). The exchange of wedding goods for burial ones was an established *topos* long before Pliny's time, beginning with Euripides' *Antigone,* becoming common in Greek and Roman epitaphs, and particularly popular with Hellenistic epigrammatists.[27] But in earlier examples, the spotlight is generally on the bride; it is she who must accept the trappings of a funeral instead of her bridal array.

---

[27] Inscriptions, e.g., *SEG* I, 567, 3–6; *CE* 383; Epigrams, e.g., *AP* 7.182 (Meleager), 649 (Anyte), 710 (Erinna). The theme appears again in the recently discovered manuscript provisionally attributed to Posidippus (9.13–18). Lucretius also evokes the theme of the tragic death of the bride, but, of course, the victim is Iphigenia, whose murder serves well his condemnation of *religio* (1.73–89).

Pliny's focus on Minicia's father is, therefore, quite unusual. The
money Fundanus had set aside for her wedding regalia must now
be spent "on incense, ointment, and spices": *quod in vestes margarita
gemmas fuerat erogaturus, hoc in tus et unguenta et odores impenderetur*
(7). With parallelism *in vestes ... in tus* and the following opposing
uses of asyndeton and polysyndeton, Pliny heightens the *pathos* of
Fundanus' sad duty. Pliny has shifted his concern effectively from
Minicia to her bereaved father.

   Pliny proceeds to characterize Minicia's father as *eruditus et sapiens*, a man who has devoted himself from his youth to *altiora studia*
(8). Fundanus was apparently well known to Pliny, whose relationship
with him seems centered on their shared political life. In the three
letters that he addresses to Fundanus, Pliny extols the value of retreat
from the hubbub of Rome (1.9) and recommends up-and-coming
young men to him (4.15, 6.6). Groag comments that Fundanus represents the high ethical culture of the leading circles of his time.[28] He
is, therefore, the ideal father of Pliny's model young woman.

   Pliny explains Fundanus' singular focus on the funeral and his
grief, whose excessive expression might expose a Roman man to serious criticism, as entirely understandable and even admirable in this
case, because Fundanus has lost a daughter who not only looked like
him but also had his character, *mores eius* (9). Pliny goes so far as to
say that "she was entirely a copy of her father in a wondrous way"
(9). Here the reader finally has an explanation for Minicia's unusual
qualities – she is the image of her father, a wise and learned man.
Pliny makes clear in several other letters that such a resemblance was
the major goal in the raising of children: he desired to help Corellius'
grandson grow to be like his grandfather, father, and uncle (3.3.2),
and Rusticus' sons were to be worthy of their father and uncle, *digni
... patre, ... patruo* (2.18.4). There was no better way for men to secure
their immortality than through children who resembled them.
Minicia had surely exceeded all expectations, becoming not just worthy of Fundanus but the very image of her father.

---

[28] Fundanus attained the suffect consulship in 107 and served as governor of Dalmatia
and proconsul of Asia. He was a friend of Plutarch and a student of philosophy,
though apparently not part of the Stoic school, but rather a follower of "modern-
ized" (so-called Middle) Platonism. See especially E. Groag, *RE* XV, Minicius 13
and Plutarch, *De cohib. ira* 6.

The complex structure and stylized language of 5.16 effectively draw the reader into Pliny's narrative as he provokes empathy for both father and daughter. In addition, the formal nature of Pliny's presentation and the exceptional language with which he describes Minicia enhance her role as an exemplum of the betrothed. Yet, unlike Pliny's characterizations of outstanding men, his portrait of Minicia is profoundly dependent on the excellence of her father. In fact, the dual focus of the letter – on deceased and bereaved – enables Pliny to consider the virtues of Minicia within the context of her father's character. She is thus immortalized as ideal child and ideal bride, as both roles are perfected by her resemblance to her outstanding father.

The Ideal Young Wife

Given Pliny's focus on presenting himself as a model Roman, it is no surprise that Pliny's wife Calpurnia is the central example in his trifold model, displaying the characteristics of an ideal young wife, both those inculcated through spotless upbringing and those acquired from the careful instruction of an older and wiser husband. What is striking about Pliny's presentation of Calpurnia is not her meritorious qualities but rather how closely they parallel ones that Pliny assigns to himself and, furthermore, how Pliny defines his wife by the alignment of their mutual ambition – his *gloria*.

Calpurnia first appears in the collection in *Epistulae* 4.1, addressed to Calpurnia's grandfather Calpurnius Fabatus, which leaves her unnamed – referring to her only as *neptis* – but signals that Pliny's personal life now includes a wife. A clear portrait of Calpurnia emerges later in the same book, when in 4.19 Pliny thanks her aunt, Calpurnia Hispulla, for his wife, praising at length the family background, the character, and the potential of his young bride. While Pliny emphasizes her suitability and growing affection for him in 4.19, his fondness for her is not stressed in the letter except through his appreciation of her qualities. The three letters that Pliny addresses to Calpurnia herself (6.4, 6.7, 7.5), however, provide ample evidence of his devotion to her. The final two letters that focus on Calpurnia, 8.10 and 8.11, deal with her unexpected miscarriage, Pliny's relief at her survival, and his hopes for their future progeny. Through these last two letters, Pliny highlights Calpurnia's despair at not providing him with the immortality he seeks through the production of an heir and the desire he shares with her to have a child. All six letters combine not only to provide a picture of Pliny's ideal young wife and their exemplary relationship but also to highlight the wisdom of Pliny's choice of wife, the efficacy of her instruction at his hands, and the potential she has for becoming a *singulare exemplum* of Roman womanhood.

LETTER 4.19. Pliny's praise of Calpurnia in 4.19 is unique in the letters. Directed as it is to Calpurnia Hispulla, it is the only tribute, among many, to be addressed to the person responsible for raising the individual acclaimed. Pliny certainly acknowledges the contribution of parents and mentors who often assume critical roles in his letters of recommendation or obituary, but his direct address of Calpurnia Hispulla requires that he include his praise both of her niece and of her. The excellence of Calpurnia's background is critical to an assessment of Pliny's choice of wife, and so praise for her aunt, serving *in loco patris*, and for the environment provided for her upbringing bears directly on Pliny's portrait of Calpurnia.

Addressing the letter to Calpurnia Hispulla offers Pliny an additional advantage, as it provides a framework within which to extol Calpurnia's quality in two phases of her life, as a suitable bride and as his eager young wife. The former requires his description of Calpurnia Hispulla's unimpeachable character and familial devotion and the latter a portrait of Calpurnia as mistress of Pliny's household. Pliny places his description of Calpurnia as his wife at the center of 4.19 and surrounds it with his praise of Calpurnia Hispulla and the laudable way in which she raised her niece.

As discussed in Chapter 3, Pliny begins the letter with the details of Calpurnia Hispulla's involvement in Calpurnia's young life, explaining that Calpurnia's parents were dead and that Calpurnia Hispulla, out of both love for her brother and his child and her sense of duty, had stepped in as her niece's surrogate parent (1). By presenting Calpurnia Hispulla as a model of devotion, Pliny assures his reader that his wife was accorded the proper guidance even though her father had not raised her. In fact, Pliny leaves no doubt that Calpurnia Hispulla has done her job remarkably well. His young wife has turned out to be deserving of all of those who raised her – father, aunt, and grandfather (1) – and as such she is suitable to carry on their line.

Later in the letter, Pliny returns to the subject of Calpurnia's tutelage and offers a more detailed account of the environment in which his young wife was reared. Pliny declares that his wife's devotion to him is entirely fitting because she had been brought up by Calpurnia Hispulla's hands and instructed according to her rules, with the result that Calpunia had seen nothing in her aunt's close company, *contubernium*, that was not *sanctum honestumque* (6). Pliny thus makes clear that Calpurnia had come to him unmarred by exposure to anything unseemly, ready to be refined according to his wishes.

Calpurnia's sheltered upbringing and her exposure only to what was proper echoes well Xenophon's requirement that a proper bride should have seen and heard as little as possible (7.4). Pliny has chosen a girl who was properly sheltered from contact with anything distasteful. She was thus suitable to be trained by him as his wife.

The importance of Calpurnia's role as head of Pliny's household is evident in Pliny's first direct statement of her abilities, which reflects her possession of the qualities that the *Oeconomicus* instructs a good manager to seek for himself and teach to his young wife. Calpurnia, Pliny declares, possesses a sharp intellect and conservative spending habits, *summum acumen* and *summa frugalitas* (2). Pliny's use of *acumen* here is unique in the letters and attests in concise form to Calpurnia's shrewd judgment. The Romans often considered such intelligence suspect in a woman, enabling sly or manipulative behavior. But here, combined with *frugalitas*, her mental acuity makes her a capable directress of Pliny's household.

Calpurnia's possession of the quality of self-restraint – *frugalitas* – aligns her not just with Roman expectations of the ideal wife but also with the character of her husband, who assigns this quality to himself when he describes his own cautious fiscal behavior in his letter to Calvina (2.4).[29] Only three other people in Pliny's letters, besides Pliny himself, are praised for their *frugalitas* – two close friends, Titius Aristo and Atilius Crescens, and Pliny's freedman Zosimus.[30] This is rare company for an exceptional virtue, one that Cicero judged to be the greatest of all virtues and defined as a combination of discretion and self-control (*modestia* and *temperantia*).[31] Her possession of *frugalitas* also connects Calpurnia to Minicia Marcella, because, as noted earlier, Pliny combines it with *verecundia* in describing the area he

[29] See Chapter 3.
[30] *Ep.* 1.22.4, 6.8.5, 5.19.9.
[31] *Deiot.* 26: *ego tamen frugalitatem, id est modestiam et temperantiam, virtutem maximam iudico.*

comes from (1.14.4), a part of the empire that preserved the conservative values of the past.[32] With this attribute, Calpurnia is defined as a
local girl who possesses personal and rural qualities that likely made
her more desirable as a wife than a sophisticated girl from Rome.[33]

The apparent reflection of Pliny's character in his portrait of
Calpurnia suggested by his use of *frugalitas* is confirmed by his immediate shift in his description of his young wife from her individual
qualities to those that she displays in her interactions with him.[34]
Rather than offering a direct assertion of her *castitas*, Pliny writes
amat me, quod castitatis indicium est (2). Her love for him is proof of her
fidelity. Thus, the quality of *castitas* is made relational rather than distinct to Calpurnia its possessor, as it is proved through her fondness
for her husband. Pliny proceeds to focus on her vicarious enjoyment
of his activities, both literary and judicial. Because of her affection for
him, she has taken up the study of literature, especially Pliny's *libelli*,
which she reads again and again and even memorizes – *meos libellos
habet lectitat ediscit etiam* (2). Just as Minicia Marcella had undertaken
intellectual pursuits because of her likeness to her studious father,
so Calpurnia is guided by her love for Pliny and has consequently
become an avid reader – but one whose interests are finely tuned to
the work of her husband. Like her *frugalitas*, Calpurnia's interest in
reading is in line with Pliny's aspirations.

Pliny's portrayal of Calpurnia as smitten with his literary accomplishments recalls his comments concerning the young wife of

---

[32] Pliny's homeland is certainly even further removed from Rome and its enticements
than Cato's Sabine land. Its distance helps it to retain the same revered and ancient
virtues of moderation and restraint that Cato highlights in his *De Agricultura* and
Plutarch remarks upon in his biography of Cato.

[33] It could be argued that rustic qualities were a standard feature in describing the
qualities of suitable wives in Pliny's time – perhaps casting back to the good old days
of the unspoiled republic and countering the wanton behavior at which Augustan
moral legislation had aimed. If so, then Juvenal, too, picks up and plays on the
topos, expressing the desire for a country girl (if he has to have any wife at all)
rather than an urban sophisticate like Cornelia, the mother of the Gracchi, who,
while an example of virtuous perfection, might feel superior to her husband and
might have unrealistic expectations (6.167–169).

[34] In her analysis of Pliny's presentation of the ideal wife, Shelton (1990) notes
repeatedly the subordination of Calpurnia's identity to Pliny's own and presents
strong evidence that marriages deemed successful by Roman men had shared that
characteristic for several hundred years before Pliny wrote his letters concerning
Calpurnia.

Pompeius Saturninus in the first book of the *Epistulae*. In the midst of 1.16, a letter whose subject is Pliny's evaluation of Saturninus' great writing and speaking abilities, Pliny inserts a rather peculiar aside concerning letters that Saturninus says were written by his wife:

(6) *Legit mihi nuper epistulas; uxoris esse dicebat. Plautum vel Terentium metro solutum legi credidi. Quae sive uxoris sunt ut affirmat, sive ipsius ut negat, pari gloria dignus, qui aut illa componat, aut uxorem quam virginem accepit, tam doctam politamque reddiderit.*

He read to me recently letters that he said were written by his wife. I thought that he was reading Plautus or Terence freed from metrical constraint. Whether they are his wife's as he claims or his as he denies, he deserves equal praise, for he either composed them or rendered his wife, whom he had married as a maiden, so educated and refined.

Pliny is clearly impressed with the quality and the apparent charm or humor of the letters, finding their style like reading Plautus or Terence in prose. Earlier in the letter, Pliny describes Saturninus' histories as having *suavitas, splendor,* and *sublimitas* and comments on the vividness of his characters (4). Pliny reports that Saturninus also writes verses in imitation of Catullus and Calvus (5).[35] Pliny's suspicion that Saturninus was the true author of the letters is thus based on Pliny's evaluation of his other writing and Saturninus' proclivity for writing in the style of earlier authors. Pliny's hesitation to attribute erudite letters to a woman may be a reflection of the rarity of accomplished writing among women of his time or, at the very least, the limited circulation of any such writing.[36]

Even if Saturninus' wife is the author of the letters that Pliny admires, it is not she to whom he offers praise. Like most wives, Calpurnia and Saturninus' wife had come to their husbands as *virgines*, likely no older than fifteen or sixteen, with very little

[35] One must, in fact, credit Pliny's wry sense of humor in suggesting that Saturninus had produced a *polita uxor*, in the same way that Catullus produced polished verses.
[36] It is difficult to surmise from our sources how much literary education Roman women in general might have had. Gillian Clark (1996b: 42–43) has noted that some might have had formal schooling and tutors, but that men may have found too much erudition in a woman distasteful. While Sallust states that Sempronia was a highly educated, witty, charming woman who also wrote poetry, he also notes her masculine boldness and her many crimes (*Cat.* 25). The message is clear – women who have too much education may overstep their bounds and become dangerous.

exposure to the world. Whatever writing skills such young women possessed were taught or at least polished under the supervision of their husbands. The opportunity to provide a literary education to a young wife might have been particularly attractive to men whose own ambitions tended to written works. Pliny has already explained that he regards Saturninus' skills so highly that he reads his friend's work before he writes anything of his own and again after he has finished a work (7). Thus, if he is himself the author of the letters, Saturninus deserves praise for his accomplished writing; as his wife's teacher, he merits it because he has conveyed a substantial measure of his own ability to her. In either case, the *gloria* belongs to Saturninus. Pliny never states directly that he set out to educate his wife but chooses instead to present Calpurnia's studies as provoked by her love for him. Yet, it is clear from his treatment of the issue in 1.16 that, just as Saturninus had with his wife, Pliny had assumed his role as Calpurnia's instructor and, therefore, deserved to reap the appropriate distinction for the education and acculturation of his young wife.

Calpurnia's fascination with Pliny's work extends far beyond the mere memorization of his works. She is also heavily invested in the acclaim he receives both as an orator and as a poet. Pliny reports that her nervousness when he is to speak at a trial is so great that she arranges for people to report to her how things have gone for him, and Pliny seems particularly pleased to tell his reader that she sits hidden by a curtain to hear him recite and others praise him for it (3). Her interests are so intertwined with his that she even composes music to which she sets the verses that he writes (4). In fact, we hear nothing of Calpurnia's activities beyond those associated with her husband's interests.

Pliny concludes his description of Calpurnia as his wife by saying that no musician has taught her to play the cithara but rather that she was taught "by love, which is the best teacher," *sed amore qui magister est optimus* (4). Just as her love was a sure sign of her *castitas*, so love compelled Calpurnia to learn skills that both highlight and complement Pliny's. Indeed, were Calpurnia to have learned music from an *artifex*, she not only would have been exposed to the influence of a man other than her husband (and the opportunity for infidelity that such teachers were thought to supply) but might even have learned to play like a professional – unseemly in a woman of her rank.[37] Calpurnia's education is limited to interests that bring only praise to her behavior – those that define her resemblance to and affection for Pliny. His successful tutelage of his young wife is reflected in the fact that her interests align with his; she is devoted exclusively to him and to his work; and it is his success in which she immerses herself.

All of Calpurnia's traits lead Pliny to the expression of his expectation for the future. Her behavior is in harmony with his, and subsequently Pliny has great hope that their *concordia* will last forever and grow even greater day by day (5). Only one other marriage in the letters is termed a *concordia*, that of Arria the Elder and Caecina Paetus (3.16.10). It too was characterized by Arria's boundless devotion to her husband, as expressed in her concern for his well-being, in her commitment to remain at his side regardless of the danger, and particularly in her determination to ensure his reputation by encouraging his honorable suicide. As he presents it, Pliny's marriage to a woman whose world revolves around his and centers on the praise others bestow upon him shows all the signs of mutual devotion, the *concordia* he so admires in Arria and Paetus.[38]

In return for her devotion, Arria received *gloria et aeternitas* (3.16.6). Together with *laus*, Pliny says, a person can receive nothing greater: *tametsi quid homini potest dari maius quam gloria et laus et aeternitas* (3.21.6). Pliny is quite consumed with the pursuit of *gloria* – that is, public recognition of praiseworthy actions or accomplishments. Pliny seeks such acclaim in court, in the writing of poetry, and in his *amicitiae*.[39] But women in the letters rarely achieve *gloria* and, like Arria the Elder, do so only through their interaction with their husbands. For example, Domitius Tullus' wife turns the blame she received for marrying an elderly invalid into *gloria* by her endless devotion to his

---

[37] See particularly Plutarch, *Pomp.* 55.1; Sallust, *Cat.* 25.2; Juvenal 6.443–456.

[38] The term *concordia* had long been used to describe the ideal state of marriage. Catullus calls the uniting of Peleus and Thetis a *concordia* (64.338) and invites young brides to establish the same with their spouses (66.87). See also Plautus, *Amph.* 475; Cicero, *Clu.* 12; Statius, *Silv.* 5.2.157.

[39] See especially 6.29.3, in which Pliny adds cases that bring fame and glory to the other types that Thrasea had called suitable for one to undertake; 7.9.10 and 9.25.2, in which Pliny discusses the *gloria* that can be gained from the writing of light verse; and 3.8.3, in which Pliny will be praised for allowing his friends either to take or to give away the office of tribune he offers them.

care (8.18.10), and Fannia is offered a share of Pliny's *gloria* in avenging the prosecution of her husband, Helvidius Priscus – presumably a final act of marital devotion (9.13.5). Pliny's wife is too young to have displayed the kind of commitment under duress shown by the wives of Paetus and Domitius Tullus, and so it is no surprise that he does not speak of Calpurnia's *gloria*. Yet, Pliny has already demonstrated with illustrations of Calpurnia's passionate concern for his *officia* that she is focused on his *gloria*. Indeed, he ends his treatment of Calpurnia with a final explanation of his confidence in their relationship, effectively summarizing her appreciation of his pursuits. She does not love his physical person, which declines and ages, but his *gloria* (5), the focus of his ambition.

As noted with regard to the *Panegyricus,* a Roman man's choice of wife and her subsequent behavior were important to his reputation, and there is no question that Pliny's characterization of his wife is of primary importance as an element in the presentation of his own character. As numerous literary works and tombstone inscriptions attest, Roman men who wrote or set up memorials to the women being immortalized believed that *castitas, pietas, sanctitas,* and *concordia* were the qualities of good women and successful marriages. Pliny does incorporate this traditional vocabulary in his praise of both women in 4.19, but he is equally concerned with establishing the quality of his own interaction with his wife and her aunt. However important Calpurnia's virtue may be to him, it is clearly her interest in his *gloria* that Pliny finds most attractive.[40] Furthermore, Pliny exploits every opportunity to insert himself into the letter: he mentions the excitement a speech of his can provoke while discussing Calpurnia's anxiety when he is to plead, *quos clamores excitarim*; his description of her eagerness to hear him reading gives Pliny an opening to speak of the praise he sometimes receives for it, *laudesque nostras;* even Pliny's expression of gratitude concerning the role of Calpurnia's aunt in Pliny's young life, as discussed in Chapter 3, provides a vehicle for him to inform his reader that his talents are innate, visible to Calpurnia Hispulla when he was still a child – *talemque qualis nunc uxori meae videor, ominari solebas* (7). Pliny's emphasis on her presence

---

[40] Aubrion (1975: 97) notes that Pliny's praise for others often reflects on his own status and includes in his list of examples Pliny's approval of Calpurnia's concern for his *gloria*.

in his young life assures the reader that Calpurnia Hispulla provided the same *sanctum honestumque* atmosphere for him as she had for his outstanding wife. In a letter purporting to be a letter of praise for his wife and her aunt, Pliny's own character and accomplishments are remarkably prominent. The reader sees Calpurnia only through the lens of her interaction with her husband, through the qualities that she shares with him and through her devotion to his goals. Indeed, after reading Pliny's description of his wife, we know nothing about Calpurnia as an individual. Rather she is a wife who has already come to resemble her husband as much as Minicia Marcella resembled her father.

THE "LOVE LETTERS" (6.4, 6.7, 7.5). While 4.19 gives the reader a clear but limited picture of his excellent young wife and her love for him, Pliny says nothing in it of his affection for Calpurnia. Pliny is not hesitant to express his fondness for others whom he characterizes in his letters, and although his praise for Calpurnia is lavish and his satisfaction with her conduct is evident, his portrait of their relationship remains incomplete without some indication of his emotional connection to her. But Pliny's omission in 4.19 is more than amply rectified by subsequent letters addressed directly to his wife.[41] These letters provide Pliny with the means to portray his marriage to Calpurnia as one filled with affection, and they offer a context that is eminently more suitable for such expression than a letter addressed to her aunt (4.19), in which Pliny would have been limited by propriety to a simple statement of his love.

Separated from Calpurnia by the illness from which she is recuperating in the country and by his duties in Rome, Pliny writes a series of three letters to her that describe his distress at their separation and his longing to see her. These absence letters are an ideal medium through which Pliny can present his relationship to Calpurnia as a love match, but they serve two other functions as well. They offer a means for Pliny to explore the function and importance of epistolary works, particularly the role of the letter as substitute for its sender, and they allow him to play with genre expectations as he incorporates *topoi* and vocabulary from love elegy.

---

[41] Because of his letters to Calpurnia, Pliny has been credited as the inventor of a new, albeit derivative genre – the love letter between husband and wife. These letters also mark the rise of the love relationship in Roman marital alliances.

In the first letter, 6.4, Pliny states his concern for Calpurnia's health, as she has traveled to Campania, *causa valetudinis* (1). He wishes to see for himself that she is better, *cupiebam, ut oculis meis crederem quid viribus quid corpusculo apparares* (2). Even if her health were not an issue, says Pliny, he would worry about her as he would anyone he loved and had no news of, *est enim suspensum et anxium de eo quem ardentissime diligas interdum nihil scire* (3). Their separation and her illness fill Pliny with fear, and he imagines all kinds of disasters, *vereor omnia, imaginor omnia* (4). He asks Calpurnia to write once or twice a day so that his worries may be allayed while he is reading her letters (5). Thus, the scene is set for Pliny to express his feelings for Calpurnia, using a genre that is particularly suited to expressing longing.

In fact, 6.4 brings to mind nothing so much as Cicero's letters to Tiro when the latter was ill and unable to return to Rome with his master. In no fewer than nineteen letters,[42] Cicero expresses his anxiety concerning Tiro's health (*magnae nobis est sollicitudini valetudo tua* – Ad Fam. 16.8.1), his distress at their separation (*non queo ad te nec libet scribere quo animo sim adfectus* – Ad Fam. 16.8.2), and his love and longing for his faithful scribe (*paulo facilius putavi posse me ferre desiderium tui, sed plane non fero* – Ad Fam. 16.1.1). He wants to see for himself that Tiro is well – *mihi maximae voluptati fore, si te firmum quam primum videro* (*Ad Fam.* 16.2). Repeatedly, he asks for Tiro to send him letters that will offer some comfort, *si me diligas, excita ex somno tuas litteras* (*Ad Fam.* 16.14.2), even asking for them daily and providing the means for Tiro to send them – *cogitavi unas litteras Marionem adferre posse, me autem crebras expectare. poteris igitur et facies, si me diligis, ut cotidie sit Acastus in portu* (*Ad Fam.* 16.5.1–2). In a single letter, Pliny echoes well the fear and desire that Cicero expresses in the letters to Tiro. Furthermore, Pliny stresses the power of letters to lessen anxiety, a recurring theme in literally dozens of letters that Cicero wrote not only to Tiro during his illness but also to friends while he was in exile. For Cicero, letters provide a lifeline, a tangible connection to his life in Rome and the friends and family for whom he expresses deep affection. Bereft of all that he loves, he

[42] Letters focused on Tiro's health constitute the majority of *Ad Familiares* 16, all of which are addressed to Tiro who, we must assume, was rarely absent from Cicero. His illness and the separation it provoked is thus a natural focus of Cicero's concern.

begs for letters and arranges for their transport as a means of sustaining his existence in Rome, if only through his correspondence. Pliny makes a similar plea, as if he, too, were in exile.

While the role of letters in allaying Pliny's fear seems natural, his separation from Calpurnia is somewhat contrived, as it is imposed upon them only by her need to recuperate rather than by war, exile, or official decree. There is no compelling reason why Pliny cannot go to her in Campania, or she to him in Rome. Pliny uses this somewhat artificial distance in order to play with otherwise unexplored aspects of his genre. Although comparison between 6.4 and Cicero's letters to Tiro suggests that Pliny intends to allude to the work of his idol, we cannot know how familiar Pliny was with particular letters written by Cicero.[43] Yet Pliny himself leaves little doubt that he sought to emulate the great orator, as he compares himself with Cicero or quotes his predecessor in a number of letters.[44] He surely was familiar with the flavor and subject matter of Cicero's letters as well as the details of his career. His separation from Calpurnia provides him the opportunity to explore the themes that arise subsequently – fear, longing, and the palliative power of letters.

Pliny, of course, has another antecedent to whom he is indebted as a model for correspondence addressing separation from a beloved: the poet Ovid, whose banishment provoked a veritable flood of exile poetry – *Tristia* and *Epistulae ex Ponto*. Together with his *Heroides*, these works address the question of distance and the role of letters (albeit in verse rather than prose) in the cultivation of relationships. In the *Heroides*, Ovid assumes the role of abandoned women who address their unfaithful lovers; in the *Tristia* and *Epistulae ex Ponto*, it is Ovid himself (or at least his own persona) who expresses his despair. All three works serve Ovid's desperate need to be present in Rome despite his exile, as his poems become his voice and allow him not to disappear entirely from his home.[45] Particularly poignant are the

---

[43] See the Introduction. For a comprehensive discussion of the circulation of Cicero's correspondence, see Nicholson (1998).

[44] Comparisons: *Ep.* 1.2, 1.5, 3.15, 4.8, 5.3, 7.4, 9.2, and 9.26. Quotations: *Ep.* 1.2, 1.20, 7.17, and 9.23.

[45] Some of Ovid's letters are intended by him to address individuals back in Rome (*Tr.* 3.7 and 5.4), while others, Ovid says, take on their own purpose, purportedly outrunning Ovid's intention (*Pont.* 2.7 and 4.15). Furthermore, Ovid makes it clear that the letters are a substitute for his presence (*Pont.* 1.7, 2.6, and 4.9).

letters that Ovid addresses to his wife – letters that express his love, his desire to see her, his regret that she too is afflicted by his exile, his praise for her loyalty, and his promise to immortalize her devotion in his poetry.[46]

In her work on the epistolary novel, Janet Altman (1984: 14–20) has examined at length the seemingly contradictory functions of letters between lovers, which both bridge and accentuate the distance between sender and recipient. This dichotomy makes the letter's author present while it increases the impact of his absence, creating a longing within its reader for his physical presence. Love and desire are thus natural subjects for the epistolary genre, in which the letter becomes a substitute for the lover – as seducer and comforter – bringing both solace and distress.

In 6.7, Pliny answers a letter from Calpurnia in which she had said that she was deeply affected by his absence – *scribis te absentia mea non mediocriter adfici* (1). The power of his writing is her only solace; indeed, his *libelli* become Pliny for her, and so in his absence she holds them as she would Pliny or sits with them in his usual place, *pro me libellos meos teneas, saepe etiam in vestigio meo colloces* (2). Calpurnia's attachment to Pliny's *libelli* has already been discussed by him in 4.19 and so seems natural as a symbol of his presence in her life. As their marriage matures, as Calpurnia matures, Pliny has made active the correlation between writing and affection that he introduced in 4.19. His writing – now including letters addressed to Calpurnia – becomes Pliny's surrogate as husband and wife are separated.

Pliny next expresses his pleasure that Calpurnia misses him and has found consolation in his *libelli,* and he says that in turn he reads her letters again and again – *invicem ego epistulas tuas lectito* (2). Calpurnia's epistles offer comfort to Pliny, but, as letters between lovers are wont to do, they have the additional effect of increasing his longing for her, *eo magis ad desiderium tui accendor* (3), the more he reads them. For, Pliny says, her letters have as much *suavitas* as conversation with her has *dulcedo* (3). They come, thereby, to represent Calpurnia's sweet company, and so they fuel Pliny's *desiderium.* The *suavitas* of Calpurnia's writing aligns her with Minicia Marcella to whom Pliny assigns the characteristic, and at the same time it equates

[46] *Tr.* 1.6, 3.3, 4.3, 5.2, 5.11, 5.14; *Pont.* 4 and 3.1.

the quality of her writing with that of some of his most admired authors whose work he extols with the term.[47]

As Cicero and Ovid had done before him, Pliny pleads with Calpurnia to write frequently and states openly for his reader the dual nature of the letters to both please and upset him – *hoc ita me delectet ut torqueat* (3). Pliny's use of *torquere*, a word found frequently in love elegy, heightens our impression of the passion that exists between him and Calpurnia. It is still a passion based on their mutual interest in his writing and their conversations both face to face and through letters, but it is no less powerful a connection for its literary foundation. Pliny has effectively used the epistolary genre to portray his now firmly established affection for Calpurnia, and with *torqueat*, the last word of the letter, he prepares the reader for his third letter to Calpurnia.

Pliny begins 7.5, the last letter addressed to his wife, with a forceful statement of his longing for her, followed by an explanation of its causes – his love for her and their unaccustomed separation – *incredibile est quanto desiderio tui tenear. in causa amor primum, deinde quod non consuevimus abesse* (1). He is now fully in the grasp of the yearning for her that he said in 6.7 was provoked by reading her letters. Here, for the first time, Pliny openly expresses the source of his desire, his *amor* for Calpurnia. It is remarkable that Pliny, who prides himself on his self-control, would admit to being enthralled by his love for his wife. Although Sherwin-White (1966: 406–407) credits Pliny as the first to write affectionate letters to his wife ("the love letter"), he dismisses Pliny's passion and sees the tone of the letter as little different from others to absent friends or from 6.4 and 6.7. In fact, the content and diction of the letter is drastically different from any others in Pliny's corpus; for here, Pliny seems not to be in control of his feelings or his actions.[48] Yet, a ready explanation for the unusual language and raw emotion of 7.5 is apparent in the letter that precedes it.

---

47 *Suavitas* is a feature of Vestricius Spurinna's Greek and Latin lyrics (3.1.7), Saturninus' histories (1.16.4), and Voconius Romanus' voice and means of expression. Pliny also uses the term to describe successful historical writing (5.8.10).

48 It is clear that Pliny is attempting what he suspected Saturninus of doing, rendering the poetry of literary forebears in prose form. Two of Pliny's three letters to Calpurnia, 6.7 and 7.5, are filled with diction and themes that seem taken directly from love elegy.

One of the many letters in which Pliny discusses his poetry, 7.4 is one of only two letters in the corpus, the other being 7.9, in which Pliny offers samples of his verse. In 7.4, Pliny speaks of his many ventures into poetry – Greek tragedy, elegiacs, hendecasyllables – but the dactylic hexameter he offers is written upon reflection on an epigram that Cicero had written about his affection for Tiro.[49] According to the verses Pliny writes, Cicero had complained that Tiro had not delivered on kisses promised to his lover, *nam queritur quod fraude mala frustratus amantem / paucula cenato sibi debita savia Tiro / tempore nocturno subtraxerit* (6). Pliny the poet proceeds to ask himself why *he* should not venture to write about love and his personal passions. Pliny credits the inspiration of his poetic response to the model offered in Cicero's epigram, which he calls the source of his motivation thereafter to write and publish a volume of hendecasyllables – presumably focused on lighthearted and personal subject matter.

Nestled between 7.4 and 7.9, which offers yet another endorsement of light verse as a proper form of relaxation for great men and a potential source of fame, as well as Pliny's epigram on the wisdom of change (11), the last letter to his wife serves as a confirmation both of the "love letters" connection with the correspondence between Cicero and Tiro and of 7.5's unique form as elegiac love poetry in prosaic form.

Having introduced the reason for his distress, Pliny explains the effect of his unquenched desire. He cannot sleep but spends most of the night thinking about her – *inde est quod magnam noctium partem in imagine tua vigil exigo.*[50] During the daytime, Pliny goes to her empty room at times when he was accustomed to visit her; indeed, he does this unconsciously, as his feet compel him – *inde quod interdiu, quibus horis te visere solebam, ad diaetam tuam ipsi me, ut verissime dicitur, pedes ducunt* (1). With these two images, he has drawn a picture of himself as consumed by his passion for Calpurnia and, therefore, unable to control his thoughts or deeds. That Pliny means to recall the themes

<hr />

[49] Pliny has found the verses in the work of Asinius Gallus (7.4.3), not in anything of Cicero, a circumstance that again brings into question the nature of his familiarity with Cicero's work.

[50] Pliny's sleepless nights bring to mind again Cicero's distress at his absence from Tiro and the paucity of information regarding his health: *itaque habui noctem plenam timoris ac miseriae* (*Fam.* 16.14.1).

of love elegy is confirmed with his next statement: *quod denique aeger et maestus ac similis excluso a vacuo limine recedo* (1). Like Ovid, Propertius, or Tibullus – the *exclusus amator* – barred from the mistress's presence, Pliny leaves her empty room. Of course, Pliny is *not* locked out. While Calpurnia is absent, she has not rejected him; on the contrary, Pliny has made clear in the preceding letter that their desire to be together is mutual, made impossible only by temporary circumstances. Still, the theme is an appealing mechanism through which Pliny may elaborate his devotion to her.

Finally, Pliny has only one source of solace for the emotional turmoil that his *desiderium* causes him – his work – and he states that he is only free from torment when he is in the Forum or in court, *unum tempus his tormentis caret, quo in foro et amicorum litibus conteror* (2). His dependence on his *officia* as a distraction sufficient to escape his misery is also a symbol of the depths to which his existence has plunged, *aestima tu, quae vita mea sit, cui requies in labore, in miseria curisque solacium* (7.5.2). Pliny's work then is a poor substitute for a fulfilled life that, Pliny implies, must include the presence of a devoted wife.

Antonio Ramírez de Verger (1988: 114–116) has pointed out that 7.5 recalls a series of motifs from love elegy besides the *exclusus amator* directly referred to by Pliny: the longing for the beloved, the emphasis on separation, the inability to sleep, love as a source of illness, the torment suffered by the lover, the relief from suffering that might be sought, and the solace gained thereby. There is no question that all of these elements are present in 7.5, one of Pliny's shortest missives. But while aptly noting the presence of such elements, de Verger fails to see that all are undermined by the reader's sure knowledge that Pliny's love is not unrequited; indeed, his explication of Calpurnia's love for him precedes the presentation of his own for her. We need not fear that the door will be closed to their reunion. Pliny thus becomes the successful lover, the antithesis of the tormented persona of the elegiac poet.

LETTERS 8.10 AND 8.11. Following 4.19 in which Pliny establishes their mutual affection and his three letters to Calpurnia that serve to reinforce the depth of their alliance, Pliny includes two letters whose tone and topic are drastically different. Had Pliny's obvious devotion to Calpurnia not already been established in the previous letters, his reader would not be so stunned by the apparent callousness with which he deals with her miscarriage in 8.10, the first of two consecutive letters regarding this topic. Addressing Calpurnius Fabatus, her grandfather, Pliny notes Fabatus' desire for a great-grandchild and bluntly reports his news: because she was young, Calpurnia did not realize she was pregnant and did not behave as she should and so lost the child (1); her error caused the miscarriage. There is no sense of concern for Calpurnia in Pliny's criticism, but rather his worry is for the potential heir she might still provide, as she has at least proved her fertility, *explorata fecunditas facit* (2). Pliny remarks that his desire for children is as great as Fabatus' for great-grandchildren, *neque enim ardentius tu pronepotes quam ego liberos cupio* (3), that his children's road to office will be easy because of their association with himself and Fabatus, *a meo tuoque latere pronum ad honores iter* (3), and that Pliny will leave them well-known names and established ancestors, *audita latius nomina et non subitas imagines relicturus* (3).

The overriding theme of the letter is neither Calpurnia's health nor Pliny's sadness. Rather, Pliny is firmly fixed on the potential of the progeny she might provide him. It is likely that Pliny's focus falls on hope for future offspring because his addressee shared that concern. In fact, Calpurnia was the only conduit through which Fabatus' family line would be secured.[51] Although it is impossible to say with any confidence whether Pliny had already received the *ius trium liberorum* whose grant would abrogate the political necessity for him to produce children, it was surely still important to Pliny to pass on the *audita nomina* to at least one child. There is no question that he is a man concerned with his own immortality, *mihi ... praemium aeternitatis ante oculos* (9.3.1), or that he believed children were an important means of securing it, because he makes this attitude abundantly clear in his concern for the sons of Arulenus Rusticus and Corellia, as discussed

---

[51] Shelton (1990: 167) points out the pressure on both Pliny and Calpurnia to provide for the continuation of their families with their offspring. Hoffer (1999: 94–97) questions Pliny's sincerity in proclaiming his desire for children and suggests that his childlessness and the liberality that it enabled were political advantages that had to be disguised in light of the efforts by the principate to ensure the production of the next generation by the upper classes. However, Hoffer's proposition is only an unsubstantiated hypothesis. Pliny's attempts to provide for the well-being of the children of others and to assume a fatherly role in their lives if only peripherally may well be reflections of his sincere concern rather than premeditated acts designed to conceal his satisfaction with his lack of an heir.

in Chapters 1 and 2. In addition, his ardent expression of his desire for children sets Pliny in accord not only with his addressee, Fabatus, but also with the state policy regarding child rearing. Yet, in exploiting the opportunity to make his wish for children and his disappointment clear, his attitude toward Calpurnia appears quite heartless.

Redemption of Pliny's rough treatment of Calpurnia follows swiftly the close of 8.10 with a second letter on the subject addressed to her aunt, Calpurnia Hispulla. The juxtaposition of the two letters assures us that they are to be read together for a proper assessment of Pliny's reaction to Calpurnia's miscarriage. Pliny begins 8.11 by recalling that Calpurnia Hispulla's affection for her niece is more tender than that of a mother, *materna indulgentia molliorem* (1). He is quick to report that the danger to Calpurnia has passed, though it was grave, *summo discrimine* (2). Pliny reminds Calpurnia Hispulla too that, although she is still without a grandchild of her brother to comfort her in her loss of him, Calpurnia's recovery offers hope that a child will be produced (3). Pliny's letter to his wife's aunt is filled with his loving concern for both its subject and recipient; Pliny, moreover, expresses his own fear and relief in anticipating these same emotions on Calpurnia Hispulla's part. Pliny closes 8.11 with a suggestion that his addressee might undertake to explain the circumstances of the miscarriage, brought on perhaps by Calpurnia's youth and the nature of an unsuspected pregnancy, to Calpurnius Fabatus (3). Pliny's affection for his wife is reasserted by his careful and caring treatment of her physical condition and his declaration of her innocence in causing the miscarriage.

Sherwin-White (1966: 459) may be correct in his conclusion that the difference in tone between 8.10 and 8.11 is predicated on the nature of their recipients; that is, Pliny modifies both the manner in which he reports his bad news and his presentation of his own emotional reaction to the loss of his child entirely on the basis of the characters of his addressees. Pliny's letter to Fabatus is harsh because the old man was harsh. The variation between the letters may also be attributable to the gender of the addressees, but such a facile explanation tends to preclude a closer examination of the combined content of the two accounts. Although the letters seem to offer contradictory portraits of Pliny's character, they may actually be viewed as complementary. In the letter to Fabatus, Pliny displays his pragmatic response to Calpurnia's miscarriage – it has happened, she is young and was unwittingly careless, Pliny wants children, this is possible because she is fertile, his children will be successful because of the connections and ancestry he has to offer them. Pliny's letter to Calpurnia Hispulla offers his emotional response to the tragedy – it has happened, Pliny was afraid Calpurnia would die, she was young and unaware, Pliny is sad at his loss but relieved that she is alive, Pliny wants children, this is still possible because she was spared. Thus, the two letters constitute a full presentation of Pliny's reaction to his loss and his hope for the future, including his rational evaluation of what has happened and what it portends and his sentimental reaction to the same event. His choice of addressee for each letter allows him to present both views of his character in credible communication, and the placement of 8.11 immediately following the harsher 8.10 permits him to quickly modify his reader's initial interpretation of his reaction to the tragedy as he reasserts his affection for Calpurnia.

Although 8.10 and 8.11 add little to our knowledge of Calpurnia's character, they do assure us that she possessed a critical quality in assuring her ultimate success as Pliny's wife – she both wanted children and was capable of getting pregnant, though her ability to deliver a child was never to be proved. Pliny's accounts of her miscarriage do serve to underline her youth; she is a work in progress, albeit a promising one. The two letters are critical to Pliny's self-portrait because they offer him a forum through which he can state unequivocally not only that he desires children but also that he has much to offer them. Finally, 8.10 and 8.11 allow the reader to see Pliny's flexibility in his interactions with others as he deals with both Calpurnia's no-nonsense grandfather and her aunt. Pliny seems just as comfortable with his rational treatment of their loss (8.10) as he is with his emotional one (8.11).

Pliny's ideal young wife, Calpurnia, was prepared for her marriage by an outstanding aunt in an unimpeachable household. While she reflected well the good character of her own forebears, like unworked clay she was ready to be shaped by Pliny into her proper form as the spouse of a politically prominent man. The result of Pliny's efforts is a wife who shares his goals, manages his household well, zealously reads his writing and has developed her own literary skills, and is committed to his work and devoted to his person. Pliny has every reason to expect that their relationship, which has brought nothing but credit to him thus far, will grow even deeper and will yet provide an heir to carry on his name. Lastly, Calpurnia's devotion to his *gloria* aligns her goals with his and contributes to his potential for *immortalitas*.

The Ideal Matron (Letter 7.19)

Clodia Fannia enjoys Pliny's affectionate devotion more than any other woman in the letters except his wife. She is more than just a friend to whom he feels obliged, as discussed in Chapter 1. In 7.19, a letter that reads much like one of his obituaries (even though Fannia is not yet dead), Pliny openly offers her as a model when he asks rhetorically who there will be for men to point to as a model for their wives after she is gone. Pliny even considers her an *exemplum fortitudinis* for himself and other men (7). With his presentation of the matron Fannia's qualities, Pliny completes his portrait of the ideal wife.

As Pliny writes 7.19, Fannia is seriously ill. Although her body is failing, her mind and spirit thrive, *animus tantum et spiritus ... viget* (3). Her strength and resolve in the face of illness bring to mind the *vigor animi* of the maiden Minicia Marcella. In fact, Pliny describes only the *animi* of Fannia and Minicia in these terms.[52] In the same breath, Pliny defines Fannia's *spiritus* as most worthy of her husband Helvidius and her father Thrasea, *Helvidio marito, Thrasea patre dignissimus* (3). Like Minicia, who was a copy of her father, and Calpurnia, who was worthy of her father, aunt, and grandfather, Fannia is an appropriate reflection of her father, in fact a superlative one, but age and experience have added an important element to her worthiness. The younger women, worthy of their upstanding forebears, may serve their spouses suitably, but Fannia is a seasoned wife who has weathered many trials with her husband. She has become most worthy of him through her devotion in the course of their married life and through her actions to preserve his *gloria* after his passing.

As if anticipating the loss of a senior statesman, Pliny bemoans the impending loss to the state of a *femina maxima* and offers his readers a list of Fannia's virtues in a single exclamation: *quae castitas illi, quae*

---

[52] The etymologically related *vigere* and *vigor* appear rarely in the letters – a total of six times: to characterize the flourishing of literature (1.13.1), to describe men's physical strength (1.14.7, 2.19.2, and 3.1.10), and to praise Minicia and Fannia (5.16.4 and 7.19.3).

sanctitas, quanta gravitas, quanta constantia (4). Near the end of a life lived properly, Fannia is assigned qualities that rank her among the outstanding men whom Pliny praises. Examination of Pliny's use of *castitas, sanctitas, gravitas,* and *constantia* as personal qualities reveals the power of the collocation of these terms in his portrayal of Fannia.

The first attribute, *castitas,* is the rarest of the four virtues assigned to Fannia. It is first and foremost an imperial virtue, one that Pliny says was *ingenita et innata* in Trajan (*Pan.* 20). It appears only six times in Pliny's letters. Two of the three uses that describe men are presented by Pliny within a list of virtues, offered one after another without conjunctions, that is, in a format similar to the one Pliny employs in 7.19.[53] The first is Titius Aristo, whose qualities are *castitas, pietas, iustitia,* and *fortitudo* (1.22.7). Earlier in his portrait of Aristo, Pliny remarks that nothing is *gravius, sanctius, doctius* than Aristo. Pliny is particularly impressed with his intellectual achievements, his vast knowledge of law and history, and his simple life-style. His erudition causes Pliny to consult Aristo on obscure matters (2). Because Aristo does not isolate himself in the gymnasia or porticos but rather takes an active role in civic life, both in *negotia* and as an advocate, Pliny ranks him first among intellectuals in all four virtues (7). Just as he was accustomed to seek out Aristo, Pliny also confers with Maturus Arrianus. In a letter of recommendation (3.2), Pliny promotes Maturus Arrianus as someone whose advice he follows in business and on literary topics (3). Here too, as with Aristo, it is both Arrianus' learning and his involvement in *negotia* that justify the virtues Pliny names – *castitas, iustitia, gravitas,* and *prudentia* (3.2.2).[54] It is the moral purity, *castitas,* of each man that Pliny places first in his list of qualities.[55] Combined with their *iustitia* and *gravis/gravitas,* it is their *castitas* that makes them worthy advisers to Pliny.

---

[53] The last man to be assigned *castitas* is Julius Genitor, the tutor whom Pliny is about to recommend for Corellia Hispulla's son, who needs to have *severitas, pudor, castitas* (3.3.3) to be suitable.

[54] Maniet (1966: 151–152) notes that when *castitas* appears in an asyndetic listing of an individual's qualities as it does for Aristo, Arrianus, and Fannia, it is the first virtue named.

[55] The Elder Seneca offers some sense of how *castitas* might best be defined as a male attribute in *Contr.* 1.2.13 where he sets the question as to "whether *castitas* should refer only to virginity or to abstinence from all things base and unseemly" – *utrum castitas tantum ad virginitatem referatur, an ad omnium turpium et obscaenarum rerum*

Castitas takes on a more specific sense when assigned to women. Besides its use in describing Fannia, the term appears two other times in descriptions of women. The first occurs in letter 1.14 to Iunius Mauricus in which Pliny presents his recommendation of a husband for Rusticus' daughter Iunia. Pliny has just offered an extended explanation of the proposed bridegroom's good looks. In fact, Acilianus is one of only a few individuals in the letters to be given any physical description. Pliny seems compelled to offer an explanation for his account of Acilianus' appearance and says that he thinks he ought to include a description, because a handsome appearance serves as a sort of reward for the chastity of girls, *debet enim hoc castitati puellarum quasi praemium dari* (1.14.8). We must assume that Iunia would be among the *puellae* who possessed *castitas*. The second to be assigned the virtue is Calpurnia, whose love for Pliny he takes as an indication of her virtue, *amat me, quod castitatis indicium est* (4.19.2), as discussed previously. It is she who receives Pliny's most expanded discussion of the quality of chastity. While it is clear that Pliny intends Iunia's and Calpurnia's *castitas* to be read as sexual purity or fidelity, the meaning of *castitas* in the listing of Fannia's virtues may not be so limited. Because it is combined with other qualities elsewhere assigned to outstanding men only and because Pliny's list is immediately followed by a recitation of Fannia's political behavior, *castitas* may be read as meaning both sexual purity and the same kind of personal integrity that Aristo and Arrianus are credited with, as she remains faithful to the memory of her husband and staunch in her opposition to Domitian's evil regime.[56]

Sanctitas, too, is an unusual attribute in Pliny's letters, reserved almost entirely for men with whom he has close ties, especially Corellius Rufus (1.12.5), Vestricius Spurinna (3.1.7), and Spurinna's son Cottius (2.7.4). Further, his mentor Corellius is *sanctissimus* (3.3.1), his memory *sacrosancta* (7.11.3). Among the women in the letters, only

---

abstinentiam. Cicero frequently uses the adjective *castus* and the adverb *caste* to characterize his clients and their behavior, but the virtue itself is found rarely in Latin literature before Pliny's time, and even when it does appear in the works of other authors, it generally refers to the virginity or fidelity of women.

[56] Hellegouarc'h (1972) includes neither *castitas* nor *castus* in his consideration of political vocabulary in the republic. Indeed, Pliny appears to be the first to use the term as a virtue for men of rank.

Fannia possesses *sanctitas*. Pliny's use of *sanctum honestumque* in praising the environment provided by Calpurnia's aunt while Calpurnia
was her charge (4.19.6) suggests that his wife has the potential to
be extolled for her *sanctitas*, but it may be a virtue that is achievable
only in mature womanhood. It is important to note that the adjective
sanctus is used as a direct attribute of only one woman, the empress
Plotina, whom Pliny calls *sanctissima* (9.28.1). Fannia, then, is in rare-
fied company. Furthermore, Fannia is the only person to have *castitas*
and *sanctitas*, both of which refer to moral purity and integrity. By
their collocation, Pliny elevates her character beyond that of everyone else in the letters.

Fannia's last two traits, *gravitas* and *constantia*, appear more frequently in the letters than *castitas* and *sanctitas*. Pliny assigns *gravitas* or uses the adjective *gravis* frequently to describe laudable men.
Gravitas appears in lists of traits possessed by several men, including
his protégé Fuscus Salinator (6.26.1) and the emperor Trajan (6.31.2).
Particularly interesting is the counterbalancing of *gravitas* with *comitas* that Pliny includes in his descriptions of Arrius Antoninus (4.3.2),
Pompeius Quintianus (9.9.2), and Trajan, because Fannia possesses
gravitas and is called *comis* later in 7.19. Joseph Hellegouarc'h (1972:
215–216) describes *comitas* as the ability to provide a sort of boon
companionship, one result of which was the elevation of the treatment of a social inferior to the level of that of an *amicus* by the possessor of *comitas*. In the moderation of *gravitas* by *comitas*, Pliny implies
that *gravitas* – the seriousness of one's conduct and the authority that
it engenders – might make for rather uncomfortable, even intimidat-
ing company in less exceptional people than those whom he praises.
While *gravitas/gravis* is commonly assigned to any man with either
mature experience or youthful potential, among women Pliny uses
the trait to describe only Fannia and Minicia Marcella. As mentioned
earlier, the *gravitas* of Minicia Marcella is qualified by the adjective
matronalis and opposed to her youthful sweetness. She has grown
beyond her years without the loss of her childlike innocence. Her
matronalis gravitas, unnaturally attained and cut short by her early
death, anticipates the true *gravitas* of a matron like Fannia.

Constantia, too, is a quality that Fannia and Minicia Marcella share,
but the quality as it pertains to Fannia is not directly connected with
her illness as it is for Minicia. Although Pliny does use *constantia* to

discuss how individuals deal with infirmity, the trait is found most often in connection with court cases, particularly in reference to Pliny's own actions. Indeed, in 6.29 when Pliny explains the three types of cases that Thrasea Paetus had said advocates should undertake, the second type involves those which no one else will take on, because they offer the means to display one's *constantia* (6.29.2). In several letters, he emphasizes his own determination in advocacy settings[57] and that of his protégés Fuscus Salinator and Ummidius Quadratus. It is only appropriate that Pliny credits Fannia, who endured her husband's exiles and doggedly pursued the preservation of his reputation long after his death, with *constantia*.

That we are meant to interpret Fannia's traits not only as the private virtues of a *materfamilias* but as the public qualities of the indomitable widow of a great man is confirmed by the sentence that follows Pliny's exclamatory list of virtues: *bis maritum secuta in exsilium est, tertio ipsa propter maritum relegata* (4). All of Fannia's qualities must be viewed through the actions that she took both with and for her husband. Pliny's repetition of *maritum ... propter maritum*, leaves no doubt as to Fannia's role as wife of a great man. Fannia's commitment extended far beyond her husband's demise, as illustrated by her request that Senecio write a biography of the elder Helvidius and by her rescue of the subsequent literary products from the destruction decreed for them by the senate (7.19.5–6).

Pliny has prepared his reader for Fannia's devotion by presenting in 3.16 the model that she followed in the person of her grandmother, Arria the Elder. As discussed in Chapter 1, Pliny recounts in detail Arria's determination to travel with Caecina Paetus as he was being returned to Rome as a prisoner, but Arria was most famous for her final actions and words, the suicide with which she encouraged that of her husband. Pliny calls her *marito et solacium mortis et exemplum* (3.16.2), a source of solace in death and a model for her husband. Arria's unflagging support of Caecina Paetus is admirable, but it is her preemptive suicide, carried out as a means to encourage her husband to do the same, that provides the model Pliny offers as a frame for her other laudable actions, all with respect to her husband. Despite Pliny's praise of her lesser known actions, it is her death that brings her immortal glory and assures not only her lasting reputation but that of her husband, whose suicide was prompted, even forced, by her own. It is clear, in fact, that she kills herself in order to bolster his courage to do what any man of honor was expected to do when he had been condemned to die. In the end, Arria's suicide is her final and most important act of support for her husband – a way to win *gloria et aeternitas* (3.16.6) for them both.

That Pliny considers Arria's behavior exemplary is confirmed by his account of similar action taken by an anonymous woman upon determining that her husband's disease was incurable. She chose to commit suicide by jumping into Lake Como and compelled her husband to follow by roping herself to him: *dux immo et exemplum et necessitas fuit; nam se cum marito ligavit abiecit in lacum* (6.24.4). The unidentified woman forces her husband to take the action appropriate to his hopeless condition. Bold and righteous action on behalf of one's husband is a source of praise, especially when it requires dying with him.

While Fannia does not die with her husband, the actions that she takes many years after his death to ensure *his gloria* are as daring as Arria's suicide, for they might have led to Fannia's condemnation and did cause her relegation. She arranged for the writing of a life of her husband and, when called to account for doing so, admitted her deeds without offering any excuses. Pliny had presented Arria by quoting her extensively, but in his quotations of Fannia, he presents her as laconic in her responses to the prosecutor's questions. Did she ask Senecio to write the *de vita Helvidi? Rogavi.* Did she lend him Helvidius' diaries? *Dedi.* Did her mother know? *Nesciente* (5). She had commissioned the biography; she had safeguarded her husband's words and then employed them to preserve his memory; she had taken full responsibility for her own actions. Her deeds are memorable, not her words. Yet, her single-word responses are powerful and leave the reader with the sense that she had stood fast before her accusers, bold in the knowledge of the rightness of what she had done. Finally, Pliny tells us, she carried into exile the very publications that caused her exile – the biography of Helvidius, written by Senecio and ordered destroyed by senatorial decree, and perhaps her husband's diaries as well. Her devotion to her husband had remained undiminished by the twenty or more years since his death.

There is no question that for Fannia doing what was necessary to assure Helvidius' *gloria* exceeded by far any concern she had for her own safety.

Pliny thus far has presented Fannia as a formidable figure, one who might easily intimidate by her bearing, determination, and virtue, but he next offers a second series of exclamations that soften his characterization of her: *eadem quam iucunda quam comis, quam denique – quod paucis datum est – non minus amabilis quam veneranda* (7). Three of the four adjectives are exceedingly rare in the letters. While *comitas* appears in depictions of the well-respected philosopher Euphrates (1.10.7), the famed jurist Neratius Priscus (7.15.3), and the emperor Trajan (6.31.2), the adjective form *comis* is used only to describe Fannia. She and Minicia Marcella are called *amabilis*, but otherwise that word is used only to describe the pleasure one finds in giving tribute to the emperor (3.18.7). Even *iucunda*, an adjective that appears frequently in the letters, applies to only one other person, Pliny's close friend Voconius Romanus, whom Pliny praises as a *iucundior sodalis* (2.13.6). With vocabulary that is unique to Fannia, Pliny draws a detailed portrait of Fannia and sets her apart from his other subjects.

Concluding his presentation of Fannia's strengths, Pliny proclaims that Fannia represents the woman that others (including Calpurnia, we must presume) should imitate, and she even serves as an exemplum of courage for men, as she embodies the virtues of the heroines of the past (7). Those heroines, of course, would include her grandmother Arria (I), who had herself served as a model for her husband.

The remainder of the letter provides details of Pliny's relationship with Fannia and his grief at her impending death as discussed in Chapter 1. Letter 7.19 is marked as unusual by Pliny's highly detailed description of Fannia and their relationship. It is exceptional among his characterizations because of the inclusion of numerous expressions of his overwhelming sorrow, which seems particularly untimely because they anticipate Fannia's demise and fail to express the customary hope for recovery that Pliny includes in similar letters about seriously ill friends. In fact, he mourns Fannia as he did the death of his own great model, Corellius Rufus. Neither his own wife nor any other's will have Fannia's example to follow after her death, but the men and wives for whom Pliny calls Fannia an exemplum will

have access to the careful portrait that Pliny draws as he immortal-
izes Fannia and preserves her image as the ideal matron: a woman
of impeccable character who is dutiful and companionable, who is
committed to her husband even in times of trouble, and who has the
fortitude to fight to preserve her husband's *gloria* for all time.

Conclusion

That Pliny places great value on the power of exempla is made clear
in his discussion of *antiquitus institutum* (8.14.4), the good old days in
the senate, when a young man modeled the conduct of his father or a
distinguished older man in his father's absence. Pliny states that good
behavior was best learned in this manner: *omnem denique senatorium
morem quod fidissimum percipiendi genus exemplis docebantur* (8.14.6). Just
a few letters later, he further emphasizes how critical models were to
a properly lived life – *nam cum aures hominum novitate laetantur, tum ad
rationem vitae exemplis erudimur* (8.18.12). That Pliny trusts the efficacy
of the example as a teaching tool is more than amply demonstrated
by his many uses of the terms *exemplum* and *exemplar* to explain why
he has included particular episodes from his own experience and
that of others in his letters.[58] A quick sampling reveals both the varied purposes of exempla and their pervasive presence in the letters:
Pliny offers Geminus a model to follow in recovering from an illness
by means of a lengthy discussion of how he coped with his own illness
(7.1.7); he justifies his interest in writing poetry by citing a number of
outstanding men who had done so with no censure in the past (5.4);
Pliny states directly that he hoped with his panegyric of Trajan to set
an example for emperors to come (3.18.2).

Pliny's models are not limited to passing references or episodic
reporting. Without question, he makes a concerted effort to present to
his reader comprehensive portraits of individual men and women in
various stages of life whose comportment may serve to enlighten and
encourage imitation. As discussed earlier, Iunius Avitus is the ideal
young man beginning his public service; Pliny himself, following the

---

[58] In fact, the letters are permeated with direct references to exempla by Pliny. The
terms appear a total of fifty-eight times in the first nine books. See also above
Chapter 1, note 42.

model set for him by Corellius Rufus (1.12), serves as an exemplar of a mature statesman for his promising protégés Fuscus Salinator and Ummidius Quadratus (6.11); and, finally, Vestricius Spurinna leads the kind of life in retirement that Pliny has set his sights on (3.1.12). Thus, Pliny's male readers have ready access to models for emulation at all stages of adult life.

Pliny offers a snapshot of Spurinna's well-ordered life, earned by his hard work (3.1.12), in which the elder statesman walks on his estate, reads, converses with friends, composes verse, exercises, bathes, eats simply, and enjoys an evening's light entertainment. But no man's life would be complete without his wife, and Spurinna's is present, though by his side only in the carriage in which he goes for a drive in the middle of the day. We do not know her name until the salutation of 3.10, a letter in which Pliny informs the couple that he has composed a piece about their recently deceased son. Cottia, we now know, was the wife whom Pliny calls a *singulare exemplum* in 3.1.5, as she rides around the estate with her husband.

How, then, does a Roman man set about obtaining so fine a wife? Here, too, Pliny offers models to follow and sets himself squarely in the middle of the process of creating for himself an ideal wife. Indeed, Pliny's arrangement of the key letters delineating the various aspects of the ideal wife repeatedly focuses the reader's attention on Calpurnia's spotless past, excellent present, and exemplary potential. Pliny introduces her as book 4 opens and then, midway through the book at 4.19, presents his portrait of her as promising young wife, highlighting near the end of the letter the purity of her upbringing. Pliny makes brief mention of Calpurnia's aunt and grandfather in 5.14.8 and then in 5.16 offers his eulogy for Minicia Marcella, whose potential is great but whose destiny will remain unfulfilled. Minicia's qualities of studiousness and sweetness bind her to Calpurnia. The reader can scarcely fail to see in this ideal bride the same unspoiled maiden that Pliny chose for himself.

Just nine letters later Pliny offers the first in his series of "love letters" to Calpurnia – 6.4, followed by 6.7 and 7.5 – through which he demonstrates the ever deepening bond he has forged with his wife along with her growing literary abilities and devotion to him. It is that devotion, as Pliny has remarked in 4.19, which both assures her *castitas* and gives him hope of *perpetua concordia*.

Both *castitas* and Calpurnia's potential to achieve the *sanctitas* that
Fannia possesses bind Pliny's young wife to the ideal matron, whose
portrait Pliny sets forth in 7.19, a letter that must also be read as the
future he projects for his own wife. Of course, Fannia's portrait also
echoes that of the lost maiden Minicia in their shared *constantia* and
matronly *gravitas*, and all three women are bound together because
they are *amabilis*. But it was surely Pliny's particular desire that
Calpurnia would display the *constantia* toward him that Fannia had to
Helvidius Priscus. Because Calpurnia was considerably younger than
Pliny, he must have expected that she would outlive him. Her devotion
to him and to his writing would have led him to hope that she would
commit herself to guarding his *gloria* and his immortality through
the preservation of his work, as Fannia had preserved Helvidius' *fama*
by commissioning and protecting Senecio's biography.

No detailed examples of faithful wives appear after Pliny's presentation of the matron Fannia. Pliny does use *singulare exemplum*, as he
had in characterizing Spurinna's wife in 3.1, to describe the recently
deceased wife of Macrinus in 8.5. While her name is left unspoken,
her qualities as a wife are extolled in sweeping exclamations by Pliny:
Macrinus' wife was excellent, even compared with women of the past.
She lived with him for thirty years without conflict (1). She was respectful to her husband, while she herself was praiseworthy. Because he
has already presented his triptych of the ideal wife with images of
Minicia, Calpurnia, and Fannia, Pliny has no need to catalog the virtues of Macrinus' wife but states instead that she had gathered and
intermingled many virtues from various stages of life, *quot quantasque
virtutes ex diversis aetatibus sumptas, collegit et miscuit* (1), presumably the
three ages for which Pliny has already offered details.

Finally Pliny brings the reader back to consideration of the character of his wife in letters 8.10 and 8.11 in which he assures the reader
that despite her childlessness, Calpurnia is both capable and desirous
of bearing his heirs. While motherhood was not critical to Pliny's
assessment of the excellence of a Roman woman – for example,
Fannia has no children of her own and yet is elevated by Pliny above
all other women in the letters – these letters assuage any doubt that
he hoped Calpurnia would yet provide him with progeny who would
preserve his memory and reflect his character. Indeed, her developing literary skills would have made her, in the tradition of Cornelia,

the mother of the Gracchi,[59] a fit educator of their offspring should Pliny die.

Pliny's reader now has an inventory of all of that he should expect of an ideal wife and guidelines to follow in choosing and training her. The qualities emphasized by Pliny are overwhelmingly masculine traits – for example, *gravitas*, *sanctitas*, and *constantia* – perhaps because those were virtues most easily understood and cultivated by Roman men or perhaps because those were the virtues that reflected the most glory on the men associated with women who bore them. No wool workers appear among Pliny's ideal wives; rather, they are all women of masculine fortitude who are deserving of their grandfathers, fathers, and husbands.

Calpurnia has already begun to display her excellence, and Pliny has signaled clearly his expectation that she will become a *singulare exemplum*, deserving of praise and especially worthy of her husband, to whom *gloria* will accrue for having shaped so fine a wife.

---

[59] Quintilian, *Inst.* 1.1.6.

5

Pliny

Arbiter of Virtue

Pliny, *Epistulae* 4.19.6

nothing unless it is virtuous and honorable

Pliny's fixation on presenting positive feminine exempla seems to leave little room for the seedier side of Roman elite existence. In his treatment of men, we do repeatedly see great villains like Domitian or Pliny's archenemy Regulus, as well as some of Pliny's other oratorical rivals and, of course, the men he prosecutes, each of whom has somehow failed to fulfill the requirements of the ideal Roman man – sometimes egregiously. But even in these considerations of disgraceful behavior, Pliny's purpose is either to highlight his own achievements or to offer the reader a stark contrast to his own character. Women of questionable reputation (with whom, of course, Pliny would not wish to be associated) are rarely considered, but they are not entirely absent from the *Epistulae*; yet none of them receives the kind of close attention that Pliny gives to his ideal wives, and only one is described at any length, Ummidia Quadratilla, whose weaknesses, while they are discussed in detail, Pliny masterfully manipulates until they become a source of strength. Each of the four women examined here serves to highlight and reinforce the political and social models Pliny so carefully crafts through his interaction with and assessment of admirable women throughout the letters.

Unseemly Women

Four of the named women in the letters (and a handful of others
mentioned in passing but not by name) exhibit behavior that does
not conform to the Roman ideal, at least as Pliny defines it. The most
important of these to Pliny's image is Ummidia Quadratilla, the
grandmother of one of his most promising protégés and the matri-
arch of a wealthy family with both a senatorial past and future imperial connections. The Vestal Cornelia appears in a letter in which, in
order to vilify Domitian, Pliny questions her condemnation for incest.
Casta seems an incidental player in Pliny's prosecution of her husband Classicus for *repetundae*, but she and her daughter allow Pliny to
consider the proper treatment of both guilty and innocent women in
the courtroom and to offer a clear example of wifely devotion gone
wrong. Finally the adulterer Gallitta provides Pliny an occasion to
consider the repercussions of failing to deal with a wayward wife as
well as to discuss his experiences as adviser to Trajan during her trial.
The letters in which these four women appear are as follows:

Letter	Women
3.9	Casta (wife of Classicus)
4.11	Vestal Cornelia (Cossa?)
6.31	Gallitta
7.24	Ummidia Quadratilla

Pliny apparently had a long-standing relationship with the people of Baetica, undertaking the prosecution of two rapacious governors of the province – Baebius Massa in 93 and Caecilius Classicus
in 99.[1] In *Epistulae* 3.9, Pliny recalls at length the details of the prosecution that was carried forth despite the fact that Classicus himself had not survived to stand trial. The intent of the trial was not
only the condemnation of the deceased but also the conviction of his

[1] For Pliny's prosecution of Baebius Massa, see *Ep.* 3.4 and 6.29, both of which also
mention Caecilius Classicus but whose focus is actually Pliny's decision to represent
the interest of the Baeticans, and *Ep.* 7.33, which focuses on Pliny's conduct when
Massa sought to reclaim his property, held as collateral by the state until repayment
of his debts.

accomplices: Baebius Probus and Fabius Hispanus, provincials who claimed to have been compelled to obey his orders, his wife Casta, his son-in-law Claudius Fuscus, and his daughter, unnamed by Pliny but presumably Caecilia. All of those accused, including Classicus himself, are unattested elsewhere, and so no details beyond the facts as reported by Pliny can be added to their backgrounds nor indeed their futures. From Pliny we can glean just a few details: Classicus was a plebian of senatorial rank and of African origin; he served as proconsul of Baetica in 97–98 and died and was condemned afterward in 99.

Ancient sources tell the story of a Vestal Cornelia's trial and condemnation by Domitian for breaking her vows of chastity, but only Pliny in *Epistulae* 4.11 casts doubt upon her guilt. Pliny's Cornelia is generally and logically identified with the Cornelia of Suetonius' *Domitian* (8.4), and her condemnation is also alluded to in Juvenal's fourth satire (8–10) and in Cassius Dio (67.3.3).[2] Several of the sources identify Cornelia as the chief Vestal; thus we may be certain that she was in the later years of her thirty-year term. Although it is not possible to determine for certain, she may be the same Cornelia whose selection to replace the deceased Laelia in 62 Tacitus mentions in *Annales* 15.22. He reports that that Cornelia was "ex familia Cossorum." Jakub Pigoń (1999: 209) calls her assignment to the Cossi a certainty, arguing convincingly that Tacitus reports Cornelia's *captio* in 62, a minor and seemingly insignificant event, because she will be a prominent figure later in the historical narrative, not because her selection was particularly newsworthy.[3] If she is identified as Cornelia Cossa, further speculation might provide the name of Cossus Cornelius Lentulus Gaetulicus for her father, a patrician senator whose own father, Gnaeus Cornelius Lentulus Gaetulicus, ordinary consul in 26, was assassinated by order of Caligula. Such a connection is tantalizing, as it would directly associate Cornelia, at least by heritage, with an enemy of bad emperors. Regardless of her identity, there can be no doubt that the story of her

---

[2] The episode is also mentioned in the Chronicle of St. Jerome (217.3). Philostratus' *Life of Apollonius* (7.6) includes a reference to Domitian's execution of three Vestals but fails to name Cornelia.

[3] In his article, Pigoń (1999: 207–210) cites a number of comparable examples of this technique in the *Annales* and points out that notices of the selection or death of Vestals were not a standard element in the composition of annals, noting Livy's inclusion of the deaths and replacement of priests, but not Vestals, and the almost complete omission of even those notices in Tacitus.

death achieved great renown, particularly because the trials involved a majority of her priestly order.

A reading of all the ancient sources indicates that there were two trials under Domitian, with three or four Vestals condemned but Cornelia acquitted in the first and Cornelia retried and found guilty in the second (Sherwin-White 1966: 282–283). The dating of the trials is a difficult matter. It seems reasonable to set 83 as the time of the first trial, on the basis of Dio's account and a much later reference in Jerome. The second trial is more problematic, occurring perhaps in 89 as the *Chronicon Paschale* suggests.[4] Jerome's *Chronicle* (215) places Cornelia's condemnation in 91 or 92, certainly a date more in keeping with the furious emperor that Pliny portrays in his account (4.11.5). The only sure *terminus post quem* that can be established rests on the presence at the second trial of Herennius Senecio defending Licinianus against the charge of incest with Cornelia, as Senecio was executed in 93.

Little can be said of the military tribune's wife, Gallitta, who appears in *Epistulae* 6.31. She had accompanied her unnamed husband to his unnamed province and had become involved in an adulterous relationship with an unnamed centurion there. We are given no further details and can only assume that she was of senatorial rank, as her husband must have been. All else remains unknown, but in fact the couple's anonymity facilitates their use as character types – unfaithful wife and indulgent husband.

Ummidia Quadratilla's death is the subject of *Epistulae* 7.24. The occasion provides Pliny the opportunity to address her less than spotless behavior as it related to her grandson, Ummidius Quadratus, a young man who had already shown great promise as an orator, much to his mentor Pliny's great delight (6.11.1). Because of her nomenclature, it is reasonable to connect her to C. Ummidius Durmius Quadratus, as the daughter of a new man who enjoyed a successful career under the emperors Tiberius, Claudius, and Nero. But, as Sir Ronald Syme pointed out in what remains the most comprehensive treatment of the Ummidii, "many hazards infest the gap" between Ummidia's father and her grandson.[5] Yet Syme's measured

---

[4] Both chronicles are, of course, late documents whose precision is dubious.

[5] Syme 1968b: 105. See also Gallivan 1978: 417; Raepsaet-Charlier 1987: Ummidia Quadratilla 829 and 830.

conjectures create a compelling narrative that would support well the rise of Pliny's protégé Ummidius Quadratus.

The family clearly had its origins at Casinum, the beneficiary of Ummidia's euergetism as attested by several inscriptions found there that mark her funding of an amphitheater and a temple and the repair of a theater.[6] The prominence and apparent wealth of the Ummidii are surely what brought C. Ummidius Durmius Quadratus to the attention of Tiberius, at the beginning of whose reign he began his *cursus* as quaestor.[7] He appears to have had at least three children: C. Ummidius (Quadratus?) Sallustius, C. Ummidius Quadratus, and Ummidia Quadratilla Asconia Secunda.[8] The first son, Syme (1968b: 77–81; 1982a: 108–109) proposes, connects the Ummidii with the Sallustii, perhaps the branch associated with the imperial family in the 40s, and the last child – Pliny's Ummidia – indicates marriage to an Asconia of the Patavian Asconii, a family that also produced the scholar Asconius Pedianus and the orator Tiberius Catius Asconius Silius Italicus.

Making the leap from Ummidia Quadratilla to her grandson is even more fraught with difficulties and the need for thoughtful inference. The greatest impediment to identifying the connecting elements – Ummidia's unnamed husband and the son or daughter to whom the grandson was born – is the fact that in Pliny's letters, the young man is called only Ummidius Quadratus, that is, by the family name of his grandmother. While it was not unusual in Pliny's time for a man to use names from the distaff side of his family, his official name had to include the name of his father's *gens*. Inscription evidence from his term as governor of Moesia assists somewhat and suggests that Ummidia's grandson's complete name was C. Ummidius Quadratus

---

[6] *CIL* vi 28526, x 5183, xv 7567. The site of Casinum also offers a structure identified by a number of scholars as the Mausoleum of Ummidia Quadratilla. In addition, Varro, who was familiar with Casinum because he had a villa there, mentions an Ummidius in the earliest literary attestation of the name (*RR* III.3.9).

[7] Having completed a term as governor of Lusitania in the late 30s, Ummidius became suffect consul in 40. His career culminated in a lengthy term in the prestigious post of governor of Syria for virtually all of the 50s, an office in which he likely died in 60. Syme (1968b: 73) proposes that Durmius is either his mother's name or an indication of his adoption, perhaps by the senator M. Durmius.

[8] Her full nomenclature appears on *CIL* vi 28526, the entablature of the amphitheater at Casinum.

Severus Sertorius (*CIL* iii 7539). Thus, either Ummidia married a Severus Sertorius and their son fathered Pliny's protégé or a daughter of Ummidia married a man by that name and did so. It is tempting but in reality merely speculation to identify this man with Pliny's fellow heir to Pomponia Galla (*Ep.* 5.1), as mentioned in Chapter 3, further connecting Pliny with the Ummidii. In any case, both of Ummidia's grandson's parents are absent from the evidence, and Pliny makes clear that it is Ummidius' grandmother who raises him.

Ummidius Quadratus Severus Sertorius, Pliny tells us, was about twenty-three years old in 107, the date of Pliny's letter, at which point he was already married, but to whom we are not told. Pliny clearly sees him as a rising star, something we could dismiss as a conceit of his mentor were it not for his service in the suffect consulship as Hadrian's colleague in 118. Syme argues convincingly for an assignment as governor of Lower Moesia in the early 120s and, on the basis of a series of inscriptions that suggest he granted citizenship to a local provincial family, the proconsulship of Africa in the mid 130s.[9] Quadratus apparently fell into disfavor in the last years of Hadrian's reign, but it seems that the interests of the family did not wane significantly as a result, if we can assume, as most scholars have, that M. Ummidius Quadratus, ordinary consul of 167, was his grandson and the offspring of a marriage between a son of Quadratus and Annia Cornificia Faustina, the younger sister of Marcus Aurelius. The final decade of the century and the reign of Commodus appear to bring an end to the male line of the Ummidii whose last member may have been involved in a conspiracy against the emperor (Syme 1968b: 102–103), but almost all details and confirming evidence of the family's history after Pliny's letters are subject to question.

Close examination of these letters about the less-than-admirable women of Pliny's letters demonstrates their value to Pliny's models both of himself and his fellow elite.

The Letters

LETTER 3.9: CASTA. Pliny actually begins his account of the trial of Classicus and his accomplices in an earlier letter, *Epistulae*

---

[9] See *CIL* viii 11029, 22693, 27936, and *AE* 1903, 0201.

3.4, in which he explains why he has undertaken the prosecution of Classicus on behalf of the Baetici and claims to seek the approval of his addressee, Caecilius Macrinus. Pliny's chief concern in the earlier letter seems to be his involvement in the condemnation of a senator, an act that might identify him with those prosecutors who assisted Domitian in his attacks on the senate. Pliny makes clear that the Baetici had requested his services from the senate, which had unanimously agreed that Pliny should assist the provincials. Freed from the fear of creating lasting enmity with a fellow senator by Classicus' death before the trial and assured of senatorial support, Pliny undertakes the prosecution, the details of which he will report in *Epistulae* 3.9.

In this second letter, Pliny recalls for his addressee Cornelius Minicianus the complicated trial of Classicus and the cases against those charged along with him. Minicianus, a man of equestrian rank whose career Pliny promoted (7.22), apparently had a particular interest in prominent court cases, as he also receives Pliny's letter about the Vestal Cornelia's death (4.11).[10] The two letters, 3.9 and 4.11, offer contrasting views of the execution of justice under good and bad emperors and set Pliny firmly among the righteous.

The charges against Classicus were prosecuted even though he had died, because it would have been difficult to convict anyone of collusion with him without his condemnation. He and two provincials who had assisted him were tried first; all were convicted and the provincials relegated for five years. What Classicus had possessed before his term as governor was given to his daughter, with all other property given back to those he had robbed (12–17). Next, his son-in-law, Claudius Fuscus, and Stilonius Priscus, one of his tribunes, were tried. The latter was convicted and banished for two years, whereas the former was acquitted (18). The third action grouped a number of individuals together, including Classicus' wife.

Right from his first mention of Casta, Pliny makes it clear that he had never thought there was enough evidence to convict her, despite

---

[10] According to Sherwin-White (1966: 391), he may also be the addressee Cornelianus of 6.31, the letter about Gallitta. While all three letters concern prosecutions and the assignment of Minicianus to 6.31 would nicely tie the letters under consideration here together, the identification of an otherwise unknown Cornelianus as Cornelius Minicianus stretches credulity past any reasonable limit.

the fact that she was strongly suspected (19), presumably either of aiding her husband or of committing her own offenses against the Baetici.[11] Pliny treats the issue of her indictment quite delicately, having already postponed it to the last of the three trials, which, he notes, grouped together people of less importance than those who had been tried in the first two (19). We may rightly wonder if Pliny's caution is prompted by the fact that it was unusual to indict a governor's wife for *repetundae*. Anthony Marshall (1990: 365) points out that Casta was the first woman against whom we can be certain that such a charge was made.[12] Whether women had been subject to prosecution for provincial extortion before Trajan's time is a greatly disputed question because of differing interpretations of a *senatus consultum* dating to 24 C.E. – one claiming that a governor is liable for his wife's offenses, the other that the two of them are jointly liable.[13] Even if charges of *repetundae* had been made against women in the past, prosecution of such cases must have been exceedingly difficult given the pervasive notion that husbands were responsible for their wives' behavior.[14]

In contrast to Pliny's suspicions about her mother, he finds no fault whatsoever in Casta's daughter, although she had been enrolled among the accused. All children of governors accused of *repetundae* may have been subject to prosecution under the *Lex Acilia Repetundae*, although the law mentions only the liability of sons.[15] Pliny not only states that the daughter was free of suspicion but pleads vigorously

[11] The debate over whether Roman wives should accompany their husbands to the provinces (see particularly Tacitus, *Ann.* 3.33–34) seems to have centered largely on women's inability to contain their rapacious natures – an accusation implying both uncontrolled material and sexual appetite – and their supposed tendency to interfere with military matters. Republican Roman governors rarely had their wives with them, but following the imperial practice of the emperor and his wife traveling to the provinces together, in the first century C.E. the presence of wives with their husbands becomes commonplace, expected rather than frowned upon. See Chapter 1, note 33, and Marshall 1975a.

[12] He notes further that the charge of *repetundae* seems never to have been made against a woman alone.

[13] Ulpian, *Dig.* 1.16.4.2: *proficisci autem proconsulem melius quidem est sine uxore: sed et cum uxore potest, dummodo sciat senatum Cotta et Messala consulibus censuisse futurum, ut si quid uxores eorum qui ad officia proficiscuntur deliquerint, ab ipsis ratio et vindicta exigatur.* For further discussion, see Marshall 1990: 334–335 n. 4.

[14] As discussed at length in Chapter 4.

[15] Sherwin-White (1966: 345–346) makes this same suggestion, but if the indictment of governor's wives is a Trajanic innovation, changes in the ways the laws pertaining to *repetundae* were administered may also have included the indictment of daughters,

with the Baetici and the senate that he should not be forced to proceed against an innocent person (21). The fact is that her husband
had already been acquitted in the second round of prosecutions.
Making a charge against her was probably not only a waste of time
but also a distraction from the other minor players whose conviction
Pliny was more likely to secure.

Pliny does not give details about the outcome of this final set of
charges except to say that some were acquitted but many convicted
and banished either temporarily or for life – a sentence that none of
the major defendants in the two earlier proceedings suffered (22).
Pliny does not tell the reader at this point whether Casta was found
guilty or innocent; instead, he recounts expressions of gratitude
from the senate for his diligence (23–27) and then recalls that he has
omitted something – noting that Homer and many others had told
things out of order but claiming that he had done so inadvertently!
Pliny's intention, of course, is to draw the reader's attention to what
was likely the most exciting and unique part of all of the proceedings
prompted by Classicus' bad behavior – the charge of *praevaricatio*
that was brought against Norbanus, an accuser from Baetica in the
case against Casta. One of the witnesses, unnamed by Pliny, made
the accusation of collusion against Norbanus so forcefully that it was
considered before Norbanus began his indictment of Casta, revers-
ing the customary order in such matters (30).[16] Additional accusations were made regarding Norbanus' behavior during the reign of
Domitian, and the enmity that such charges aroused provoked his
immediate trial without time to prepare, followed by a quick verdict
of guilty and sentence of banishment (31–34).

Norbanus' conviction must have seemed a boon to Pliny's case
against Casta, and indeed Pliny says he stressed in his prosecution
of her that Norbanus had been found guilty of *praevaricatio* with
her, but nevertheless she was acquitted. Pliny calls it an unusual and

who had not been subject to prosecution in the past. For a reconstruction of the *Lex
Acilia* from a number of bronze fragments, see Girard and Senn 1977.
[16] Pliny remarks that the charge of collusion would naturally be considered after the
prosecution of the accused with whom the prosecutor was charged with colluding
so that the latter's honesty might be properly judged (30). Otherwise, we might
suppose, the prosecutor might be unfairly convicted of something he had no intention of carrying out. The charge of *praevaricatio* would assume that Norbanus had
colluded with Casta to weaken the case against her.

unprecedented result that her accomplice should be convicted but she released (34). The implication, of course, is that the woman Pliny chose to prosecute was in fact guilty, despite her acquittal. After his lengthy argument regarding Classicus' daughter and the cruelty of pursuing her prosecution when she was clearly innocent, Pliny must feel the need to report Casta's acquittal while justifying the charges against her.

Finally, Pliny adds yet another supposed omission – that on the final day of the trial an accusation was made against the rest of the Baetican delegates for not proceeding against all of those whom the province had instructed them to charge. Pliny reports that he successfully defended them and that they had escaped being caught up in the whirlwind because of him (36). This final addendum again suggests the righteousness of Pliny's prosecution, implying that those charged were selected from a larger pool of people involved in illegal activities, and thus they are either more guilty than those who were not charged or at least more likely to be convicted.

Of all those who were caught up in the prosecutions surrounding Classicus, Pliny identifies only three as escaping conviction, although he hints that there were others: Classicus' son-in-law, daughter, and wife. Pliny gives no details about the charges against any of the three, nor does he comment on the acquittal of either Classicus' daughter or her husband. But he leaves no doubt that he believes Casta to be guilty, even though the only convincing evidence he offers is the conviction of her supposed colluder, Norbanus. Does Pliny assume that a wife must be guilty if her husband is guilty? I would suggest instead that Pliny's assessment of Casta has more to do with her character than it does with any indictable behavior on her part. Pliny convicts her of failing her husband, by choosing to live after he had died. In the contest to display *constantia*, Casta must be compared with the women of the next letter in the corpus to consider the loyalty of wives – 3.16. As discussed in Chapter 1, Vibia and Arria, both of whom are wives of men charged with serious crimes, indeed treasonous rebellion, are drastically different in their reactions to the condemnation of their husbands: Vibia chooses to live and even to betray her husband by giving witness to his revolt, while the noble Arria ends her own life as testament to her devotion. Though Pliny does not say so, it is possible that Casta testified on her own behalf or that her defense included statements that further besmirched her husband's reputation, in spite of her duty to defend it. She, like Vibia, is to be condemned for her disloyalty. Pliny is uncertain whether Classicus had killed himself to avoid prosecution or died of some other cause, but, as the contrast with Arria makes clear, a faithful wife would have followed him in death. His *gloria* was her *gloria*, his disgrace, her disgrace. Despite her acquittal on charges of *repetundae*, Casta cannot escape Pliny's verdict of failure as a wife.

Just a few letters later in book 4, Pliny recalls another contrast to his treatment of Casta and her daughter. In 4.2, he reminds his reader about Regulus, the despicable legacy hunter – preying on vulnerable women rather than defending them.[17] Pliny, by comparison, even when serving as prosecutor, persistently concerns himself with just behavior and fair treatment; he is a model of the restraint of power and adherence to the principles of justice he so commends in his praise of Trajan (*Pan.* 80).

LETTER 4.11: VESTAL CORNELIA. With 4.11 Pliny shifts back to Domitian's time, where he is an observer, not a participant in the judicial system. Just as with the prosecutions of the Stoics, Pliny is passive – noting the brutality and injustice of Domitian's actions, condemning him for them, but remaining himself absolved of blame. Nowhere in the letters is Pliny's revision of the past in service to the vilification of Domitian more evident than in his treatment of the execution of the Vestal Cornelia. While he had sanitized the political activities of the Stoics to make them seem wrongly convicted and had altered the timing of Corellius' death to align it with the demise of Domitian as a defiant act, in 4.11 Pliny arguably creates a work of historical fiction, making innocent and noble a woman firmly condemned by all other sources.

There is no question that the sanctity of the Vestal Virgins, whose chief duty it was to maintain the hearth of the Roman world, was imperative for the safety of the state.[18] In his thoughtful treatment of this topic, Holt Parker (2004: 587) notes that the bodies of all Vestals, even those condemned for *incestum*, were buried inside the *pomerium*, the sacred boundary of the city, and that we can thereby

[17] See Chapter 3 on Pliny's legacy letters.
[18] See the first section of Chapter 4 on the importance of control of women to the preservation of Roman rule.

conclude that the body of every Vestal was sacred and that its burial brought protection to Rome. Accounts of the execution of Vestals are virtually always connected with times of crisis for the state, whether brought on by war, famine, disease, or social strife, with the Vestal's death seeming to restore divine favor. There is no obvious crisis, however, with which to connect the trial and execution of the Vestals in 83.[19] We are merely told by Suetonius that Domitian wanted to address a problem that both his father Vespasian and brother Titus had ignored – *incesta Vestalium virginum* (*Dom.* 8.4). In fact, Suetonius places his report of the emperor's harsh treatment of Cornelia and the other Vestals between consideration of the actions Domitian took to address immoral behavior – including adultery, inappropriate themes in theatrical productions, and misbehavior by men of rank – and the destruction of a tomb because it had been built with stones intended for the Temple of Capitoline Jupiter (*Dom.* 8.3 and 8.5). In this context, Domitian's treatment of the Vestals simply seems part of a plan to restore traditional Roman values rather than an act provoked by crisis. Indeed, if we date Cornelia's execution to 89 or 90, it would have followed the emperor's celebration of a double triumph over the Chatti and the Dacians, victories that, while they did not signal lasting control of the conquered territories, certainly belie any great threat to Roman security.

Pliny's retelling of the condemnation and execution of Cornelia begins almost casually, not with the Vestal herself, but with the news that Valerius Licinianus is teaching rhetoric in Sicily, banished because he had admitted committing incest with a Vestal Virgin. Pliny remarks that Licinianus' fate is a just punishment for the crime, but he then casts doubt upon his guilt with the suggestion that the exiled senator might have pleaded guilty to avoid a more serious charge from an emperor who was determined to bury Cornelia alive but was short on witnesses (5). Pliny's intimation of a false confession seems quite improbable, a proposition colored by Domitian's later violent suppression of senatorial opponents. But Pliny's characterization of the emperor in a state of fury (*fremebat ... aestuabat*) is clearly

[19] Nor does there seem to be any particular crisis in 213 when Caracalla buried three Vestals alive and another committed suicide. Both emperors were, however, thoroughly condemned for their cruelty, and we might see in the story of Caracalla the casting of the tale through the inimical lens of Domitian's biographers.

intended to set up the heart of the letter in which Pliny creates a showcase for Domitian's cruelty, as the emperor subjects Cornelia to what was arguably the most horrifying form of capital punishment in the ancient world.

It might, in fact, be argued that Pliny saw Domitian's actions against the Vestals as entirely unnecessary, given the lack of a state crisis, and he says quite directly that Domitian undertook the charges in order to make his reign memorable (6). Pliny was also quite perturbed by the way in which her prosecution was handled; the tyrannical emperor, he says, called the pontifices not to the Regia but to his own Alban villa, where Cornelia was condemned *in absentia* and without the oppor- tunity to speak in her own defense (6). Sherwin-White (1966: 283) comments that Pliny may be trying to suggest that Domitian held the trial in secret, but in fact there was no customary place for such trials. Furthermore, we have no specific evidence from other sources either that the Vestal had to be present for her to be tried or that she had to be permitted to speak. The trial of a Vestal was both a religious and judicial matter at the same time, and its process was undoubtedly quite unique in Roman jurisprudence.[20] Domitian as both pontifex maxi- mus and chief judicial officer of the Roman state surely had the power to condemn a Vestal regardless of her social status, just as a *paterfamil- ias* might a wayward daughter. But Pliny's aim is to establish Cornelia's treatment as a gross injustice, if not in verdict, then at least in process.

From Pliny's viewpoint, Domitian is himself a criminal for the man- ner in which Cornelia was tried (*nec minore scelere quam quod ulcisci vid- ebatur* [6]), regardless of her guilt or innocence. Such a charge opens the door for Pliny's next accusation – that Domitian himself not only had committed incest with his niece Julia, the daughter of Titus, but had even been the cause of her death following a miscarriage (6).[21]

---

[20] For a discussion of the legal status of Vestals on trial, see Parker 2004: 583–585. If, as Parker concludes, the execution of a Vestal was a form of human sacrifice, the objectification and deracination of the Vestal was surely critical to Roman ability to consider it otherwise. Much the same can be said of the oath of subjection taken by the gladiator and the *infamia* that adhered to those who would lose their lives in the arena.

[21] The tale of Domitian's familial violation is also mentioned by Juvenal (2.28–35) and Suetonius (*Dom.* 22). Pliny will refer obliquely to the episode again in the *Panegyricus* when he mentions the dirtying of the statues of the gods in the Temple of Jupiter Optimus Maximus by the presence of images of the incestuous emperor (52.3).

Pliny, of course, is suggesting that the condemnation of a Vestal for incest by an incestuous emperor was hypocritical, despite the fact that Pliny would hardly have approved if the emperor had chosen to ignore the violation of a Vestal.

Pliny next reports that Domitian sent the pontifices to carry out the sentence immediately – to bury Cornelia alive. Now suddenly Cornelia is present in the narrative as if she had been at the trial, with no indication of where the priests found her. Pliny's narrative becomes highly dramatic, as he has Cornelia invoking the goddess for whom she had cared for so many years and has her repeating *frequentissime*, "Caesar thinks that I have committed incest, I by whose performance of the sacred rites he has been victorious, he has triumphed" – *me Caesar incestam putat, qua sacra faciente vicit triumphavit* (7). Pliny claims not to know why she chose these words – perhaps out of irritation or contempt or in hope of release or simple confidence in herself (8). Of course, the words are not attested elsewhere, and whether or not they were actually spoken by Cornelia, in their recounting Pliny has managed to politicize an event that might to this point have been merely a matter of broken vows of chastity. Cornelia had fulfilled her responsibilities and done so effectively, for Domitian had conquered the enemy and celebrated his triumphs. The chief reason for the execution of Vestals – danger to the state – is patently absent as attested by Cornelia herself.

Lest the reader believe Pliny to be credulous in suggesting that Cornelia was wrongly convicted, he says carefully that he does not know if she was innocent, but she seemed it. The final scene in Pliny's tale of her demise brings us to her underground chamber, the site of her execution, where, Pliny suggests, the purity of her person was so important to her that, as she descended into the chamber, she drew away from being touched in order to maintain her *sanctitas* (9). Despite Pliny's declaration of his uncertainty regarding her guilt, he leaves his reader with the image of the intact Vestal, going to her death with dignity.

After a brief mention of similar protestations of innocence by an equestrian named Celer who was charged with being Cornelia's accomplice (10), Pliny returns to the story of Licinianus that frames the letter, saying that following Cornelia's death, Domitian was enraged by the damage to his reputation that her execution had

caused, and he had Licinianus arrested for hiding a freedwoman of
Cornelia on his estate. Licinianus was subsequently advised to with-
draw his defense, save his possessions, and go into exile, which he
did, leaving Herennius Senecio, speaking for him in absentia, to
report his withdrawal (11–13).[22] Licinianus' reward, Pliny says, was an
easy exile and later, under Nerva, permission to move to Sicily (13).
We must note that he was not permitted to return to Rome, which we
can safely assume he would have preferred. There can have been no
real evidence of his innocence, despite Pliny's insinuations, because
Nerva decides to keep him away from the center of power.

The letter concludes with epistolary small talk that suggests
Licinianus' move to Sicily was recent and asks for news from Pliny's
addressee, making Pliny's historical account seem like the local gossip,
and thus perhaps not to be taken as established fact. But, indeed, this
is the only letter in Pliny's corpus in which Domitian is a vivid part of
the narrative. Despite the many references to him in the letters about
the Stoics or in Pliny's interaction with Corellius, Domitian himself
is not actually present. The condemnation of the Vestal Cornelia,
reported in the midst of his gossip about Licinianus, has given Pliny
an ideal opportunity to show Domitian in action – angry, belligerent,
secretive, more concerned with the legacy of his age than with justice.
In truth, Domitian was likely justified in condemning Cornelia and
her three fellow Vestals, for the violation of the vow of chastity would
surely have been seen as a threat to the state in itself, even without
external peril or internal discord to provoke it. Had such action been
taken by Trajan, we can be sure that Pliny would have reported it
as a return to ancient Roman values. As Parker (2004: 576) points
out, "though Pliny hated Domitian … he could not bring himself to
believe that the charge was utterly without foundation." We might
wonder what would have made Cornelia's condemnation acceptable
to Pliny. Perhaps Domitian should have conducted the trial in the
Regia, permitted Cornelia to commit suicide, or treated all of the

---

[22] As Sherwin-White (1966: 284) notes, that neither Cornelia nor Licinianus is present at her or his trial suggests that this was normal procedure in the trial of a
Vestal for incest. The problem with his supposition is, of course, that this is a single case, reported by a staunch opponent of Domitian, who may leave defendants
out of the courtroom as a way to further condemn the bad behavior of the hated
emperor.

Vestals equally by burying all of them alive. Despite her guilt or innocence Pliny has presented his version of a historical event, in highly
dramatic format, to cast doubt upon the conviction and particularly
on the judicial process while blackening the emperor's character –
precisely the kind of bad press the hated Domitian was trying to
avoid.

LETTER 6.31: GALLITTA. In stark contrast to Domitian's seemly
capricious administration of justice, three times in his nine-book
corpus Pliny reports his own experiences serving *in consilium*, that
is, as an adviser to Trajan on judicial matters. In the first two, 4.22
and 6.22, the judicial council is merely a venue within which Pliny
may discuss other matters.[23] Trajan is present naturally, but there is
no real interaction between him and Pliny nor is there any lengthy
discussion of the cases under consideration. *Epistulae* 6.31, however,
not only gives details of three cases considered by Trajan and his *consilium* but discusses Pliny's firsthand observations of the emperor's
judicial abilities and judgment, as well as Trajan's hospitality outside
of the courtroom. Thus, 6.31 is the only letter published by Pliny in
which he is interacting directly with Trajan or involved with him in
any intimate way.[24]

While the charges being brought in each case heard by the *consilium* are varied, all are complicated by some legal misconduct on the
part of the accusers, who either bring charges inappropriately or fail
to follow through on them. Such cases were surely of great importance
to the emperor in his determination to counter the terrible memories
of senators charged by informers and convicted by Domitian. Sorting
through guilt and innocence, calling for just and rational action, and
demanding appropriate prosecution are Trajan's obvious concerns.
The centerpiece of the letter is the case of the patently guilty Gallitta,

[23] In 4.22, Pliny has been called to serve the emperor at an inquiry into the abolishing
of a gymnastic contest at Vienna; however, the focus of that letter is not so much the
legal proceedings as it is the characterization of a fellow adviser, Iunius Mauricus
(discussed at length in Chapter 1) and his forthright manner. *Ep.* 6.22 reports
a case of treachery between provincial colleagues and serves to admonish those
embarking on provincial duties to be self-reliant whenever possible.
[24] Clearly book 10 of the letters constitutes an entirely different type of interaction
between Trajan and Pliny, that of emperor and provincial legate. Thus, there is
little or no intimacy in these formal communiqués, though certainly some expressions of fondness.

the adulterous wife of a military tribune, whose trial is framed by cases whose circumstances are considerably less clear.

Pliny reports that on the first day, the *consilium* heard the charges against Claudius Ariston of Ephesus. Precisely what he was accused of, Pliny does not say, only that Ariston was a generous man, whose position had aroused envy and the procurement of an informer against him (3). Pliny's terse account implies the brevity of the proceedings and a quick acquittal, and yet the case against Ariston must surely have been strong enough to warrant its consideration by the emperor. It may be that, as a Roman citizen, Ariston was exercising his right to be tried in Rome rather than risk having his case heard by men whose hostility toward him had brought the charge to begin with. Regardless of his motives, Ariston had chosen wisely, as the emperor saw through the false charges and acted accordingly.

For Gallitta, accused of adultery with a centurion, there is no question of false charges and apparently no question of innocence, but rather insufficient action taken in response to her disgraceful behavior. Her husband was just about to seek office, Pliny reports, but she had stained both her own and her husband's *dignitas* (4), thus potentially ruining his candidacy and political future. It is not so much her adultery that would have damaged him, we must assume, but the way in which he dealt with his errant wife. As required, the legate had reported her adultery to the governor, who in turn told the emperor. Trajan had cashiered and relegated the centurion in accordance with the *Lex Julia de Adulteriis* (5). But while her husband had begun the required proceedings, he had not seen them through. The Julian Law required that he both divorce and prosecute Gallitta within sixty days of discovering her offense. Pliny comments that his love for his wife held him back, and that he was satisfied to keep her in his house once he had removed his rival. The legate was admonished to complete the process and make the charge against his wife, which he did unwillingly, and it was the case against Gallitta that Pliny's *consilium* heard. She was subsequently condemned and sentenced under the Julian law, which would have meant her relegation to an island.[25] The

---

[25] The law may also have required her to forfeit one-third of her property and half of her dowry (*Sententiae Pauli* 2.26.4) in addition to her relegation to an island (Tacitus, *Ann.* 2.85 et al.); she was also forbidden to remarry (*Dig.* 48.5.12.13). See also Sherwin-White 1966: 394.

emperor then made a statement about military discipline and named the centurion (although Pliny does not), so that not all cases of this kind would be referred to him (6).

Without a doubt one of the major reasons the charges against Gallitta were made with Trajan as judge was that she and her husband were of senatorial rank and the centurion was not. Trajan was annoyed by the case – likely for several reasons: lack of military discipline (the adultery probably occurred in camp), the husband's fecklessness, and the failure of the governor to deal with the matter. But we must also wonder who Gallitta's husband was. If Trajan was determined to enforce adultery laws strictly, the tribune could have been charged with *lenocinium* for his failure to carry out his duties under the law. Was the tribune treated leniently because he had at least reported the adultery or because of his rank? Given the paucity of examples in our sources of individuals actually charged with *lenocinium* under the Julian precepts, it is perhaps easier to imagine that the potential of a charge was frequently used as a threat to compel reluctant husbands to take proper action against their wives. So Gallitta's husband was chastised but not punished, except by his loss of her. The anonymity Pliny provides him may have left this negligent husband's future political aspirations at least somewhat intact and certainly insulated Pliny from any lasting enmity with him.

With its prominent location in the letter and following Pliny's presentation of his own wife's character and particularly her *castitas*, the case of Gallitta and its many social implications are compelling. Pliny has already set the standard for a good wife and made clear a husband's role in the creation and maintenance of her excellence. The Gallitta episode illustrates well what might happen to a man who fails to meet societal expectations of his marriage and thus reinforces Pliny's instruction of his readers. Furthermore, the emperor's treatment of Gallitta's husband and his impatience at having to hear the case make clear his stand on the need for men to control their wives and adhere to the stringent laws compelling them to do so.

The final case considered by the *consilium* was not nearly as clearcut as the first two. The will of Julius Tiro contained clauses said to be forged, and so his heirs complained and begged Trajan to make an inquiry, but, when the emperor agreed to do so, he found that some of the heirs did not want to appear, because one of those they were charging was an imperial freedman. Trajan had adjourned the case previously and now was hearing it again (8–9). Only two heirs appeared and asked that the emperor either compel the appearance of the others or permit them to drop the case, while the advocates for the defendants pleaded for a hearing so that their clients might be exonerated. Trajan is concerned that he might appear high-handed and so asks for his council's advice (10–11), upon which he acts, ruling that all heirs be summoned to proceed with the accusations or to explain sufficiently why they were dropping them; otherwise, they themselves would be declared guilty of filing false charges (12). Here Pliny demonstrates Trajan's cautious approach to dispensing justice and to avoiding the appearance of tyrannical or hasty behavior. The care with which Trajan handles both accusers and defendants in this case serves to highlight his forceful rebuke of the laggard husband of Gallitta, who received no such tender treatment.

Despite Pliny's claim that his days on the *consilium* were devoted to serious matters, none of the three cases seems to be of great import. Indeed, he offers little information on the first, and the last remains unresolved. Pliny's concern is to showcase his proximity and service to a good emperor, as important to his reputation as his determined avoidance of any personal connection with Domitian. The letter also provides negative exempla that offer sharp contrasts to Pliny's own integrity – in court, in his marriage, and in legacy disputes. Indeed, the outcome of each case is cautionary, warning against informers, those more consumed by emotion than duty, and accusers who fail to follow through, with the wayward husband receiving the harshest reprimand of all.

LETTER 7.24: UMMIDIA QUADRATILLA. While Pliny's skillful prose convicts the acquitted Casta and casts doubt upon the guilt of the Vestal Cornelia, he brings the full force of his rhetorical genius to his character assessment of the recently deceased Ummidia Quadratilla, successfully creating virtue out of her vices and salvaging her reputation and more importantly that of her grandson. Despite her feminine weakness, Ummidia is the embodiment of qualities Pliny has extolled in other women – particularly those responsible for overseeing the upbringing of proper Roman children. She is unique in Pliny's corpus: in age, in bearing, and in her singular ability to be highly praiseworthy despite her sometimes indecent activities.

Epistulae 7.24 is addressed to Rosianus Geminus, a protégé of Pliny who served as his quaestor in 100 C.E. and later as consul and governor of Cappadocia (A. Birley 2000: 85). Pliny recommends him to Trajan for advancement (10.26) and sends a number of letters to him focused on various human weaknesses and strengths of both body and mores. Because its recipient is one of Pliny's rising stars, 7.24 must be viewed as offering an exemplum of character and comportment.[26]

Most of Pliny's obituary letters commence with an expression of his own distress or sorrow,[27] but 7.24 begins directly with Ummidia Quadratilla's name in the nominative case, a most unusual opening. In fact, only ten letters in all of the nine-book collection begin with a name, of which four are letters of recommendation and two requests for favors for the individual named.[28] Pliny's reader, then, would perhaps expect that Pliny was writing about Ummidia Quadratilla in hopes of garnering some type of positive support for her, only to find that Pliny is reporting her death; yet, the letter can easily be read as a commendation.

Having reported Ummidia's demise at nearly eighty years of age, Pliny then includes a surprising comment on her physical form – being vigorous right until her final illness, Ummidia possessed a body that was well set and strong (*compactus et robustus*). Pliny is quite disinclined to discuss anyone's physique, beyond general comments regarding the beauty (*forma* or *pulchritudo*) of young bachelors, the vigor of the old, or the infirmity of the ailing. His physical description of Ummidia is unique in the letters, and furthermore he adds that her body is *ultra matronalem modum* – beyond what is customary of matrons (1). Thus, we are advised immediately that she is no ordinary woman, and we are assured that her life-style has not led to any sort of dissipation.

---

[26] For other examples of letters to protégés, see Chapter 1's discussion of *Ep.* 1.5 and 9.13 and Chapter 3, *Ep.* 6.33.

[27] See *Ep.* 1.12, 3.21, 4.21, 5.16, 5.21, 8.5, 8.23. Two other letters open with a statement that Pliny has just heard about a death, and thereafter he comments upon the meaning of the loss for him – *Ep.* 3.7 and 5.5.

[28] The letters are as follows: recommendation – 1.24, 4.4, 7.16, 7.31; requesting favors – 4.28 and 6.8. The other three letters include: 4.2, a letter about Regulus (Pliny's enemy) and the death of his son; 4.5, a letter about oratory that begins with the name of Aeschines; and 6.29, a letter to Ummidius Quadratus regarding the types of cases it is suitable to undertake.

Next Pliny notes that, when she died, she did so with a properly written will. The importance of Roman wills is discussed more fully in Chapter 3, but it is most interesting that Ummidia Quadratilla is the only woman in Pliny's letters to write a proper will. All other female testators in the corpus have difficulty in assuring the proper dispersal of their estates; they are subject to captation and manipulation and guilty of writing wills that are unclear or that disinherit close family members. The suggestion is that leaving a proper will was a masculine virtue, perhaps only to be aspired to by women but not expected of them.[29] In any case, Ummidia has properly made her grandchildren her heirs, with two-thirds of the estate going to her grandson and one-third to her granddaughter, and thus she displays an intellectual acuity equal to her physical fortitude.

Pliny then admits knowing the grandchildren – the girl in passing but the boy quite intimately (2). He then describes the young man as someone who has done all the right things: avoiding any bad reports of his conduct as a youth despite his good looks, marrying before age twenty-four as required by law, wishing for though not yet blessed with children (3) – all the hallmarks of a properly raised young man. The reader might wonder why his excellence is particularly remarkable, until Pliny proceeds to explain that he had been raised not just by a woman – as Calpurnia Hispulla and Plinia had overseen the childhoods of Calpurnia and Pliny[30] – but by Ummidia, his self-indulgent grandmother, *avia delicata*. Indeed, *delicata* can also suggest addiction to pleasure and certainly signals that she has habits of which Pliny disapproves. As a result, her grandson was in the difficult position of needing to be obedient to her while maintaining his own decorum. Pliny immediately suggests that he has managed to do just this by characterizing his childhood as both very strict and yet compliant – *vixit in contubernio aviae delicatae severissime, et tamen obsequentissime* (3).

The explanation of the most troublesome of Ummidia's pleasures follows Pliny's declaration of her grandson's good behavior – she owns pantomime actors, and she treasures them more than is suitable for a woman of her status (4). In fact, association with performers was a problem for anyone of senatorial rank, with pantomime

---

[29] Sherwin-White (1966: 431) calls Ummidia's proper will a counterpart of that of Domitius Tullus in *Ep.* 8.18 (see Chapter 3) – "bad man makes good will."
[30] See Chapter 3.

actors attracting perhaps the most reasons for censure because
they were seen to embody moral turpitude.[31] Of course, upper-class
Roman men had always been involved with the games, raising horses
for the *ludi circenses* and owning gladiatorial troupes, among other
activities, but the performances of pantomime actors were often sex-
ually explicit, and liaisons between elite Romans and lowly performers were a regular topic of lurid historical and biographical accounts
of elite moral corruption. David Sick (1999: 342–343) has recently
suggested that Ummidia's possession of performers was not just an
idle pastime but a lucrative source of income.[32]

Because of the overwhelmingly negative opinion of those who
associated with entertainers and particularly because Ummidius was
a handsome young man who might attract rumors of sexual impropriety, it was imperative that he be kept from any contact with her pantomimes. Indeed, immediately after reporting Ummidia's unseemly
affection for her actors, Pliny states that the young man had never
seen them, either at home or in the theater, and that his grandmother never compelled him to do so (4). Pliny's statement suggests
that Ummidia might have chosen to force her grandson to watch the
pantomimes perform or might have permitted it had he asked, but
this would have stained his reputation. In truth, despite the fact that
Ummidius had not been involved with the pantomimes, we can safely
assume that he might have been affected by public knowledge of her
patronage of performers whom she would have provided for both
public and private venues. Pliny would scarcely need to emphasize
the young man's purity otherwise.

Now we come to the heart of the letter and the chief reason why
Pliny has undertaken its composition: Pliny reports that Ummidia

[31] The connection between pantomimes and bad character is attested by the Younger
Seneca (*Ep.* 47.17), the Elder Pliny (*Nat.* 7.184), Suetonius (*Cal.* 36.1, 55.1), and the
Younger Pliny (*Pan.* 46.4), as well as a number of later sources. In addition, there
were legal restrictions on association with pantomimes and on their performances,
like those of the *Lex Julia Theatralis* (e.g., Tacitus, *Ann.* 1.77), as well as episodes of
rioting in Rome centered around those performances, often followed by expulsion of the performers from Rome (e.g., Tacitus, *Ann.* 14.21). See Jory 1984 and
Slater 1994 for full consideration of the circumstances surrounding these riots and
banishments.

[32] Sick considers a number of inscriptions of entertainers with female owners or
patrons and suggests that some families may have made substantial investment in
the business of entertainment.

208

Pliny: Arbiter of Virtue

had asked him to be her grandson's tutor (5). Clearly Pliny agreed, and the young man became one of his outstanding protégés, as we have already been told in *Epistulae* 6.11, a letter in which Pliny's effusive praise for Ummidius' oratorical skill is matched only by his delight at having been the young man's teacher and model.[33] Here it becomes clear that Pliny is no longer a detached observer of Ummidius' upbringing but rather a mentor with great interest in protecting his reputation. At the time that Ummidia had engaged him to teach her grandson, Pliny says, she had told him how she occupied her free time, playing board games (*lusus calculorum*) or watching her mimes. Pliny carefully includes in her statement the words *ut feminam in illo otio sexus* (5) – an ambiguous phrase that might mean either that as an elite woman she naturally had leisure time or that the ways in which she amused herself were acceptable for women. There is no question of the impropriety of a man's association with actors, and playing with *calcula* was also an activity that was frowned upon among the upper classes and was associated, particularly in rhetoric, with other licentious behavior.[34] Nicholas Purcell (1995: 15–16) suggests several reasons for the bad reputation of games that employed dice or markers, the most compelling of which are their persistent popularity with the lower classes and their connection with the inappropriate use of *otium*. Because elite women were removed from the expectations of *negotium*, their leisure activities were undoubtedly less open to censure than those of their male relatives.[35]

We can imagine the interview in which Pliny and Ummidia discussed her pastimes, and perhaps Pliny is also imagining it. Being tutor for a young man from so prominent a family must have been enticing. Perhaps Pliny would have wanted some assurance of the young

[33] Pliny goes so far as to invoke the gods to sustain his joy: *quod gaudium ut perpetuo capiam deos oro* (6.11.4).

[34] Pliny's hero and model Cicero makes this charge, among many others, against Catiline (2.23 – *in his gregibus omnes aleatores, omnes adulteri, omnes inpuri inpudicique versantur*) and Antony (*Phil.* 3.35 – *libidinosis, petulantibus, impuris, impudicis, aleatoribus, ebriis servire;* 8.26 – *cavet mimis, aleatoribus, lenonibus, Cafoni etiam et Saxa cavet, quos centuriones pugnaces et lacertosos inter mimorum et mimarum greges collocavit;* 13.24 – *in lustris, popinis, alea, vino tempus aetatis omne consumpsisses*).

[35] Sherwin-White (1966: 431) suggests that Ummidia's tastes are Neronian, not yet reflecting the shift under Trajan toward restraint. Yet Trajan had, in fact, permitted the return of pantomime competition. Moreover, there is nothing to suggest that Ummidia's leisure time activities were not commonplace among elite women.

man's purity before taking him on, but the family's involvement with
the games was surely public knowledge. In any case, Pliny implies that
Ummidia shared the information in response to his inquiry about
her grandson's exposure to her questionable activities before Pliny
agreed to become the boy's tutor, thus suggesting his cautious concern for his own *fama*. That assurance came, according to Pliny, with
Ummidia's explanation that she had been careful to keep Ummidius
apart from her leisurely pursuits, always sending him away to study
(5). With this statement she absolves from blame both Ummidius,
because he had not been corrupted, and herself, because she had
kept him from disgrace. Pliny adds that Ummidia removed him from
her *otium* because she both loved and respected Ummidius (5); thus,
she had both grandmotherly affection for him and an acute awareness of his rank and the reputation it demanded.

Are we really expected to believe that Ummidius had not had any
exposure to those freedmen mimes performing under his own roof?
Pliny continues the letter with the words *miraberis, et ego miratus sum*
(6). The recipient of the letter is expected to be surprised, amazed,
bewildered, perhaps by the episode that Pliny will next report but
also surely by the possibility that Ummidius had had no prior contact with grandma's fancies. The letter then recounts an episode
from the recent sacerdotal games that opened with a performance
by Ummidia's pantomimes. Pliny and Ummidius were leaving the
games together, when Ummidius commented to him, *scis me hodie primum vidisse saltantem aviae meae libertum* – "do you know that today is
the first time that I have seen a freedman of my grandmother danc-
ing?" (6) Here Pliny presents direct evidence – the young man had
not seen even one of her pantomime actors before this public performance – that provides clear proof of Ummidius' innocence and
his grandmother's proper treatment of him. Pliny then calls him *hoc
nepos*, recalling that Ummidius is her heir, which leads into the next
element of the anecdote and brings the reader into the theater.

In order to separate Ummidius even further from corrupting contact with the pantomimes, Pliny offers a stark contrast to his protégé's behavior – *hoc nepos. at hercule alienissimi homines* ... (7). As Pliny
and Ummidius are leaving the games, men of another type entirely,
whom Pliny separates from Ummidius with the exclamation *at hercule* and calls *alienissimi* – a word that can mean both unfamiliar and

distasteful – are dashing into the theater to honor Ummidia (Pliny says it shames him to call it honor) with bits of pantomime meant to reflect her own gestures (7). Such behavior would naturally be *alienum* to Ummidius. Pliny's *alienissimi*, who do not just applaud, but sing, dance, and mimic Ummidia, can be no others than her pantomime actors, who performed in competition individually, but after the competition appear together in a show of honoring their mistress.[36] Their praise of her in so open and public a setting assured that everyone in the community must have known her as their patron. In stark contrast, Pliny then notes that these same men will receive a tiny legacy, a final tip for their hired applause from her heir – *qui non spectabat* – "who was not used to watching them."[37] That Pliny ends his anecdote with these three words makes clear his purpose in telling the story – to exonerate his protégé. Furthermore, Ummidia's mention of the actors in her will is in appropriate proportion to their importance in her life – a minor amusement in an otherwise impeccable existence.

To conclude at this point would make the letter's defensive nature entirely too obvious. Instead, Pliny makes light of its contents thus far as merely a bit of amusing news (8), for he was pleased by Ummidia's *pietas* and by the honor given to the *optimus iuvenis*. Instead he ends the letter by noting that Ummidia's house, once owned by C. Cassius, founder of the Cassian school of jurisprudence, will now serve a master as great as Cassius had been. Quadratus will properly fill it and will return it to its former greatness – without pantomime actors, we must assume – because he will be as fine an orator as Cassius was a jurisconsult (9). In this last sentence of the letter, Pliny leaves no doubt as to his personal interest in Ummidia's heir, calling him *meus Quadratus*. The reader will surely recall the young man from

---

[36] Some translations of this passage suggest that these men are a separate group of hired applauders, who meant nothing to Ummidia (Radice 1969: vol. II, 537). This seems an unnecessary and unlikely complication, as Pliny uses *alienissimi* not to indicate their strangeness to Ummidia but to her grandson. Furthermore, it is clearly her pantomimes to whom Ummidius paid the required *corollarium* (7).

[37] It is tempting to see Pliny's use of the words *theatralis operae corollarium*, which does evoke an image of claqueurs hired for a specific occasion, as an attempt to minimize the importance of the pantomimes to Ummidia. She has left them the smallest token in her will. But Pliny has just finished an elaborate description of the zeal they displayed for their mistress in the theater, after which it is difficult to exonerate her behavior. Nor does Pliny have to do so, as long as he can successfully separate Ummidius from any contact with them beyond paying her legacy.

the previous book of letters: *Epistulae* 6.11, praising his emerging rhetorical skills, and *Epistulae* 6.29, where Pliny offers him (as recipient) guidelines for choosing which cases to undertake. Yet to come is perhaps the greatest indication of Ummidius' importance to Pliny, his receipt of *Epistulae* 9.13, the account of what Pliny considered his greatest oratorical triumph, his vindication of Helvidius Priscus.[38]

A seemingly newsy and lighthearted letter, then, has serious implications for both Ummidius and Pliny and serves as a defense of the young man's honor, of Ummidia's ability to set appropriate boundaries in her household to protect the grandson who bore her name, and especially of Pliny's choice to serve as his mentor and guide. For a childless man like Pliny, the impeccable character of his protégé as a reflection of his own was critical to his *immortalitas*. Under Pliny's careful hand, Ummidia's questionable activities become part of her grandson's success rather than a stain on his reputation because she is an exceptional woman, of formidable physique and character, who manages to keep her feminine weaknesses from affecting his future.

Conclusion

Pliny's model Romans are all clear-cut examples of excellence, with occasional endearing human quirks but no questionable character traits or episodes of misbehavior. Minicia, Calpurnia, and Fannia are all virtue; Corellius and his family are proper Romans, defying tyrants and conforming to social expectations; the Stoics are innocent victims, cleansed of any iniquity; Pliny's family members are devoted, loyal, and above repute; even the women of the legacy letters, who have sometimes been less than diligent in securing their estates, are vulnerable and without guile. There is little room in the world Pliny portrays for ambiguity of character or momentary human weakness.

Pliny creates an empire of drastic contrasts – virtue and vice, loyalty and deceit, safety and peril – drawing consistent comparisons between his past under Domitian and his present under Trajan. Critical to his presentation of a changed Rome is the distance that Pliny emphasizes between proper and miscreant behavior, not just in his persistent pairing of the actions of Domitian and Trajan, who

---

[38] See Chapter 1.

is always acutely aware of his need to be as un-Domitianic as possible, but in the way that he separates all those behaving badly from the righteous. Thus, Pliny strips the Vestal Cornelia of her wickedness and clothes her in rectitude so that he may compare her unsullied person to Domitian's villainy; and, to maintain social balance, Trajan and Pliny must compensate for the unnamed tribune's failure to distance himself from his adulterous wife Gallitta. Even Casta, acquitted of the charges against her but clearly guilty, should have separated herself from her innocent daughter by dying with her husband. It seems that only Ummidia managed to maintain both upright and distasteful portions of her life, enjoying her board games and pantomimes while keeping her grandson removed from them. Pliny makes the best of her vices by praising her thoughtful concern for Ummidius, and, in reality, in Pliny's letter she too has conformed to the need for complete detachment from her pantomimes and her grandson's future prospects, by dying and leaving him to restore the grandeur of her abode.

In the world of Pliny's letters, where any contact with unacceptable behavior – barring the role of prosecutor – taints an upright Roman, Pliny must separate himself and associate only with exemplary men and women. In each of his stories of unseemly women, there is no doubt where Pliny's judgment falls, and he distances himself accordingly from any questionable activities.

This is not to say that Pliny does not make the most of the opportunities presented to him by feminine misbehavior. Pliny stains Casta with her husband's blatant guilt; in fact, she serves as a reflection of her husband, shaped, we must assume, by his bad character just as an excellent wife is the creation of her admirable husband. Pliny thus justifies his prosecution of Casta, despite her acquittal, just as convincingly as he argues for the injustice of prosecuting her innocent daughter. Good wives are not associated with disreputable husbands, although the opposite is most certainly possible, as in the case of Gallitta, whose husband would not have been exposed to any criticism had he carried to completion his full responsibilities in dealing with her adultery. In a collection that offers many examples of exemplary wives and makes clear how crucial a husband is in creating a wife of good character, the reluctance of Gallitta's husband to divorce and prosecute her and the censure he endured serve as a clear warning to the man who does not take his duty seriously. While Pliny never identifies the cuckolded husband, it is hard to imagine a bright political future for him, under an emperor who emphasized a return to traditional morality and whose modest and demure wife Pliny praises so highly in the *Panegyricus*.[39]

There is no husband unwilling to bring his adulterous wife to task in the story of the Vestal Cornelia's condemnation. While Pliny cannot bring himself to call her innocent, he does his best to characterize Domitian's treatment of her as unjust and cruel. Ironically, as pontifex maximus, Domitian has a responsibility to Cornelia similar to the one Gallitta's husband had to his wife. He must punish the errant behavior of a Vestal and maintain the integrity of his household – in this case, the Roman state itself. In this historical vignette, Pliny successfully draws a fine distinction between Domitian's justifiable reaction and Cornelia's horrifying punishment and manages to plant just a seed of doubt as to the Vestal's guilt by criticizing the judiciary process and by emphasizing Cornelia's dignity and bearing.

The story of Ummidia Quadratilla, on the other hand, is no mere anecdote or casual tale. On the contrary, Ummidia's patronage of pantomime actors and deep involvement in the business of entertainment, at the very least in the building and restoration of facilities devoted to the games, and Pliny's close connection to her grandson make his characterization of the grand dame a necessity in his self-portrait. We may be sure, however, that Pliny would never have connected himself with Ummidia at all had he not needed to insist that his protégé – and, by association, Pliny himself – had remained untouched by her unfortunate behavior.

---

[39] See particularly Chapter 4.

Conclusions

*ego beatissimum existimo qui bonae mansuraeque
famae praesumptione perfruitur.*

Pliny, *Epistulae* 9.3

I consider that man to be the most fortunate who enjoys the
expectation of an enduring good reputation.

In the idyllic world of Pliny's letters there are no argumentative
wives, no disagreeable children, no battles, no calamities; the guilty
are condemned, the wrongly accused avenged, the needy assisted,
the weak protected; good never succumbs to temptation, and the
empire is secure in the hands of an emperor who acknowledges the
importance of elite support and an elite that shoulders its burden
of responsibility for the maintenance of Roman honor and integrity. The villains of Tacitus' *Annales* and *Historiae*, who cared more
for their own pleasures and power than for the state, are part of the
past, and those few that remain, like Regulus and Certus, die off and
leave the empire in the hands of those who guard its survival and
adhere to its rules. Gone too are women who usurp power, who overstep their boundaries, who abandon their modesty; they are replaced
by women who are no less formidable, but who, like the husbands and
fathers by whom they were guided, zealously conform to propriety
and thus ensure the stability and happiness of all. Pliny cleaves the
idealized present from the dreadful past so thoroughly it is hard to
imagine that he and Tacitus inhabited the same Roman world. It is

not that in his naiveté Pliny cannot see evil, error, or dysfunction, but rather that he chooses to model excellence so forcefully and with just enough negative exempla to accentuate the positive that his reader will be compelled to follow his lead and to become more Plinian than Pliny himself.

In assembling his collection of letters, Pliny institutes a new genre, using the centuries-old tradition of epistolography not only to promote himself as a model elite Roman but also to carve out his own literary niche where he can display his formidable writing skills. Pliny's new genre creates and populates a world that is at the same time genuine and fictional, with identifiably real characters and situations that can either be scrubbed clean or sullied as required by the author's design. It is this very ambiguity that makes Pliny's correspondence so hard to pin down as either "authentic" or contrived. Each letter is complete without any need of reply, unlike "real" correspondence, which would generally require or at least request some response, if only to confirm its safe arrival, and yet each seems credible – a true account of some piece of Pliny's life.

As we have seen, even the briefest of the letters is a rhetorical masterpiece, carefully refined and placed within the corpus to create interlocking narratives about various aspects of Pliny's life, culminating in a complete portrait of their author, while at the same time masquerading as a casual collection of varied personal correspondence. Cicero can hardly have envisioned creating anything like Pliny's grand assemblage when he considered publishing a selection of letters. It is easy to imagine the premier orator pulling together letters that demonstrated his involvement in historical moments of great importance, examples of his fortitude and beneficence, but certainly not anything that revealed his inner world. History in Pliny's time, however, was controlled largely by whoever held the principate; the emperor's biography was also Rome's life story, as we can certainly see in all of the historical accounts of writers like Tacitus and Cassius Dio.

Having chosen letters as his medium, Pliny is not constrained by the requirements of history – sequential or topical reporting and at least some attempt to recount the facts. While he demurs to write history, he certainly does provide a number of historical vignettes, the most famous of which are 6.16 and 6.20 about the eruption of Vesuvius, and there are a number of letters in which Pliny reports on courtroom proceedings in which he is either actor or observer. Pliny the reporter offers brilliantly dramatic historical accounts of the action but with a particular emphasis that skews the reader's perception. He can do this without fault in a medium that expects the sentiment of the author to color his point of view and gives credence to firsthand observations.

Of course, historical writing is by no means the only genre with which Pliny engages. Rhetoric is well represented in almost all of Pliny's letters but particularly those recommending tutors, husbands, or lesser men for promotion. More interesting are letters in which Pliny speaks of his own oratory – sending speeches for assessment or setting the scene for his Demosthenic triumphs. While we might wish for the speeches themselves, Pliny's reports tell us much more about his character than the speeches ever could.

To these genres we could certainly add tragedy and many others,[1] as letters had traditionally provided a venue for virtually any kind of interpersonal relationship. Indeed, the *Typoi Epistolikoi* of Pseudo-Demetrius includes twenty-one types of letters with which one could console, blame, praise, accuse, thank, or be ironic, among other possibilities,[2] without any particular generic constraint other than including an addressee and a greeting. Pliny's real innovation comes in the disposition of letters within the collection in service to its over-all aims and in the addition of a new type of correspondence, the love letter, which owes as much to elegy as to any of its potential epis-tolary forebears. Perhaps Pliny's careful arrangement of letters was prompted by the many works of poets like Propertius and Statius that gathered together short poems with great attention to variety and interplay among persistent themes within the collection. The result for Pliny is a literary pastiche that engages and holds his reader's attention and enables his complex self-presentation.

Finding venues in which to display excellence – whether in the courtroom, in the forum, or in literary circles – had always been a strong component of competition among the elite of Rome. Furthermore, detailed examination by its members of one another's behavior was critical in counteracting inappropriate actions or the seizing of power.[3] Ideally, the opening of all aspects of a man's life to

---

[1] Including didactic, pastoral, technical treatise, tragedy, and philosophy.

[2] See Malherbe 1988.

[3] As noted by Riggsby 1997: 52, among others.

public scrutiny assured the community of his proper comportment – no backroom dealing, no ulterior motives – and so any activity that concerned the community was to be conducted in public view. In reality, of course, a man could create a respectable image and still find the means to hide socially unacceptable behavior.

Perhaps the most extreme example of the threat posed by elite clandestine activity is Catiline as seen through Cicero's account of the conspiracy created by his political rival, which was thwarted only by inside information. In the first Catilinarian, Cicero asks his enemy what there is left to hope for if his conspiracy cannot be contained by the walls of a private house (1.2). Activities that threatened the very existence of the state could be conducted in the dark recesses of a *domus*, and secrecy was always suspect. Sallust reports that Cicero was able to defeat Catiline by obtaining information from a spy with access to the inner circle of conspirators (*BC* 23). In fact, the original informer was a woman, Fulvia, the mistress of Quintus Curius. His mistreatment of her prompted her to question him and then to report the conspirators' plans. We are led to the clear conclusion that Romans were to behave as if the walls of the *domus* were permeable, and one's conduct within them had to be able to withstand examination.

However, the Roman house into which clients came on a daily basis could hardly be considered private. More useful to an understanding of the Roman terms *privatus* and *publicus* is to view places thus designated as what Andrew Riggsby (1997: 36) calls "loci of responsibility" rather than as markers of openness and intimacy.[4] The expectations that Roman society placed upon an individual varied according to the nature of the space in which he acted – the senate, the lawcourts, his hometown, his *domus*, or his villas. Pliny's letter 1.9 illustrates this well. Here, he contrasts life in the city – where he is expected to attend to any number of civic and social obligations – with that in the countryside, where he can choose his own activities.[5] Each venue has its own acceptable behavior. Any real privacy must have been nearly

[4] Riggsby (1997: 49) remarks further that the Roman concept reverses our modern expectations where public (not-private) is "derivative" from private. In Rome the public took precedence over the private, and "Community had ethical primacy over individual."

[5] Pliny's description of Spurinna's life in retirement (3.1) reinforces the nature of life away from civic duties.

impossible in city houses with their relatively open and ready access for their masters' business and social contacts, but even the villa, although it was much further removed from the eyes of others, with its staff of slaves and regular visitors lacked the kind of intimacy that modern readers associate with private residences.

Pliny's collection of letters enables him both to permit access to every aspect of his life in the most natural way possible, through seemingly everyday communication with people in his life, and to exert full control over the impressions gained through that access. The words are Pliny's, arranged as he sees fit, with no other voices except those quoted by Pliny. Even Pliny's "love letters," whose openness and intensity give them a sense of authenticity greater than any other letters in the collection, must be treated cautiously. Do they set Pliny's marriage in the midst of what Michel Foucault (1986: 72–80) sees as an evolution in the marital relationship from a union defined by the economic and political necessities of the household to one based on partnership and affection, or does Pliny want his readers to see him as someone in the vanguard of that evolution? The collective effect of his correspondence with and about his wife would suggest true affection and not just its image, which is of course precisely what Pliny wants us to believe.

Whether Pliny's affection for Calpurnia is real or contrived, she is certainly crucial to a full assessment of his character, as are the many women with whom he associates. Indeed, the importance of women to Pliny's personal political identity and to elite male status in general should compel a reassessment of the prominence of women in the age of Trajan, during which they have too often been viewed as suppressed and silent compared with the brash women of the Julio-Claudian and Flavian eras. Trajan's concerted effort to separate his principate from those that came before surely determined the way in which his wife and sister were presented to the Roman populace. Yet, Pliny's letters expose the reality that elite women in his day are persistently independent and powerful players in Roman social, economic, and political circles.

In all of his interactions with women in the letters, Pliny assumes the role of guide, mentor, aide, or patron; he is never overbearing but always in charge; however, the women with whom he associates can scarcely be seen as subordinated to his control, or indeed to the control of any man, despite the fact that a number of them are married to men of rank. Strong matriarchs like Ummidia Quadratilla or Corellia Hispulla, women with influential forebears, assume prominent roles in the education of their male heirs, in both the absence and presence of male relatives. Women like Pompeia Celerina and Corellia control considerable wealth and exercise autonomous economic and social power; cultivation of *amicitia* with them offered access to their influence, as well as to the men in their lives. In addition, Pliny's women have literary aspirations, make wills, and support and even foment political dissent.

The picture of Pliny's milieu that emerges is one in which elite men regularly interacted with self-reliant women of rank in their daily activities regardless of the setting – business, judicial, educational, domestic, or otherwise. Pliny does not consult with Corellia's husband regarding the purchase price of property, nor does he confer with her niece's husband regarding a tutor for their son.[6] His mother-in-law Pompeia Celerina's money is placed at his disposal without any mention of anyone else's consent.[7] Of course, Pliny may present this picture of female autonomy in order to highlight his trustworthiness and integrity, but it is hard to imagine that he would empower these women with authority that they did not possess. In fact, these powerful matrons of Trajan's time are displaying precisely the same sort of fiscal freedom exercised by Cicero's wife, Terentia, over her property and even over Cicero's estates in his absence.[8] Such control went hand in hand with political influence that may have gone underground in response to the perceived excesses of the Julio-Claudian women but was little diminished in actual practice, as the activities of Fannia and even of Pompeia Plotina herself clearly indicate.[9]

Although female independence seems at first to fly in the face of Pliny's clear sense that men must cultivate their wives, we must conclude that properly trained women were thought to be perfectly capable of making important decisions without constant oversight by their male relatives. Naturally, then, it is only these refined women

---

[6] See *Ep.* 7.11, 7.14, and 3.3, respectively, and Chapter 2.
[7] See *Ep.* 3.19 and Chapter 3.
[8] See particularly Cicero, *Att.* 2.4, 2.15, 12.32; *Fam.* 14.1. For a thorough consideration of Terentia's personal estate, see Treggiari 2007.
[9] It is, after all, Plotina who announces Trajan's death and the adoption of Hadrian.

with whom Pliny would or could do business, as women who were less exemplary would not have been granted the freedom to engage in important matters independently, nor would they have had the necessary qualities to make interaction with them rewarding or even appropriate.

As would have been true in any man's life, there must have been other women in Pliny's milieu: the fish monger, the laundress, wives of middle- and lower-class men with whom he did business, even slaves in his own household. It is, I believe, quite telling that we hear nothing of those women. Pliny's careful selection of the women included suggests that elite men were expected to limit the kinds of contact they had with women, in order, we must suspect, to avoid any stain on their reputation. Pliny presents an image of himself as interacting only with women of impeccable character and status and, beyond that, women with whom he has particular reasons for contact. Either they are affiliated with his family, his patrons, his protégés, or his close friends, or he has been called upon to represent their interests in court. He may maintain those relationships, he may even further cultivate them as he seems to do with his former mother-in-law and the sister of Corellius Rufus, but he apparently decided to avoid the discussion of any interactions with women outside of these parameters.

We might argue that he was simply not interested in women beyond his intimate circle of family and close friends, but there are hints of friendships unexplored in the letters. Particularly tantalizing are his testatory benefactors Pomponia Galla and Sabina, the women who named him as an heir. Had he been of particular assistance to their families? Were there long-standing ties of *amicitia* that caused them to designate Pliny? While we will never know the answer, we may be assured that there is much more to his relationships with those women than he cares to report and that there were many other women in Pliny's life whom he omits entirely from his correspondence. What remains is a portrait of the author's best side, the most positive exemplum he can provide, and an image meant to gain the prize that Pliny sought – his *aeternitas.*

Appendix A

Stemmata

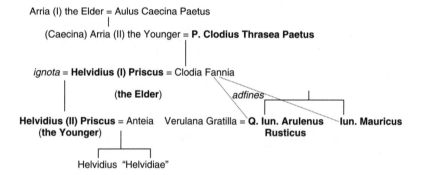

FIGURE 1. Family of Thrasea Paetus (members of the Stoic opposition in bold)

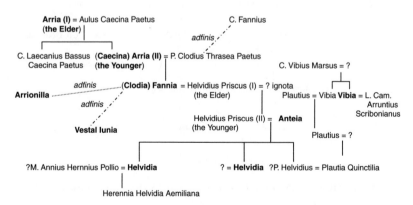

FIGURE 2. Clodia Fannia – Helvidii Stemma (women related to Helvidius Priscus (II) in bold)

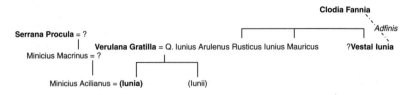

FIGURE 3. Clodia Fannia – Iunii Stemma (women related to Arulenus Rusticus in bold)

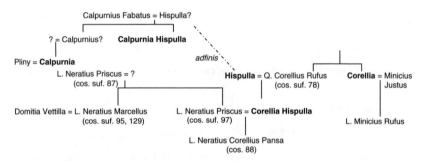

FIGURE 4. The Corellii and Calpurnii (women related to Corellius Rufus and Calpurnius Fabatus in bold)

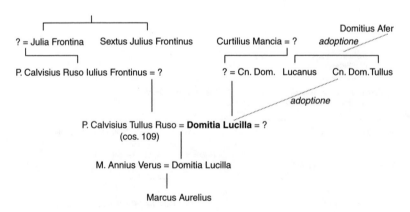

FIGURE 5. Family of Domitia Lucilla (the heiress Domitia Lucilla in bold)

Appendix B

Women in Pliny's Letters

Letter	Women
1.4	Pompeia Celerina – *recipient*
1.5	Arrionilla
1.12	(Corellia Hispulla) (Hispulla)
1.14	(Iunia, daughter of Q. Iunius Arulenus Rusticus) Serrana Procula
1.16	Wife of Pompeius Saturninus
1.18	(Pompeia Celerina)
1.19	(Plinia)
1.22	Wife of Titius Aristo Daughter of Titius Aristo
2.4	Calvina – *recipient*
2.15	(Plinia)
2.20	Verania Gemina Aurelia
3.1	Wife of Vestricius Spurinna
3.3	Corellia Hispulla – *recipient*
3.9	Casta Mistress of Classicus (Caecilia, daughter of Classicus)

(continued)

(continued)

Letter	Women
3.10	Cottia – *co-recipient*
3.11	Arria the Younger Clodia Fannia Verulana Gratilla
3.16	Arria the Elder Vibia
3.19	(Pompeia Celerina)
4.1	(Calpurnia) (Calpurnia Hispulla)
4.2	Former wife of Regulus
4.4	Sister of C. Calvisius
4.10	Sabina
4.11	Vestal Cornelia Freedwoman of Vestal Cornelia (Iulia, daughter of Emperor Titus)
4.15	Wife of Asinius Rufus
4.17	Corellia Hispulla
4.19	Calpurnia Hispulla – *recipient* (Calpurnia) (Plinia)
4.21	(The Helvidiae)
5.1	Pomponia Galla
5.14	(Calpurnia) (Calpurnia Hispulla)
5.16	(Minicia Marcella)
5.17	Mother of Calpurnius Piso
5.18	Wife of Macer
5.21	Mother of Iulius Avitus Sisters of Iulius Avitus
6.3	Pliny's nurse
6.4	Calpurnia – *recipient*
6.7	Calpurnia – *recipient*
6.10	(Pompeia Celerina)
6.16	Rectina (Plinia)
6.20	(Plinia)

Letter	Women
6.24	Anonymous wife
6.26	(Julia Paulina, daughter of Iulius Servianus) Mother of Fuscus Salinator
6.31	Gallitta
6.32	Daughter of Quintilianus/granddaughter of Tutilius
6.33	Attia Viriola Stepmother of Attia Viriola
6.34	Wife of Maximus
7.3	Wife of Praesens
7.5	Calpurnia – *recipient*
7.6	Anonymous mother
7.11	Corellia
7.14	Corellia – *recipient*
7.19	Clodia Fannia Arria the Younger Vestal Iunia
7.24	Ummidia Quadratilla
8.5	Wife of Macrinus
8.10	(Calpurnia)
8.11	Calpurnia Hispulla – *recipient* (Calpurnia)
8.18	(Domitia Lucilla) Wife of Domitius Tullus
8.19	(Calpurnia)
8.23	Mother of Iunius Avitus Wife of Iunius Avitus Daughter of Iunius Avitus
9.13	Clodia Fannia Arria the Younger Anteia (Helvidia, daughter of Anteia and Helvidius Priscus)
9.28	Pompeia Plotina
9.36	(Calpurnia)
10.4	Mother of Romanus
10.5	Antonia Maximilla Hedia Harmeris Antonia Harmeris

(continued)

(continued)

Letter	Women
10.6	(Hedia Harmeris) (Antonia Harmeris)
10.11	Ancharia Soteris Stratonice
10.51	(Pompeia Celerina)
10.59	Furia Prima
10.60*	Furia Prima
10.81	Wife of Dio
10.96	Deaconesses
10.107	Daughter of Aquila
10.120	(Calpurnia) (Calpurnia Hispulla)
10.121*	(Calpurnia)

Note: Parentheses indicate that woman is not named by Pliny.
*Trajan's reply to preceding letter.

Appendix C

Frequency of Personal Pronouns and Possessive Adjectives in Pliny's Letters, by Total Frequencies per 100 Words

Letter	No. of Words	Ego	1st Pro	1st Adj	1st Total	Frequency/100	Tu	2nd Pro	2nd Adj	2nd Total	Frequency/100	1st & 2nd Total	Total/100
9.31	85		2		2	2.4		12	1	13	15.3	15	17.6
1.4	107	1	3	7	10	9.3		1	5	6	5.6	16	14.9
6.28	87	1	4	3	8	9.2		1	4	5	5.7	13	14.9
6.9	43	1	3		4	9.3		2		2	4.7	6	14.0
6.12	129	2	9	1	12	9.3	3	1	2	6	4.7	18	14.0
6.3	52		1	3	4	7.7	1	2		3	5.8	7	13.5
9.24	67	1	2	2	4	6.0		4	1	5	7.4	9	13.4
6.7	75		2	3	6	8.0	1	1	2	4	5.3	10	13.3
9.8	54	1	1	1	3	5.5	1	2	1	4	7.4	7	13.0
6.1	85	3	4		7	8.2	2	1	1	4	4.7	11	12.9
8.7	83	2	2		4	4.9	2	2	2	6	7.3	10	12.2
7.28	83	1	5	3	9	10.8		1		1	1.2	10	12.0
7.14	67	1	2	1	4	6.0	1	3		4	6.0	8	11.9
9.28	190	1	6	1	8	4.2		11	3	14	7.4	22	11.6

(continued)

(continued)

Letter	No. of Words	Ego	1st Pro	1st Adj	1st Total	Frequency/100	Tu	2nd Pro	2nd Adj	2nd Total	Frequency/100	1st & 2nd Total	Total/100
1.19	113	1	3	2	6	5.3	1	4	2	7	6.2	13	11.5
7.16	115	3	5	2	10	8.7	1	2		3	2.6	13	11.3
3.8	141	1	3	2	6	4.3		5	5	10	7.1	16	11.3
7.11	217	3	9	10	22	10.1		1		1	0.5	23	10.6
5.11	104		3	1	4	3.8		3	4	7	6.7	11	10.6
5.1	402	3	16	10	29	7.2		11	2	13	3.2	42	10.4
5.10	100		1	3	4	4.0	2	2	2	6	6.0	10	10.0
6.6	296	5	9	8	22	7.4		5	2	7	2.4	29	9.8
1.7	193	1	8	3	12	6.2	1	2	4	7	3.6	19	9.8
1.21	51	1	1		2	3.9		1	2	3	5.9	5	9.8
4.19	217	1	6	5	12	5.5		3	6	9	4.1	21	9.7
1.11	52	2	3		5	9.6				0	0.0	5	9.6
2.9	200	3	6	7	16	8.0	1	2		3	1.5	19	9.5
9.21	149		4	2	6	4.0		5	3	8	5.4	14	9.4
4.18	64			2	2	3.1		3	1	4	6.3	6	9.4
7.32	67		2	1	3	4.5		3		3	4.5	6	9.0
4.26	78		2	1	3	3.8	1	3		4	5.1	7	9.0
9.12	100	1			1	1.0	3	3	2	8	8.0	9	9.0
2.4	157	1	3	3	7	4.5		4	3	7	4.5	14	8.9
6.18	90	1		2	3	3.3	1	3	1	5	5.5	8	8.9

Letter	No. of Words	Ego	1st Pro	1st Adj	1st Total	Frequency/100	Tu	2nd Pro	2nd Adj	2nd Total	Frequency/100	1st & 2nd Total	Total/100
7.20	208	1	4	2	7	3.4	3	6	2	11	5.3	18	8.7
6.14	59		2	1	3	5.1	1	1		2	3.4	5	8.5
7.5	83		1	1	2	2.4	1	1	3	5	6.0	7	8.4
2.16	120	2	5	1	8	6.7	1		1	2	1.7	10	8.3
5.12	98		4	1	5	5.1	1	1	1	3	3.1	8	8.2
3.17	73	2	1		3	4.1	2		1	3	4.1	6	8.2
2.18	176		3	1	4	2.3		4	6	10	5.7	14	8.0
4.6	76		3	1	4	5.3	1	1		2	2.6	6	7.9
1.18	191	1	5	3	9	4.7	3	1	2	6	3.1	15	7.9
8.10	126	2	1	1	4	3.2	1	2	3	6	4.8	10	7.9
1.3	165			1	1	0.6	2	5	5	12	7.3	13	7.9
2.15	51		1		1	2.0		1	2	3	5.9	4	7.8
9.3	91	2	3		5	5.5	1	1		2	2.2	7	7.7
3.15	130	1	3	2	6	4.6		1	3	4	3.1	10	7.7
3.2	132	1	4	1	6	4.5	1	2	1	4	3.0	10	7.6
9.20	66		2	1	3	4.5		1	1	2	3.0	5	7.6
6.4	121		3	3	6	5.0		2	1	3	2.5	9	7.4
6.8	302	4	10	5	19	6.3		2	1	3	1.0	22	7.3
9.38	41	1	1		2	4.9	1			1	2.4	3	7.3
6.11	139		8	1	9	6.5	1			1	0.7	10	7.2

(continued)

Letter	No. of Words	Ego	1st Pro	1st Adj	1st Total	Frequency/100	Tu	2nd Pro	2nd Adj	2nd Total	Frequency/100	1st & 2nd Total	Total/100
4.4	70		2	1	3	4.3		1	1	2	2.9	5	7.1
7.33	308	2	8	1	11	3.6	2	3	6	11	3.6	22	7.1
6.26	99		1	1	2	2.0		3	2	5	5.1	7	7.1
1.15	115		2	1	3	2.6	2	3		5	4.3	8	7.0
9.18	57			1	1	1.8		2	1	3	5.3	4	7.0
6.32	86		1		1	1.2		1	4	5	5.8	6	7.0
8.13	58			1	1	1.7		2	1	3	5.2	4	6.9
9.17	117	1	1		2	1.7	3	2	1	6	5.1	8	6.8
7.22	76		1	2	3	3.9		2		2	2.6	5	6.6
5.18	60	1	1		2	3.3		2		2	3.3	4	6.6
7.13	47				0	0.0	1	2		3	6.4	3	6.4
9.15	80		1	3	4	5.0	1			1	1.3	5	6.3
7.2	64			1	1	1.6		3		3	4.7	4	6.3
2.10	223	2		1	3	1.3		9	2	11	4.9	14	6.3
7.23	65	1	1		2	3.1		2		2	3.1	4	6.2
1.5	618	5	17	4	26	4.2	1	11+3q		12+3	1.9	38+3q	6.1
8.3	82		1	1	2	2.4		2	1	3	3.7	5	6.1
4.20	66				0	0.0	1	1	2	4	6.1	4	6.1
9.34	100	1	2	3	6	6.0				0	0.0	6	6.0

Letter	No. of Words	Ego	1st Pro	1st Adj	1st Total	Frequency/100	Tu	2nd Pro	2nd Adj	2nd Total	Frequency/100	1st & 2nd Total	Total/100
6.27	166	2	3	2	7	4.2		2	1	3	1.8	10	6.0
7.1	182		5	1	6	3.3		3	2	5	2.7	11	6.0
2.13	301	3	3	3	9	3.0	3	3	3	9	3.0	18	6.0
6.30	116	2			2	1.7	2		3	5	4.3	7	6.0
9.23	202	1	7	3	11	5.4		1		1	0.5	12	5.9
5.14	275	1	8	5	14	5.1		1	1	2	0.7	16	5.8
6.23	138		2	3	5	3.6	1		2	3	2.2	8	5.8
7.8	53		2		2	3.8		1		1	1.9	3	5.7
5.19	265	2	4	2	8	3.0		3	4	7	2.6	15	5.7
9.25	88		2		2	2.3	1	1	1	3	3.4	5	5.7
4.17	374	3	13	4	20	5.3		1		1	0.3	21	5.6
3.10	197		7	3	10	5.1		1		1	0.5	11	5.6
3.6	232	3	6	1	10	4.3	1	2		3	1.3	13	5.6
7.12	160		2	1	3	1.9	1	3	2	6	3.8	9	5.6
3.4	307	1	8	6	15	4.9	1		1	2	0.7	17	5.5
8.15	55		1	1	2	3.6		1		1	1.8	3	5.5
4.3	183	1	2		3	1.6	1	4	2	7	3.8	10	5.5
4.14	294	4	2	3	9	3.1	1	3	3	7	2.4	16	5.4
2.2	94	1	3		4	4.3		1		1	1.1	5	5.3

(continued)

Letter	No. of Words	Ego	1st Pro	1st Adj	1st Total	Frequency/100	Tu	2nd Pro	2nd Adj	2nd Total	Frequency/100	1st & 2nd Total	Total/100
4.1	150	1	2	2	5	3.3		1	2	3	2.0	8	5.3
9.37	171	1	3	1	5	2.9		2	2	4	2.3	9	5.3
5.7	188	1	1	3	5	2.7		3	2	5	2.7	10	5.3
1.2	189	1	3	1	5	2.6	1		4	5	2.6	10	5.3
9.11	76			1	1	1.3		1	2	3	3.9	4	5.3
4.21	134	1	1	4	6	4.5		1		1	0.7	7	5.2
1.14	347	3	6	3	12	3.5	1	3	2	6	1.7	18	5.2
9.14	58	1			1	1.7		2		2	3.4	3	5.2
1.24	117	1	1	2	4	3.4		2		2	1.7	6	5.1
9.7	158	2	1	1	4	2.5	1	3		4	2.5	8	5.1
3.3	254		4	1	5	2.0	5	3		8	3.1	13	5.1
4.28	99			1	1	1.0		2	2	4	4.0	5	5.1
7.30	141	1	3	2	5	3.5	1		1	2	1.4	7	5.0
7.3	142		1		1	0.7	1	5		6	4.2	7	5.0
8.1	83		1	3	4	4.8				0	0.0	4	4.8
9.29	83	2	2		4	4.8				0	0.0	4	4.8
7.7	84		2		2	2.4		1	1	2	2.4	4	4.8
4.15	428	3	3	4	10	2.3	3	5	3	10	2.3	20	4.7
5.3	394	3	10	3	16	4.1		1	1	2	0.5	18	4.6

Letter	No. of Words	Ego	1st Pro	1st Adj	1st Total	Frequency/100	Tu	2nd Pro	2nd Adj	2nd Total	Frequency/100	1st & 2nd Total	Total/100
1.9	195		5	1	6	3.1	1	2		3	1.5	9	4.6
4.27	199	1	4+2p	2+1p	7+3p	3.5		2		2	1.0	9+3p	4.5
2.5	374	1	4		5	1.3	4	6	2	12	3.2	17	4.5
5.15	45	1			1	2.2			1	1	2.2	2	4.4
9.19	277	1	4	2	7	2.5	1+1q	3		4+1q	1.8	11+1q	4.3
9.1	140				0	0.0		6		6	4.3	6	4.3
1.23	165		4		4	2.4	1	2		3	1.8	7	4.2
8.11	118		1		1	0.8		2	2	4	3.4	5	4.2
6.34	96				0	0.0	1	3		4	4.2	4	4.2
8.12	170	2	4	1	7	4.1				0	0.0	7	4.1
7.4	322	2+1p	5	3	10+1p	3.4		2		2	0.6	12+1p	4.0
4.24	152		3	1	4	2.6		2		2	1.3	6	3.9
4.23	103		1	1	2	1.9		1	1	2	1.9	4	3.9
9.16	51		1		0	0.0		2		2	3.9	2	3.9
4.13	426	3	5	6	14	3.3		1	1	2	0.5	16	3.8
8.19	106		2	1	3	2.8			1	1	0.9	4	3.8
1.1	52		1		1	1.9		1		1	1.9	2	3.8
6.17	185		1	1	2	1.1	1	3	1	5	2.7	7	3.8
9.2	136		1	1	2	1.5		2	1	3	2.2	5	3.7
4.10	112		2	1	3	2.7		1		1	0.9	4	3.6
9.5	83		1		1	1.2	1		1	2	2.4	3	3.6

(continued)

(continued)

Letter	No. of Words	Ego	1st Pro	1st Adj	1st Total	Frequency/100	Tu	2nd Pro	2nd Adj	2nd Total	Frequency/100	1st & 2nd Total	Total/100
2.6	226	2	2	2	6	2.7		1+2q	1	2+2q	0.9	8+2q	3.5
4.16	86		1	1	2	2.3		1	1	1	1.2	3	3.5
4.12	173	1	1		2	1.2	1		2	4	2.3	6	3.5
7.24	292	2	6	2	10	3.4				0	0.0	10	3.4
9.22	146	2	3		5	3.4	1			0	0.0	5	3.4
5.8	473	1	10	4	15	3.2				1	0.2	16	3.4
4.8	174		4	1	5	2.9		1		1	0.6	6	3.4
8.4	269	1	2		3	1.1		2	4	6	2.2	9	3.3
8.23	308		4	6	10	3.2				0	0.0	10	3.2
1.10	380	4	6		10	2.6		2		2	0.5	12	3.2
3.21	219		3+1p	1	4+1p	1.8	1	1	1+1p	3+1p	1.4	7+2p	3.2
7.6	387	3	7		10	2.6		2		2	0.5	12	3.1
7.17	457	3	7	2	12	2.6		2		2	0.4	14	3.1
6.25	127	1		2	3	2.4			1	1	0.8	4	3.1
7.18	127		2	1	3	2.4		1		1	0.8	4	3.1
5.21	160	2	1	1	3	1.9		1	1	2	1.3	5	3.1
6.10	160		2	1	3	1.9	1	1	1	2	1.3	5	3.1
8.24	389		1	1	2	0.5		8	2	10	2.6	12	3.1
5.5	263		5	2	7	2.7		1		1	0.4	8	3.0
7.19	331	2	6	1	9	2.7		1		1	0.3	10	3.0

Letter	No. of Words	Ego	1st Pro	1st Adj	1st Total	Frequency/100	Tu	2nd Pro	2nd Adj	2nd Total	Frequency/100	1st & 2nd Total	Total/100
9.13	981	4	14	4	22	2.2		3+3q	1	4+3q	0.7	26+3q	3.0
1.6	104	1	1	1	3	2.9				0	0.0	3	2.9
6.20	661	4	9	3	16	2.4		3	2q	3+2q	0.5	19+2q	2.9
5.13	381	2	3	3	8	2.1		2		3	0.8	11	2.9
7.26	106		2		2	1.9	1	1		1	0.9	3	2.8
3.16	399	2	4	1	7	1.8		3	1	4	1.0	11	2.8
1.12	443		7	5	12	2.7				0	0.0	12	2.7
3.11	295		5	2	7	2.4		1		1	0.3	8	2.7
6.33	332		2	3	5	1.5		3		4	1.2	9	2.7
7.10	73		1		1	1.4	1	1		1	1.4	2	2.7
9.9	148		1		1	0.7		1	2	3	2.0	4	2.7
9.35	73				0	0.0			2	2	2.7	2	2.7
8.2	265	1	6		7	2.6				0	0.0	7	2.6
3.18	380	2	4	3	9	2.4		1		1	0.3	10	2.6
1.8	654	1	6	4	11	1.7		4	2	6	0.9	17	2.6
8.21	276	1	4	1	6	2.2		1		1	0.4	7	2.5
1.20	905	6	9	3	18	2.0	2	2	1	5	0.6	23	2.5
1.22	401	1	5	2	8	2.0	2			2	0.5	10	2.5
8.16	165		2	1	3	1.8			1	1	0.6	4	2.4
4.29	82			1	1	1.2				1	1.2	2	2.4
7.15	82				0	0.0	1	2		2	2.4	2	2.4

(continued)

235

Letter	No. of Words	Ego	1st Pro	1st Adj	1st Total	Frequency/100	Tu	2nd Pro	2nd Adj	2nd Total	Frequency/100	1st & 2nd Total	Total/100
9.36	263		5	1	6	2.3				0	0.0	6	2.3
7.25	172	1	1	1	3	1.7		1		1	0.6	4	2.3
9.30	128	1	1		2	1.6			1	1	0.8	3	2.3
2.1	396		5	1	6	1.5		2	1	3	0.8	9	2.3
9.10	86				0	0.0	1		1	2	2.3	2	2.3
1.16	279	1	3	1	5	1.8		1		1	0.4	6	2.2
9.40	90			1	1	1.1		1		1	1.1	2	2.2
7.31	227	1	1		2	0.9		2	1	3	1.3	5	2.2
3.13	136	1	1		1	0.7		2		2	1.5	3	2.2
6.16	717	2	3	4	9	1.3	2	2	2	6	0.8	15	2.1
3.19	283		1	2	3	1.1		3		3	1.1	6	2.1
4.5	102		1	1	2	2.0				0	0.0	2	2.0
5.2	50				0	0.0			1	1	2.0	1	2.0
6.22	204				0	0.0		4		4	2.0	4	2.0
8.9	52		1		1	1.9				0	0.0	1	1.9
9.4	52		1		1	1.9				0	0.0	1	1.9
3.1	411	1	5	1	7	1.7		1		1	0.2	8	1.9
6.29	318	1	4		5	1.6			1	1	0.3	6	1.9
3.5	639	1	4	2	7	1.1		4	1	5	0.8	12	1.9
3.7	414		4		4	1.0	1	2	1	4	1.0	8	1.9

Letter	No. of Words	Ego	1st Pro	1st Adj	1st Total	Frequency/100	Tu	2nd Pro	2nd Adj	2nd Total	Frequency/100	1st & 2nd Total	Total/100
5.17	210		2		2	1.0		2		2	1.0	4	1.9
4.9	718	3	6	4	13	1.8				0	0.0	13	1.8
6.15	114	1+1q	1		2+1q	1.8				0	0.0	2+1q	1.8
7.27	604	2	5	1	8	1.3		1	2	3	0.5	11	1.8
9.39	166		1		1	0.6	1	1		2	1.2	3	1.8
6.24	116		2		2	1.7				0	0.0	2	1.7
9.26	726	5	4	1	10	1.4	1	1		2	0.3	12	1.7
6.21	116		1		1	0.9		1		1	0.9	2	1.7
8.20	375		3	1	4	1.1		2		2	0.5	6	1.6
4.30	244		1	1	2	0.8	1	1		2	0.8	4	1.6
2.14	329		2	3	5	1.5				0	0.0	5	1.5
2.11	864	2	5	3	10	1.2		1	2	3	0.3	13	1.5
3.9	1216	3	12		15	1.2		3		3	0.2	18	1.5
8.8	269	1	1		2	0.7	1		1	2	0.7	4	1.5
1.13	210		3		3	1.4				0	0.0	3	1.4
5.6	1523	2	5	6	13	0.9		7	2	9	0.6	22	1.4
6.13	142			1	1	0.7	1			1	0.7	2	1.4
4.11	507	1	1+1q		2+1q	0.4		4	1	5	1.0	7+1q	1.4
4.25	139				0	0.0		2		2	1.4	2	1.4
7.9	483				0	0.0	3	4		7	1.4	7	1.4
9.6	152	1		1	2	1.3				0	0.0	2	1.3

(continued)

Letter	No. of Words	Ego	1st Pro	1st Adj	1st Total	Frequency/100	Tu	2nd Pro	2nd Adj	2nd Total	Frequency/100	1st & 2nd Total	Total/100
2.19	304	1	1		2	0.7		2		2	0.7	4	1.3
6.19	150				0	0.0	1	1		2	1.3	2	1.3
2.8	86		1		1	1.2				0	0.0	1	1.2
2.17	1106	1	3	6	10	0.9	1	1	1	3	0.3	13	1.2
8.14	1122	5	2	2	9	0.8	1	3	1	5	0.4	14	1.2
4.7	254			1	1	0.4	1	1		2	0.8	3	1.2
2.20	367		3		3	0.8		1		1	0.3	4	1.1
6.2	353		1	1	2	0.6	1		1	2	0.6	4	1.1
7.21	90				0	0.0		1		1	1.1	1	1.1
2.12	206				0	0.0	1	1	1	2	1.0	2	1.0
7.29	110		1		1	0.9				0	0.0	1	0.9
8.17	230		1	1	1	0.4		1		1	0.4	2	0.9
2.7	249	1	1		2	0.8				0	0.0	2	0.8
5.20	254		2		2	0.8				0	0.0	2	0.8
8.6	773		4		4	0.5		2		2	0.3	6	0.8
5.4	121				0	0.0			1	1	0.8	1	0.8
8.22	139	1			1	0.7				0	0.0	1	0.7
2.3	355	1			1	0.3	1			1	0.3	2	0.6
3.20	337				0	0.0		2		2	0.6	2	0.6

Letter	No. of Words	Ego	1st Pro	1st Adj	1st Total	Frequency/ 100	Tu	2nd Pro	2nd Adj	2nd Total	Frequency/ 100	1st & 2nd Total	Total/ 100
5.9	210		1		1	0.5				0	0.0	1	0.5
6.5	204		1		1	0.5				0	0.0	1	0.5
5.16	304				0	0.0		1		1	0.3	1	0.3
9.33	399				0	0.0	1			1	0.3	1	0.3
6.31	506		1		1	0.2				0	0.0	1	0.2
8.18	462				0	0.0	1			1	0.2	1	0.2
3.14	255				0	0.0				0	0.0	0	0.0
1.17	110				0	0.0				0	0.0	0	0.0
3.12	100				0	0.0				0	0.0	0	0.0
4.2	191				0	0.0				0	0.0	0	0.0
4.22	214				0	0.0				0	0.0	0	0.0
8.5	93				0	0.0				0	0.0	0	0.0
9.27	76				0	0.0				0	0.0	0	0.0
9.32	37				0	0.0				0	0.0	0	0.0

Note: Pro = pronoun, Adj = adjective, p = in poem, q = in quotation.
Letters numbered in bold are sent to women; those in italic mention women.

Bibliography

Abrams, M. H. (1983). *The Mirror and the Lamp.* New York: Oxford University Press.

Adcock, Frank Ezra (1959). *Roman Political Ideas and Practice.* Ann Arbor: University of Michigan Press.

Ahl, Frederick (1984). "The Art of Safe Criticism in Greece and Rome." *AJP* 105: 174–208.

Alföldy, Géza (1983). "Ein Tempel des Herrscherkultes in Comum." *Athenaeum* 61: 362–373.

——— (1982). "Senatoren aus Norditalien." In *Epigrafia e Ordine Senatorio II,* Colloquio Internazionale AIEGL, 309–368. Rome: Edizioni di Storia e Letteratura, Tituli 5.

——— (1980). "Ein Senator aus Vicetia." *ZPE* 39: 255–266.

——— (1977). *Konsulat und Senatorenstand unter den Antoninen.* Bonn: Rudolf Habelt.

——— (1969). *Fasti Hispanienses.* Wiesbaden: Franz Steiner.

——— (1968). *Die Hifstruppen der römischen Provinz Germania Inferior.* Düsseldorf: Rheinland-Verlag.

Allen, Walter, Jr. (1954). "Cicero's Conceit." *TAPA* 85: 121–144.

Alston, Richard (1998). *Aspects of Roman History, A.D. 14–117.* London: Oxford University Press.

Altman, Janet Gurkin (1984). *Epistolarity: Approaches to a Form.* Columbus: Ohio State University Press.

Andermähr, Anna Maria (1998). *Totus in Praediis.* Bonn: Rudolf Habelt.

Anderson, William S. (1982). *Essays on Roman Satire.* Princeton: Princeton University Press.

André, J. M. (1975). "Pensée et Philosophie dans les *Lettres* de Pline le Jeune." *REL* 53: 225–247.

Andrews, A. Carleton (1938). "Pliny the Younger, Conformist." *CJ* 34: 143–155.

Archer, Leonie J., Susan Fischler, and Maria Wyke, eds. (1994). *Women in Ancient Societies*. New York: Routledge.

Armisen-Marchetti, Mireille (1990). "Pline le Jeune et le sublime." *REL* 68: 88–98.

Asdrubali Pentiti, Giovanna (1978). "Iscrizioni inedite della 'gens Neratia' di 'Saepinum.'" *StudRom* 26: 544–548.

Ash, Rhiannon (2003). "'Aliud est enim epistulam, aliud historiam...scribere' (Epistles 6.16.22): Pliny the Historian?" *Arethusa* 36: 211–225.

Aubrion, Étienne (1990). "La 'Correspondance' de Pline le Jeune: Problèmes et orientations actuelles de la recherche." *ANRW* II 33.1: 204–374.

——— (1975). "Pline le Jeune et la rhétorique de l'affirmation." *Latomus* 34: 90–130.

Augoustakis, Antony (2005). "*Nequaquam Historia Digna?* Plinian Style in *EP*. 6.20." *OJ* 100: 265–273.

Balsdon, J. P. V. D. (1962). *Roman Women*. New York: John Day Company.

Barrett, Anthony A. (1996). *Agrippina*. New Haven: Yale University Press.

Barton, Carlin (1994). "All Things Beseem the Victor; Paradoxes of Masculinity in Early Imperial Rome." In *Gender Rhetorics*, ed. Richard Trexler, 83–92. Binghamton, NY: Medieval and Renaissance Texts and Studies.

Bauman, Richard A. (1992). *Women and Politics in Ancient Rome*. London: Routledge.

——— (1974). *Impietas in Principem*. Munich: Beck.

Bell, Albert A. (1990). "Pliny the Younger: The Kinder, Gentler Roman." *CB* 66: 37–41.

——— (1989). "A Note on Revision and Authenticity in Pliny's Letters." *AJP* 110: 460–466.

Benario, Herbert W. (1980). *A Commentary on the Vita Hadriani in the Historia Augusta*. Chico, CA: Scholars Press.

——— (1975). *An Introduction to Tacitus*. Athens: University of Georgia Press.

Bergener, Alfred (1965). *Die führende Senatorenschicht im frühen Prinzipat*. Bonn: Rudolf Habelt.

Bernand, Yves (1975). "Sénateurs et chevaliers romains originaires de la cité de Nîmes." *MEFR* 87: 681–791.

Best, Edward E. (1970). "Cicero, Livy and Educated Roman Women." *CJ* 65: 199–204.

Bettini, Maurizio (1991). *Anthropology and Roman Culture*. Trans. John Van Sickle. Baltimore: Johns Hopkins University Press.

Beutel, F. (2000). *Vergangenheit als Politik. Neue Aspekte im Werk des Jüngeren Plinius*. Frankfurt: Lang.

Birley, Anthony (2000). *Onomasticon to the Younger Pliny*. Leipzig: K. G. Saur.

——— (1981). *The Fasti of Roman Britain*. Oxford: Clarendon Press.

——— (1966). *Marcus Aurelius*. London: Eyre & Spottiswoode.

Birley, Eric (1983). "The Enigma of Calvisius Ruso." *ZPE* 51: 263–269.

Biscardi, A., J. Modrzejewski, and H. J. Wolff, eds. (1984). *Mneme Georges A. Petropoulos*. Athens: A. N. Sakkoulas.

Blakely, M. Aloysius (1931). "The Younger Pliny Discloses the Social Life of His Day." *Classical Weekly* 25: 57–60.

Blok, Josine, and Peter Mason, eds. (1987). *Sexual Asymmetry*. Amsterdam: Gieben.

Boatwright, Mary T. (1991). "The Imperial Women of the Early Second Century A.D." *AJP* 112: 513–540.

Bodel, John (n.d.). *The Publication of Pliny's Letters*. Brown University. Unpublished manuscript.

——— (1995). "Minicia Marcella: Taken before Her Time." *AJP* 116: 453–460.

Bosworth, A. B. (1973). "Vespasian and the Provinces: Some Problems of the Early 70's A.D." *Athenaeum* 51: 49–78.

Braginton, Mary V. (1943–1944). "Exile under the Roman Emperors." *CJ* 39: 391–407.

Braund, Susanna H. (1992). "Juvenal – Misogynist or Misogamist?" *JRS* 82: 71–86.

——— (1989). *Satire and Society in Ancient Rome*. Exeter Studies in History No. 23. Exeter.

Briscoe, John (1981). *A Commentary on Livy Books XXXIV–XXXVII*. Oxford: Clarendon.

Brown, Robert (1995). "Livy's Sabine Women and the Ideal of *Concordia*." *TAPA* 125: 291–319.

Bruère, Richard T. (1954). "Tacitus and Pliny's *Panegyricus*." *CP* 49: 161–179.

Burck, E. (1969). *Die Frau in der griechisch-römischen Antike*. Munich: Hermeran Verlag.

Burnand, Y. (1982). "Senatores Romani ex provinciis Galliarum orti." In *Epigrafia e Ordine Senatorio II*, Colloquio Internazionale AIEGL, 387–437. Rome: Edizioni di Storia e Letteratura, Tituli 5.

Bütler, V. (1970). *Die Geistige Welt des jüngeren Plinius*. Heidelberg: C. Winter.

Cairns, J. W., and P. J. du Plessis (2007). *Beyond Dogmatics. Law and Society in the Roman World*. Edinburgh, Edinburgh University Press.

Cameron, Averil, and Amelie Kuhrt, eds. (1983). *Images of Women in Antiquity*. Detroit: Wayne State University Press.

Camodeca, Giuseppe (1982a). "Sui Senatori Romani d'Origine Flegrea: Qualche Addendum." *Puteoli* 6: 55–65.

——— (1982b). "Italia: Regio I, II, III." In *Epigrafia e Ordine Senatorio II*, Colloquio Internazionale AIEGL, 101–163. Rome: Edizioni di Storia e Letteratura, Tituli 5.

——— (1976). "La carriera del giurista L. Neratius Priscus." *AAN* 87: 19–38.

Cantarella, Eva (1981). *Pandora's Daughters*. Trans. Maureen B. Fant. Baltimore: Johns Hopkins University Press.

Carcopino, Jérôme (1940). *La vie quotidienne à Rome à l'apogée de l'empire*. Trans. E. O. Lorimer. New Haven: Yale University Press.

Carp, Teresa (1981). "Two Matrons of the Late Republic." In *Reflections of Women in Antiquity*, ed. Helene P. Foley, 343–354. New York: Gordon and Breach.

Casquero, Manuel-Antonio Marcos (1983). "Epistolografia Romana." *Helmantica* 34: 377–406.

Castagna, Luigi, and Eckard Lefèvre (2003). *Plinius der Jüngere und seine Zeit.* Munich and Leipzig: K. G. Saur.

Cébeillac-Gervasoni, Mireille (1972). *Les "Quaestores Principis et Candidati" aux Ier et IIème siècles de l'Empire.* Milan: Cisalpino-Goliardica.

    (1982). "Italia: Regio I." In *Epigrafia e Ordine Senatorio II,* Colloquio Internazionale AIEGL, 59–99. Rome: Edizioni di Storia e Letteratura, Tituli 5.

Champlin, Edward (2001). "Pliny's Other Country." In *Aspects of Friendship in the Graeco-Roman World,* ed. Michael Peachin, 121–128. Journal of Roman Archaeology Supplementary Series, no. 43. Portsmouth, RI.

    (1992). "Death and Taxes: The Emperor and Inheritance." *SIFC* 10: 899–905.

    (1991). *Final Judgments Duty and Emotion in Roman Wills.* Berkeley: University of California Press.

    (1986). "Miscellanea Testamentaria." *ZPE* 62: 247–255.

    (1983). "Figlinae Marcianae." *Athenaeum* 61: 257–264.

    (1981). "Owners and Neighbours at Ligures Baebiani." *Chiron* 11: 239–264.

Chantraine, Heinrich (1980). "Freigelassene und Sklaven kaiserlicher Frauen." In *Studien zur antiken Sozialgeschichte,* ed. Werner Eck, Hartmut Galsterer, and Harmut Wolff, 389–416. Cologne: Böhlau.

Chastagnol, André, Ségolène Demougin, and Claude Lepelley (1996). *Splendidissima Civitas.* Paris: Publications de la Sorbonne.

    (1980). "Les homines novi entrés au sénat sous le règne de Domitian." In *Studien zur antiken Sozialgeschichte,* ed. Werner Eck, Hartmut Galsterer, and Harmut Wolff, 269–282. Cologne: Böhlau.

Chevallier, R. (1993). "Notes de lecture 359. Quelle immortalité?" *Latomus* 52: 419.

Chilver, G. E. F. (1979). *A Historical Commentary on Tacitus' Histories I and II.* Oxford: Clarendon.

Ciampoltrini, Giulio (1980). "Un nuovo frammento di CIL, *XI, 1735.*" *Epigraphica* 42: 160–165.

Cizek, Eugen (1990). "La littérature et les cercles culturels et politiques à l'époque de Trajan." *ANRW* II 33.1: 3–35.

Claassen, Jo-Marie (1999). *Displaced Persons: The Literature of Exile from Cicero to Boethius.* Madison: University of Wisconsin Press.

    (1998). "The Familiar Other: The Pivotal Role of Women in Livy's Narrative of Political Development in Early Rome." *AClass* 41: 71–104.

    (1996). "Documents of a Crumbling Marriage: The Case of Cicero and Terentia." *Phoenix* 50: 208–232.

    (1992). "Cicero's Banishment: *Tempora et Mores.*" *AClass* 35: 19–47.

Clark, Gillian (1996a). "Introduction." In *Women in Antiquity,* ed. Ian McAuslan and Peter Walcot, 1–17. Oxford: Oxford University Press.

(1996b). "Roman Women." In *Women in Antiquity*, ed. Ian McAuslan and Peter Walcot, 36–55. Oxford: Oxford University Press.

(1989). *Women in the Ancient World*. New York: Oxford University Press.

Clerc, Jean-Benoît (1998). "Pour se protége du *fascinum* (Pline le Jeune, *Lettres* VI, 2)." *Latomus* 57: 634–643.

Coleman, Kathleen M. (1990a). "Latin Literature after AD 96: Change or Continuity?" *AJAH* 15: 19–39.

(1990b). "The Emperor Domitian and Literature." *ANRW* II 32.5: 3087–3115.

Colloquio Internazionale AIEGL (1982). *Epigrafia e Ordine Senatorio I & II*. Rome: Edizioni di Storia e Letteratura, Tituli 4 & 5.

Connolly, Joy (1998). "Mastering Corruption." In *Women and Slaves in Greco-Roman Culture*, ed. Sandra Joshel and Sheila Murnaghan, 130–151. London: Routledge.

Corbier, Mireille (1995). "Male Power and Legitimacy through Women: The *domus Augusta* under the Julio-Claudians." In *Women in Antiquity*, ed. Richard Hawley and Barbara Levick, 178–193. London: Routledge.

(1991a). "Family Behavior of the Roman Aristocracy, Second Century B.C.–Third Century A.D." In *Women's History and Ancient History*, ed. Sarah B. Pomeroy, 171–196. Chapel Hill: University of North Carolina.

(1991b). "Constructing Kinship in Rome: Marriage and Divorce, Filiation and Adoption." In *The Family in Italy*, ed. David I. Kertzer and Richard P. Saller, 127–144. New Haven: Yale University Press.

(1981). "La Tavola Marmorea de Bolsena." *MEFR* 93: 1063–1112.

(1974). *L'Aerarium Saturni et L'Aerarium Militare*. Rome: École Française de Rome.

Cornell, Tim (1986a). "The Value of the Literary Tradition concerning Archaic Rome." In *Social Struggles in Archaic Rome*, ed. Kurt Raaflaub, 52–76. Berkeley: University of California Press.

(1986b). "The Formation of the Historical Tradition of Early Rome." In *Past Perspectives*, ed. I. S. Moxon, J. D. Smart, and A. J. Woodman, 67–86. Cambridge: Cambridge University Press.

Cotton, Hannah M. (1984). "Greek and Latin Epistolary Formulae: Some Light on Cicero's Letter Writing." *AJP* 105: 409–425.

Courtney, Edward (1980). *A Commentary on the Satires of Juvenal*. London: Athlone Press.

Cugusi, P. (1983). *Evoluzione e forma dell'epistolographie latine*. Rome: Herder.

Culham, Phyllis (1986). "Ten Years after Pomeroy." *Helios* 13: 9–20.

(1982). "The *Lex Oppia*." *Latomus* 41: 786–793.

D'Ambra, Eve (1998). "Representing Roman Women." *JRA* 11: 546–553.

Damon, Cynthia, and Sarolta Takács, eds. (1999). *The Senatus consultum de Cn. Pisone patre*. *AJP* 121: 1–186.

De Blois, Lukas (2001). "The Political Significance of Friendship in the *Letters* of Pliny the Younger." In *Aspects of Friendship in the Graeco-Roman*

World, ed. Michael Peachin, 129–134. Journal of Roman Archaeology Supplementary Series, no. 43. Portsmouth, RI.

(1994). "Traditional Virtues and New Spiritual Qualities in Third Century Views of Empire, Emperorship and Practical Politics." *Mnemosyne* 47: 166–176.

DeForest, Mary, ed. (1993). *Women's Power; Man's Game.* Wauconda, IL: Bolchazy-Carducci.

De Grassi, Attilio (1952). *I Fasti Consolari dell'Impero Romano.* Rome: Edizioni di Storia e Letteratura.

De Lacy, Phillip H. (1977). "The Four Stoic *Personae.*" *ICS* 2: 163–172.

Demougin, Ségolène (1975). "*Splendidus Eques Romanus.*" *Epigraphica* 37: 174–187.

den Boer, W., P. G. van der Nat, C. M. J. Sicking, and J. C. M. van Winden, eds. (1973). *Romanitas et Christianitas.* Amsterdam: North Holland.

De Pretis, Anna (2003). "'Insincerity,' 'Facts,' and 'Epistolarity': Approaches to Pliny's *Epistles* to Calpurnia." *Arethusa* 36: 127–146.

DeVerger, Antonio Ramírez (1999). "Erotic Language in Pliny, *Ep.* VII 5." *Glotta* 74: 114–116.

De Vivo, Arturo (1980). *Tacito e Claudio.* Naples: Liguori.

Deroux, Carl (1979, 1980, 1998). *Studies in Latin Literature and Roman History I, II & IX.* Collection Latomus 164, 168, and 244. Brussels.

Des Bouvrie, Synnøve (1984). "Augustus' Legislation on Morals – Which Morals and What Aims?" *SO* 59: 93–113.

Dessau, H. (1913). "A Roman Senator under Domitian and Trajan." *JRS* 3: 301–309.

Devijver, H. (1977). *Prosopographia Militiarum Equestrium quae fuerunt ab Augusto ad Gallienum.* Leuven: Universitaire Pers.

Devreker, J. (1977). "Le Consilium Principis sous les Flaviens." *AncSoc* 8: 223–243.

Dixon, Suzanne (1993). "The Meaning of Gift and Debt in the Roman Elite." *EMC* 12: 451–464.

(1991). "The Sentimental Ideal of the Roman Family." In *Marriage, Divorce and Children*, ed. Beryl Rawson, 99–113. Oxford: Oxford University Press.

(1988). *The Roman Mother.* Norman: University of Oklahoma Press.

(1983). "A Family Business: Women's Role in Patronage and Politics at Rome 80–44 B.C." *C&M* 34: 91–112.

Dobson, Elizabeth Spalding (1982). "Pliny the Younger's Depiction of Women." *CB* 58: 81–85.

Dominick, William J. (1997). *Roman Eloquence.* London: Routledge.

Donaldson, James (1907). *Woman: Her Position and Influence in Ancient Greece and Rome and among the Early Christians.* New York: Longmans, Green.

Döpp, Siegmar (1989). "*Nec Omnia apud Priores Meliora* Autoren des frühen Principats über die eigene Zeit." *RhM* 132: 73–101.

Dorey, T. A., ed. (1969). *Tacitus.* New York: Basic Books.

Ducos, Michèle (2003). "Pline acteur et témoin des procès dans le Livre VI de la *Correspondance.*" *VL* 168: 57–69.

Dudley, Donald R. (1968). *The World of Tacitus.* London: Secker and Warburg.

Dyck, Andrew R. (1996). *A Commentary on Cicero* De Officiis. Ann Arbor: University of Michigan Press.

Dyson, Stephen L. (1992). "Age, Sex, and Status: The View from the Roman Rotary Club." *EMC* 36: 369–385.

Earl, Donald (1969). *The Moral and Political Tradition of Rome.* Ithaca: Cornell University Press.

Eck, Werner (1985). *Die Statthalter der germanischen Provinzen vom 1.–3. Jahrhundert.* Cologne: Rheinland-Verlag.

(1983). "Zur Familie der Neratii aus Saepinum." *ZPE* 50: 195–201.

(1982a). "Die fistulae aquariae der Stadt Rom: Zum Einfluss des sozialen Status auf adminstratives Handeln." In *Epigrafia e Ordine Senatorio I*, Colloquio Internazionale AIEGL, 197–225. Rome: Edizioni di Storia e Letteratura, Tituli 4.

(1982b). "Prokonsuln von Asia in der flavisch-traianischen Zeit." *ZPE* 45: 139–153.

(1980). "Die Präsenz senatorischer Familien in den Städten des Imperium Romanum bis zum späten 3. Jahrhundert." In *Studien zur antiken Sozialgeschichte*, ed. Werner Eck, Hartmut Galsterer, and Harmut Wolff, 283–322. Cologne: Böhlau.

(1978). "Zum neuen Fragment des Sogenannten Testamentum Dasumii." *ZPE* 30: 277–295.

(1975). "Ergänzungen zu den Fasti Consulares des 1. u. 2. Jh. n. Chr." *Historia* 24: 324–344.

(1971). "Prosopographische Bermerkungen." *ZPE* 8: 81–92.

(1970). *Senatoren von Vespasian bis Hadrian.* Munich: Beck.

Eck, Werner, Antonio Caballos, and Fernando Fernández (1996). *Das Senatus consultum de Cn. Pisone patre.* Munich: Beck.

Edwards, Catherine (1997). "Self-Scrutiny and Self-Transformation in Seneca's Letters." *G&R* 44: 23–38.

(1993). *The Politics of Immorality in Ancient Rome.* Cambridge: Cambridge University Press.

Evans, J.A.S., ed. (1974). *Polis and Imperium: Studies in Honour of Edward Togo Salmon.* Toronto: Hakkert.

Evans, John (1991). *War, Women and Children in Ancient Rome.* London: Routledge.

Evenepoel, Willy (1999). "Pliny, *Epist.*, 3, 5, 18." *AC* 68: 287–288.

Fantham, Elaine (1994). *Women in the Classical World.* New York: Oxford University Press.

Ferguson, John (1958). *Moral Values in the Ancient World.* New York: Barnes & Noble.

Ferrero, Guglielmo (1925). *The Women of the Caesars.* New York: Century.

Finley, Moses I. (1983). *Politics in the Ancient World*. Cambridge: Cambridge
    University Press.
    (1968). *Aspects of Antiquity*. New York: Viking Press.
Fischler, Susan (1994). "Social Stereotypes and Historical Analysis: The
    Case of the Imperial Women at Rome." In *Women in Ancient Societies*, ed.
    Leonie J. Archer, Susan Fischler, and Maria Wyke, 115–133. New York:
    Routledge.
Flory, Marleen B. (1995). "The Deification of Roman Women." *AHB* 9:
    127–134.
Focardi, Gabriella (1980). "Il termine 'maiestas' e la matrona." *SIFC* 52:
    144–163.
Foley, Helene P., ed. (1981). *Reflections of Women in Antiquity*. New York:
    Gordon and Breach.
Fora, Maurizio (1992). "Ummidia Quadratilla ed il Restauro del Teatro di
    Cassino (per una Nuova Lettura di *AE* 1946, 174). *ZPE* 94: 269–273.
Foucault, Michel (1986). *The Care of the Self*. Trans. Robert Hurley. New York:
    Pantheon Books.
Franke, Peter Robert (1979). "Zur Chronologie der Statthalter von
    Cappadocia-Galatia." *Chiron* 9: 377–382.
Franklin, James L. (1987). "Pantomimists at Pompeii: Actius Anicetus and
    His Troupe." *AJP* 108: 95–107.
Friedlander, L. (1969). *Friedlander's Essays of Juvenal*. Trans. John R. C.
    Martyn. Amsterdam, Adolf M. Hankert.
    (1907–1913). *Roman Life and Manners under the Early Empire*. Trans. Leonard
    Magnus. London: Routledge and Kegan Paul.
Gaggiotti, M., and L. Sensi (1982a). "Italia: Regio VI." In *Epigrafia e Ordine
    Senatorio II*, Colloquio Internazionale AIEGL, 245–274. Rome: Edizioni
    di Storia e Letteratura, Tituli 5.
    (1982b). "La gens Neratia" In *Saepinum – Museo documentario dell'Altilia*,
    41–49. Campobasso: Soprintendenza Archeologica e per i Beni
    Architettonici Artistici e Storici del Molise/Istituto di Archeologica
    dell'Università di Perugia.
Galinsky, Karl (1982). "Augustus' Legislation on Morals and Marriage."
    Philologus 125: 126–144.
Gallivan, Paul (1981). "The Fasti for A.D. 70–96." *CQ* 31: 186–220.
    (1978). "The *Fasti* for the Reign of Claudius." *CQ* 28: 407–426.
Gamberini, Federico (1983). *Stylistic Theory and Practice in the Younger Pliny*.
    New York: Olms-Weidmann.
Garcia, Carmen Castillo (1984). "Los senatores de la Bética: Onomástica y
    parentesco." *Gerión* 2: 239–250.
    (1982). "Los Senadores Beticos. Relaciones familiares y sociales." In
    Epigrafia e Ordine Senatorio II, Colloquio Internazionale AIEGL, 465–
    519. Rome: Edizioni di Storia e Letteratura, Tituli 5.
Gardner, Jane F. (1982). *Women in Roman Law and Society*. Bloomington:
    Indiana University Press.
Garlick, Barbara, Suzanne Dixon, and Pauline Allen (1992). *Stereotypes of
    Women in Power*. New York: Glenwood Press.

Giangrande, Giuseppe (1975). "Catullus' Lyrics on the Passer." *MPL* 1: 137–146.

Gibson, Roy K. (2003). "Pliny and the Art of (in)Offensive Self-Praise." *Arethusa* 36: 235–254.

Girard, P. F., and F. Senn (1977). *Le lois des Romains*. Naples: Jovene.

Goetz, Rainald M. (1978). "Freunde und Feinde des Kaisers Domitian." Ph.D. diss., Ludwig-Maximilians.

Gordon, Arthur E. (1952). *Quintus Veranius Consul A.D. 49*. Berkeley: University of California Press.

Gow, A. S. F., and D. L. Page, eds. (1965). *The Greek Anthology*. Cambridge: Cambridge University Press.

Gray-Fow, Michael J. G. (1988). "The Wicked Stepmother in Roman Literature and History: An Evaluation." *Latomus* 47: 741–757.

Griffin, Miriam (2003). "*De Beneficiis* and Roman Society." *JRS* 93: 92–113.

—— (1999). "Pliny and Tacitus." *SCI* 18: 139–158.

Groag, Edmund (1935). "Zu neuen Inschriften." *JOAI* 29: 179–182.

—— (1931). "Prosopographische Bemerkungen." *WS* 49: 157–161.

Gros, Pierre (1980). "Une dedicace carthaginoise sur le Forum de Bolsena." *MEFR* 92: 977–989.

Guillemin, Anne Marie (1929). *Pline et la vie littéraire de son temps*. Collection d'Études Latines 4. Paris.

Gunderson, Erik (1997). "Catullus, Pliny and Love-Letters." *TAPA* 127: 201–231.

Gurlitt, Ludwig (1888). "Genera Usitata Epistularum." *NJ* 137: 863–866.

Haberman, Lidia (1980). "Sexual Morality and Politics in the Early Books of Livy." *CB* 57: 8–11.

Habinek, Thomas N. (1998). *The Politics of Latin Literature*. Princeton: Princeton University Press.

Hahn, Ulrike (1994). *Die Frauen des römischen Kaiserhauses*. Saarbrücker Studien zur Archäologie und Alten Geschichte 8. Saarbrücken.

Hallett, Judith P., and Marilyn B. Skinner, eds. (1997). *Roman Sexualities*. Princeton: Princeton University Press.

—— (1990). "Perspectives on Roman Women." In *From Augustus to Nero*, ed. Ronald Mellor, 132–144. East Lansing: Michigan State University Press.

—— (1989). "Women as *Same* and *Other* in Classical Roman Elite." *Helios* 16: 59–78.

—— (1984). *Fathers and Daughters*. Princeton: Princeton University Press.

Hallissy, Margaret (1997). *Venomous Woman*. New York: Greenwood Press.

Hanslik, Rudolph (1954). "Prosopographische Bermerkungen." *JOAI* 41: 159.

Hawley, Richard, and Barbara Levick, eds. (1995). *Women in Antiquity*. London: Routledge.

Heberlein, Friedrich, and Wolfgang Slaby, eds. (1991). *Concordantiae in C. Plinii Caecilii Secundi Opera*. Hildesheim: Olms-Weidmann.

Heil, Matthäus (1989). "M. Hirrius Fronto Neratius Panza, legatus exercitus Africae." *Chiron* 19: 165–184.

Hellegouarc'h, Joseph (1972). *Le vocabulaire latin des relations et des partis politiques sous la République*. Paris: les Belles Lettres.

(1964). *Le monosyllable dans l'hexamètre verbale*. Paris: Librairie C. Klincksieck.

Henderson, John (2003). "Portrait of the Artist as a Figure of Style: P.L.I.N.Y.'s Letters." *Arethusa* 36: 115–125.

(2002a). "Knowing Someone through Their Books: Pliny on Uncle Pliny ("Epistles" 3.5)." *CP* 97: 256–284.

(2002b). *Pliny's Statue: The* Letters, *Self-Portraiture and Classical Art*. Exeter: University of Exeter Press.

(2002c). "Funding Homegrown Talent: Pliny *Letters* 1.19." *G&R* 49: 212–226.

Herman, Arthur (1997). *The Idea of Decline in Western History*. New York: Free Press.

Hershkowitz, Debra (1995). "Pliny the Poet." *G&R* 42: 168–181.

Heubner, Heinz (1971). "Vater oder Tochter." *RhM* 114: 265–268.

Highet, Gilbert (1954). *Juvenal the Satirist*. Oxford: Clarendon Press.

Hillard, Tom (1992). "On the Stage, Behind the Curtain: Images of Politically Active Women in the Late Roman Republic." In *Stereotypes of Women in Power*, ed. Barbara Garlick, Suzanne Dixon, and Pauline Allen, 37–64. New York: Glenwood Press.

(1989). "Republican Politics, Women, and the Evidence." *Helios* 16: 165–182.

Hoffer, Stanley E. (1999). *The Anxieties of Pliny the Younger*. Atlanta: Scholar's Press.

Hoffsten, Ruth B. (1939). "Roman Women of Rank of the Early Empire." Ph.D. diss., University of Pennsylvania.

Hotter, Monica, and Peta Tancred (1991). *(En)gendering Knowledge*. Montreal: McGill Centre for Research and Teaching on Women.

Hutchinson, G. O. (1998). *Cicero's Correspondence: A Literary Study*. Oxford: Clarendon.

(1993). "Ciceros Briefe als Literatur (Ad Att. 1,16)." *Hermes* 121: 441–451.

Inwood, Brad (1985). *Ethics and Human Action in Early Stoicism*. Oxford: Clarendon.

Jal, Paul (1993). "Pline épistolier, écrivain superficiel? Quelques remarques." *REL* 71: 212–227.

Jocelyn, H. D. (1980). "On Some Unnecessarily Indecent Interpretations of Catullus 2 and 3." *AJP* 101: 421–441.

Jones, Brian (1992). *The Emperor Domitian*. London: Routledge.

(1979). *Domitian and the Senatorial Order*. Philadelphia: American Philosophical Society.

(1973). "Domitian's Attitude to the Senate." *AJP* 94: 79–91.

Jones, C. P. (1968). "A New Commentary on the Letters of Pliny." *Phoenix* 22: 111–142.

Jones, Nicholas F. (2001). "Pliny the Younger's Vesuvius *Letters* (6.16 and 6.20)." *CW* 95: 31–48.

Jory, E.J. (1984). "The Early Pantomime Riots." In *Maistor, Classical, Byzantine and Renaissance Studies for Robert Browning*, ed. Ann Moffatt, 57–66. Canberra: Australian Association for Byzantine Studies.

Joshel, Sandra (1995). "Female Desire and the Discourse of Empire: Tacitus's Messalina." *Signs* 21: 50–82.

Joshel, Sandra, and Sheila Murnaghan, eds. (1998). *Women and Slaves in Greco-Roman Culture*. London: Routledge.

Kaplan, M. (1979). "Agrippina Semper Atrox." In *Studies in Latin Literature and Roman History I*, ed. Carl Deroux, 410–417. Collection Latomus 164. Brussels.

Kenney, E.J. (1963). "Juvenal: Satirist or Rhetorician?" *Latomus* 22: 704–720.

Kertzer, David I., and Richard P. Saller, eds. (1991). *The Family in Italy*. New Haven: Yale University Press.

Kiefer, O. (1934). *Sexual Life in Ancient Rome*. Trans. Gilbert Highet and Helen Highet. London: Routledge.

King, Karen (1997). *Women and Goddess Traditions in Antiquity and Today*. Minneapolis: Fortress Press.

Kneissl, Peter, and Volker Losemann, eds. (1998). *Imperium Romanum: Studien zur Geschichte und Rezeption*. Stuttgart: Franz Steiner.

Koestermann, Erich (1968). *Cornelius Tacitus Annalen*, Vols. I–IV. Heidelberg: Carl Winter.

Königer, Hans (1966). "Gestalt und Welt der Frau bei Tacitus." Ph.D. diss., Erlangen-Nurnberg.

Kornemann, E. (1942). *Große Frauen des Altertums*. Wiesbaden: Dieterich.

Koskenniemi, Heikki (1954). "Cicero über die Briefarten." *Arctos* 1: 97–102.

Kötting, Bernhard (1973). "'Univira' in Inschriften." In *Romanitas et Christianitas*, ed. W. den Boer, P. G. van der Nat, C. M. J. Sicking, and J. C. M. van Winden. Amsterdam: North-Holland.

Krasser, Helmut (1993a). "Laszives Vergnügen oder philosophisches Gespräch? Zum Text von Plinius Epist. 5,3,2." *Hermes* 121: 254–258.

(1993b). "*Claros Colere Viros* oder über engagierte Bewunderung." *Philologus* 137: 62–71.

(1993c). "extremos pudeat rediise – Plinius im Wettstreit mit der Vergangenheit zu Vergilzitaten beim jüngeren Plinius." *A&A* 39: 144–154.

Kraus, C.S., and A.J. Woodman (1997). *Latin Historians*. Oxford: Oxford University Press.

Kreiler, B. (1976). "*Die Statthalter Kleinasiens unter den Flaviern* (J. Devreker) – Review." *Epigraphica* 38: 179–188.

Kumaniecki, Kazimierz (1969). "A propos de la 'Consolatio' perdue de Cicéron." *Annales de la Faculté des Lettres et Sciences humaines d'Aix* 46: 369–402.

Lambrechts, Pierre (1938). "La famille des Ummidii Quadrati." *AC* 7: 85–90.

Lattimore, Richmond (1942). *Themes in Greek and Latin Epitaphs.* Urbana: University of Illinois Press.

Leach, Eleanor Winsor (2003). "*Otium* as *Luxuria*: Economy of Status in the Younger Pliny's *Letters.*" *Arethusa* 36: 147–165.

  (1990). "The Politics of Self-Presentation: Pliny's Letters and Roman Portrait Sculpture." *ClAnt* 9: 14–39.

Lefèvre, Eckard (1996a). "Plinius-Studien VII: Cicero das unerreichbare Vorbild." *Gymnasium* 103: 333–353.

  (1996b). "Plinius-Studien VI: Der große und der kleine Plinius." *Gymnasium* 103: 193–215.

  (1989). "Plinius-Studien V: Vom Römertum zum Ästhetizismus." *Gymnasium* 96: 113–128.

Lefkowitz, Mary R. (2001). "New Hellenistic Epigrams about Women." *Diotima: Materials for the Study of Women and Gender in the Ancient World,* 22 January 2002, www.stoa.org/diotima/anthology/epigrams.shtml.

  (1996). "Wives and Husbands." In *Women in Antiquity,* ed. Ian McAuslan and Peter Walcot, 67–82. Oxford: Oxford University Press.

  (1983). "Influential Women." In *Images of Women in Antiquity,* ed. Averil Cameron and Amelie Kuhrt, 49–64. Detroit: Wayne State University Press.

  (1981). *Heroines and Hysterics.* London: Duckworth.

Lefkowitz, Mary R., and Maureen Fant, eds. (1977). *Women in Greece and Rome.* Toronto: Samuel-Stevens.

Levick, Barbara (1994). "Roman Women in a Corporate State." *Ktèma* 19: 259–267.

  (1990). *Claudius.* New Haven: Yale University Press.

  (1978). "Pliny in Bithynia – and What Followed." *G&R* 26: 119–131.

Lewis, A.D.E. (2007). "The Dutiful Legatee: Pliny, Letters V.1." In *Beyond Dogmatics,* ed. J.W. Cairns and P. J. du Plessis, 125–38. Edinburgh: Edinburgh University Press.

Lewis, Martha W. Hoffman (1955). *The Official Priests of Rome under the Julio-Claudians.* Rome: American Academy.

Licordari, A. (1982). "Italia: Regio I." In *Epigrafia e Ordine Senatorio II,* Colloquio Internazionale AIEGL, 9–57. Rome: Edizioni di Storia e Letteratura, Tituli 5.

Lilja, Saara (1978). "Descriptions of Human Appearance in Pliny's Letters." *Arctos* 12: 55–62.

Liou, Bernard (1969). *Praetores Etruriae XV Populorum.* Brussels: Latomus.

Loven, Lena Larsson (1998). "Woolworking and Female Virtue." In *Aspects of Women in Antiquity,* ed. Lena Larsson Loven and Agneta Stromberg, 85–95. Jonsered: Astroms.

Luce, T.J., and A.J. Woodman, eds. (1993). *Tacitus and the Tacitean Tradition.* Princeton: Princeton University Press.

Luck, George (1961). "Brief und Epistel in der Antike." *Altertum* 7: 77–84.

Ludolph, Matthias (1997). *Epistolographie und Selbstdarstellung.* Tübingen: Gunter Narr.

Luppe, Wolfgang (1991). "Ein verderbtes Vergil-Zitat bei Plinius." *Hermes* 119: 123–124.

MacMullen, Ramsay (1986). "Women's Power in the Principate." *Klio* 68: 434–443.

——— (1981). "Woman in Public in the Roman Empire." *Historia* 29: 208–218.

——— (1974). *Roman Social Relations: 50 B.C.–A.D. 584*. New Haven: Yale University Press.

Malherbe, Abraham J. (1988). *Ancient Epistolary Theorists*. Atlanta: Scholars Press.

Malitz, Jürgen (1985). "Helvidius Priscus und Vespasian." *Hermes* 113: 231–246.

Malmoux, Jean (1975). "C. Helvidius Priscus." *PP* 160: 23–39.

Maniet, Andrée (1966). "Pline le Jeune et Calpurnia." *AC* 35: 149–185.

Manning, C.E. (1985). "Liberalitas – the Decline and Rehabilitation of a Virtue." *G&R* 32: 73–83.

Marshall, Anthony J. (1990). "Women on Trial before the Roman Senate." *EMC* 34: 333–366.

——— (1984). "Ladies in Waiting: The Role of Women in Tacitus' Histories." *AncSoc* 15: 167–184.

——— (1975a). "Tacitus and the Governor's Lady: A Note on Annals iii.33–4." *G&R* 22: 11–18.

——— (1975b). "Roman Women and the Provinces." *AncSoc* 6: 109–127.

Martin, Ronald (1981). *Tacitus*. Berkeley: University of California Press.

May, James M. (1988). *Trials of Character*. Chapel Hill: North Carolina Press.

Mayer, Roland (2003). "Pliny and Gloria Dicendi." *Arethusa* 36: 227–234.

McAlindon, D. (1956). "Senatorial Opposition to Claudius and Nero." *AJP* 77: 113–132.

McAuslan, Ian, and Peter Walcot, eds. (1996). *Women in Antiquity*. Oxford: Oxford University Press.

McDermott, William C. (1971–1972). "Pliny the Younger and Inscriptions." *CW* 65: 84–94.

McInerney, Jeremy (2003). "Plutarch's Manly Women." In *Andreia*, ed. Ralph Rosen and Ineke Sluiter, 319–345. Leiden: Brill.

McNamara, Jo Ann (1999). "Gendering Virtue." In *Plutarch's Advice to the Bride and Groom and a Consolation to His Wife*, ed. Sarah B. Pomeroy, 151–161. New York: Oxford University Press.

Mellor, Ronald (1993). *Tacitus*. London: Routledge.

——— ed. (1990). *From Augustus to Nero: The First Dynasty of Imperial Rome*. East Lansing: Michigan State University Press.

Meyer, Elizabeth A. (1999). "Epistolary Ethos: A Rhetorical Analysis of Cicero's Letters." Ph.D. diss., Boston University.

Miles, Gary B. (1995). *Livy: Reconstructing Early Rome*. Ithaca: Cornell University Press.

Misch, Georg (1950). *A History of Autobiography in Antiquity*. 2 vols. London: Routledge.

Moffatt, Ann, ed. (1984). *Maistor, Classical, Byzantine and Renaissance Studies for Robert Browning.* Canberra: Australian Association for Byzantine Studies.

Molin, Michel (1989). "Le *Panégyrique de Trajan:* Éloquence d'apparat ou programme politique néo-stoïcien?" *Latomus* 48: 785–797.

Molisani, G. (1982). "Due note senatorie." In *Epigrafia e Ordine Senatorio I,* Colloquio Internazionale AIEGL, 495–497. Rome: Edizioni di Storia e Letteratura, Tituli 4.

Morello, Ruth (2003). "Pliny and the Art of Saying Nothing." *Arethusa* 36: 187–209.

Moxon, I. S., J. D. Smart, and A. J. Woodman, eds. (1986). *Past Perspectives.* Cambridge: Cambridge University Press.

Mullens, H. G. (1941). "The Women of the Caesars." *G&R* 11: 59–67.

Murgia, Charles E. (1985). "Pliny's Letters and the *Dialogus.*" *HSCP* 89: 171–206.

Nadeau, Yves (1984). "Catullus' Sparrow, Martial, Juvenal and Ovid." *Latomus* 43: 861–868.

Nadjo, Léon, and Élisabeth Gavoille (2004). *Epistulae Antiquae III.* Louvain: Peeters.

Nakanishi, Wendy Jones (1990). "Classical and 'Augustan' Notions of the Literary Letter." *English Studies* 71: 341–352.

Nawotka, Krzysytof (1993). "Imperial Virtues of Galba in the *Histories* of Tacitus." *Philologus* 137: 258–264.

Nichols, John (1980). "Pliny and the Patronage of Communities." *Hermes* 108: 365–385.

  (1978). *Vespasian and the Partes Flavianae.* Wiesbaden: Franz Steiner.

Nicholson, John (1998). "The Survival of Cicero's Letters." In *Studies in Latin Literature and Roman History IX,* ed. Carl Deroux: 63–105. Collection Latomus 244. Brussels.

  (1994). "The Delivery and Confidentiality of Cicero's Letters." *CJ* 90: 33–63.

Niemirska-Pliszczynska, Joanna (1955). "De Elocutione Pliniana." Ph.D. diss., Lublin.

Noguerol, Elizabeth (2003). "Le traitement des figures du père et de la mère dans le livre VI de la *Correspondance* de Pline le Jeune: Preuves et épreuves." *VL* 168: 82–93.

Nolte, A. (1968). "Plinius Minor en Tacitus." *Hermeneus* 39: 254–265.

Orentzel, Anne E. (1980). "Pliny and Domitian." *CB* 56: 49–52.

  (1978). "Declamation in the Age of Pliny." *CB* 54: 65–68.

Ortner, Sherry B. (1978). "The Virgin and the State." *Feminist Studies* 4: 19–35.

Panciera, S. (1972–1973). "L. Pomponius L. F. Bassus." *RPAA* 45: 105–131.

Parker, Holt (2004). "Why Were the Vestals Virgins? Or the Chastity of Women and the Safety of the Roman State." *AJP* 125: 563–601.

  (1998). "Loyal Slaves and Loyal Wives." In *Woman and Slaves in Greco-Roman Culture,* ed. Sandra Joshel and Sheila Murnaghan, 152–173. London: Routledge.

Paul, G. M. (1985). "Sallust's Sempronia: The Portrait of a Lady." *PLLS* 5: 9–22.

Pausch, Dennis (2004). *Biographie und Bildungskultur*. Berlin: Walter de Gruyter.

Peachin, Michael (2001). *Aspects of Friendship in the Graeco-Roman World.* Journal of Roman Archaeology Supplementary Series, no. 43. Portsmouth, RI.

Peradotto, John, and J. P. Sullivan, eds. (1984). *Women in the Ancient World: The Arethusa Papers*. Albany: State University of New York Press.

Peter, Hermann (1901). *Der Brief in der römischen Litteratur*. Leipzig: Teubner.

Pflaum, H.-G. (1978). *Les Fastes de la province de Narbonnaise*. Paris: Centre National de la Recherche Scientifique.

(1963–1964). "Q. PLANIUS SARDUS L. VARIUS AMBIBULUS, légat de la *legio IIIa Augusta*, à la lumière de découvertes récentes." *BACTH* 1966: 143–151.

(1960). *Les carrières procuratoriennes équestres sous le Haut-Empire Romain*. Paris: Librairie Orientaliste Paul Geuthner.

Philips, Jane E. (1978–1979). "Roman Mothers and the Lives of Their Adult Daughters." *Helios* 6: 69–80.

Pigoń, Jakub (1999). "The Identity of the Chief Vestal Cornelia (*PIR²* C1481): Some Suggestions." *Mnemosyne* 52: 206–213.

(1992). "Helvidius Priscus, Eprius Marcellus, and *Iudicium Senatus*: Observations on Tacitus, *Histories* 4.7–8." *CQ* 42: 235–246.

Pistor, Hans-Henning (1965). "Prinzeps und Patriziat." Ph.D. diss., Albert-Ludwigs-Universität.

Plass, Paul (1988). *Wit and the Writing of History*. Madison: University of Wisconsin Press.

Pomeroy, Sarah (1999). *Plutarch's Advice to the Bride and Groom and a Consolation to His Wife*. New York: Oxford University Press.

(1994). *Xenophon Oeconomicus: A Social and Historical Commentary*. Oxford, Clarendon.

ed. (1991). *Women's History and Ancient History*. Chapel Hill: University of North Carolina Press.

(1975). *Goddesses, Whores, Wives, and Slaves*. New York: Schocken Books.

Porter, S. E. (1997). *Handbook of Classical Rhetoric in the Hellenistic Period*. Leiden: Brill.

Powell, Anton, ed. (1992). *Roman Poetry and Propaganda in the Age of Augustus*. London: Bristol.

Powell, J. G. F., ed. (1995). *Cicero the Philosopher*. Oxford: Clarendon.

Purcell, Nicholas (1995). "Literate Games: Roman Urban Society and the Game of Alea." *P&P* 147: 3–37.

(1986). "Livia and the Womanhood of Rome." *PCPS* 32: 77–105.

Quinn, Kenneth (1973). *Catullus: The Poems*. London: St. Martin's Press.

Raaflaub, Kurt A. (1987a). "Grundzüge, Ziele und Ideen der Opposition gegen die Kaiser im 1. Jh. n. Chr.: Versuch einer Standortbestimmung." In *Opposition et résistances à l'empire d'Auguste à Trajan*, ed. Kurt Raaflaub, 1–55. Geneva: Fondation Hardt.

256 Bibliography

ed. (1987b). *Opposition et résistances à l'empire d'Auguste à Trajan.* Geneva: Fondation Hardt.

Rabinowitz, Nancy Sorkin, and Amy Richlin, eds. (1993). *Feminist Theory and the Classics.* New York: Routledge.

Radice, Betty, ed. (1969). *Pliny Letters and Panegyricus.* Vols. I and II. Cambridge, MA: Harvard University Press.

(1968). "Pliny and the *Panegyricus.*" *G&R* 15: 166–172.

(1962). "A Fresh Approach to Pliny's Letters." *G&R* 9: 160–168.

Radicke, Jan (1997). "Die Selbstdarstellung des Plinius in seinen Briefen." *Hermes* 125: 447–461.

Raditsa, Leo Ferrero (1980). "Augustus' Legislation concerning Marriage, Procreation, Love Affairs and Adultery." *ANRW* II 13: 278–339.

Raepsaet-Charlier, Marie-Thérèse (1987). *Prosopographie des femmes de l'ordre sénatorial (Ier–IIe siècles).* Leuven: Aedibus Peeters.

(1984). "L'origine sociale des Vestales sous le Haut-Empire." In *Mneme Georges A. Petropoulos,* ed. A. Biscardi, Georgios Andrea Petropoulos, Joseph Modrzejewski, Hans Julius Wolff, and Panagiotes D. Demakes, 253–270. Athens: A. N. Sakkoulas.

(1983a). "*Venulei* et *Pompei* d'Étrurie." *Latomus* 42: 422–423.

(1983b). "L'inscription *CIL* XI 1735 complétée et les *Venulei.*" *Latomus* 42: 152–155.

(1982). "Epouses et familles de magistrats dans les provinces romaine aux deux premiers siècles de l'Empire." *Historia* 31: 56–69.

(1981–1982). "Ordre sénatorial et divorce sous le Haut-Empire: Un chapitre de l'histoire des mentalités." *ACD* 17–18: 161–173.

Raschke, Wendy J. (1990). "The Virtue of Lucilius." *Latomus* 49: 352–369.

Rawson, Beryl, ed. (1991). *Marriage, Divorce and Children.* Oxford: Clarendon Press.

ed. (1986). *The Family in Ancient Rome.* Ithaca: Cornell University Press.

Rawson, Elizabeth (1987). "*Discrimina Ordinum:* The *Lex Julia Theatralis.*" *PBSR* 55: 83–114.

Reekmans, Tony (1971). "Juvenal's Views on Social Change." *AncSoc* 2: 117–161.

Rees, Roger (2001). "To be and not to be: Pliny's Paradoxical Trajan." *BICS* 45: 149–168.

Rehm, Rush (1994). *Marriage to Death.* Princeton: Princeton University Press.

Rémy, Bernard (1983). "La carrière de *P. Calvisiou Ruso Iulius Frontinus,* gouverneur de Cappadoce-Galatie." *MEFR* 95: 163–182.

Reynolds, L.D., ed. (1983). *Texts and Transmission.* Oxford: Clarendon Press.

Richlin, Amy (1992a). *The Garden of Priapus.* 2nd ed. New York: Oxford University Press.

ed. (1992b). *Pornography and Representation in Greece and Rome.* New York: Oxford University Press.

(1992c). "Julia's Jokes, Galla Placida and the Roman Use of Women as Political Icons." In *Stereotypes of Women in Power*, ed. Barbara Garlick, Suzanne Dixon, and Pauline Allen, 65–91. New York: Glenwood Press.

(1984). "Invective against Women in Roman Satire." *Arethusa* 17: 67–80.

(1981). "Approaches to the Sources on Adultery at Rome." In *Reflections of Women in Antiquity*, ed. Helene P. Foley, 379–404. New York: Gordon and Breach.

Riggsby, Andrew M. (2003). "Pliny in Space (and Time)." *Arethusa* 36: 267–186.

(1998). "Self and Community in the Younger Pliny." *Arethusa* 31: 75–97.

(1997). "'Public' and 'Private' in Roman Culture: The Care of the *cubiculum*." *JRA* 10: 36–56.

(1995). "Pliny on Cicero and Oratory: Self-Fashioning in the Public Eye." *AJP* 116: 123–135.

Roche, P.A. (2002). "The Public Image of Trajan's Family." *CP* 97: 41–60.

Rogers, Robert Samuel (1960). "A Group of Domitianic Treason-Trials." *CP* 55: 19–23.

(1931). "Quinti Veranii, Pater et Filius." *CP* 26: 172–177.

Roller, Matthew (1998). "Pliny's Catullus: The Politics of Literary Appropriation." *TAPA* 128: 265–304.

Rosen, Ralph M., and Ineke Sluiter, eds. (2003). *Andreia*. Leiden: Brill.

Rosivach, Vincent (1994). "*Anus*: Some Older Women in Latin Literature." *CW* 88: 107–117.

Rudd, Niall (1992). "Stratagems of Vanity, Cicero, *Ad familiaries* 5.12 and Pliny's Letters." In *Author and Audience and Latin Literature*, ed. Tony Woodman and Jonathan Powell, 18–32. Cambridge: Cambridge University Press.

(1976). *Lines of Enquiry*. Cambridge: Cambridge University Press.

Saller, Richard (1998). "Symbols of Gender and Status Hierarchies in the Roman Household." In *Women and Slaves in Greco-Roman Culture*, ed. Sandra Joshel and Sheila Murnaghan, 85–91. London: Routledge.

(1991). "Roman Heirship Strategies in Principle and in Practice." In *The Family in Italy*, ed. David I. Kertzer and Richard P. Saller, 26–47. New Haven: Yale University Press.

(1989). "Patronage and Friendship in Early Imperial Rome: Drawing the Distinction." In *Patronage in Ancient Society*, ed. Andrew Wallace-Hadrill, 49–62. London: Routledge.

(1982). *Personal Patronage under the Early Empire*. Cambridge: Cambridge University Press.

Sandbach, F.H. (1975). *The Stoics*. New York: Norton.

Santoro L'hoir, Francesca (1992). *The Rhetoric of Gender Terms*. New York: Brill.

Saxonhouse, Arlene W. (1985). *Women in the History of Political Thought*. New York: Praeger.

Scheid, John (1996). "Pline le Jeune et les santuaires d'Italie." In *Splendidissima Civitas*, ed. André Chastagnol, Ségolène Demougin, and Claude Lepelley, 241–258. Paris: Publications de la Sorbonne.

(1983). "Note sur les Venuleii Aproniani." *ZPE* 52: 225–228.

(1975a). "Scribonia Caesaris et les Julio-Claudiens." *MEFR* 87: 349–375.

(1975b). *Les Frères Arvales*. Paris: Presses Universitaires de France.

Schuller, Wolfgang (1995). *Frauen in der griechischen und römischen Geschichte*. Konstanz: Universitats verlag Konstanz.

Schuster, M. (1928). "Tacitus und der jungere Plinius." *WS* 46: 234–240.

Scott, James M. (1998). "The Rhetoric of Suppressed Speech." *AHB* 12: 8–18.

Scullard, H. H. (1951). *Roman Politics*. Oxford: Clarendon.

Seaford, Richard (1987). "The Tragic Wedding." *JHS* 107: 106–130.

Seltman, C. (1956). *Women in Antiquity*. London: Thames & Hudson.

Setälä, Päivi (1977). "Private Domini in Roman Brick Stamps of the Empire." Ph.D. diss., Helsinki.

Serviez, Jacques Roergas de (1718). *Lives of the Roman Empresses*. New York: Wise.

Shackleton Bailey, D. R. (1981). "Notes on the Younger Pliny." *PCPS* 207: 50–57.

Shelton, Jo-Ann (1990). "Pliny the Younger and the Ideal Wife." *C&M* 41: 163–186.

(1987). "Pliny's Letter 3.11: Rhetoric and Autobiography." *C&M* 38: 121–139.

Sherk, Robert K. (1980). "Roman Galatia." *ANRW* II 7.2: 955–1052.

Sherwin-White, A. N. (1969a). "Pliny, the Man and His Letters." *G&R* 16: 76–90.

(1969b). *Fifty Letters of Pliny*. Oxford: Oxford University Press.

(1966). *The Letters of Pliny*. Oxford: Oxford University Press.

(1957). "Pliny's Praetorship Again." *JRS* 47: 126–130.

Sick, David H. (1999). "Ummidia Quadratilla: Cagey Businesswoman or Lazy Pantomime Watcher?" *ClAnt* 18: 330–348.

Skinner, Marilyn B. (1986). "Rescuing Creusa." *Helios* 13: 1–8.

(1983). "Clodia Metelli." *TAPA* 113: 273–287.

Slater, W. J. (1994). "Pantomime Riots." *CA* 13: 120–144.

Smethurst, S. E. (1950). "Women in Livy's *History*." *G&R* 19: 80–87.

Spelman, Elizabeth V. (1982). "Woman as Body: Ancient and Contemporary Views." *Feminist Studies* 8: 109–131.

Starr, Raymond (1990). "Pliny the Younger on Private Recitations and C. Titius on Irresponsible Judges." *Latomus* 49: 464–472.

Stein, Arthur (1983). *Der römische Ritterstand*. Munich: Beck.

Steinby, Margareta (1974–1975). "La cronologia delle Figlinae Doliari Urbane." *BullCom* 84: 48–55.

Stower, S. K. (1986). *Letter Writing in Greco-Roman Antiquity*. Philadelphia: Westminster.

Strobel, Karl (2003). "Plinius und Domitian: Der willige helfer eines Unrechtssystems?" In *Plinius der Jüngere und seine Zeit*, ed. Luigi Castagna and Eckard Lefèvre, 303–314. Munich and Leipzig: K. G. Saur.

Susini, Giancarlo (1971). "Nuova iscrizione onoraria di Plinio il Giovane." *Epigraphica* 33: 183–184.

Syme, Ronald (1991). *Roman Papers*. Ed. Anthony R. Birley. Oxford: Clarendon Press.

(1985a). "Correspondents of Pliny." *Historia* 34: 324–359.

(1985b). "The Testamentum Dasumii: Some Novelties." *Chiron* 15: 41–63.

(1985c). "The Dating of Pliny's Latest Letters." *CQ* 35: 176–185.

(1985d). "Curtailed Tenures of Consular Legates." *ZPE* 59: 265–279.

(1985e). "Superior Suffect Consuls." *ZPE* 58: 235–243.

(1984a). "Hadrian and the Senate." *Athenaeum* 62: 31–60.

(1984b). "P. Calvisius Ruso. One Person or Two?" *ZPE* 56: 173–192.

(1983a). "Problems about Proconsuls of Asia." *ZPE* 53: 191–208.

(1983b). "Domitian: The Last Years." *Chiron* 13: 121–146.

(1983c). "Spanish Pomponii. A Study in Nomenclature." *Gerión* 1: 249–266.

(1982a). "Eight Consuls from Patavium." *PBSR* 51: 102–124.

(1982b). "Partisans of Galba." *Historia* 31: 460–483.

(1982c). "Clues to Testamentary Adoption." In *Epigrafia e Ordine Senatorio I*, Colloquio Internazionale AIEGL, 397–410. Rome: Edizioni di Storia e Letteratura, Tituli 4.

(1981). "Governors Dying in Syria." *ZPE* 41: 125–144.

(1980a). *Some Arval Brethren*. Oxford: Clarendon Press.

(1980b). "Guard Prefects of Trajan and Hadrian." *JRS* 70: 64–80.

(1979a). "Juvenal, Pliny, Tacitus." *AJP* 100: 250–278.

(1979b). "Ummidius Quadratus, *Capax Imperii*." *HSCP* 83: 287–310.

(1979c). *Roman Papers*. Vols. I–VII. Oxford: Clarendon Press.

(1971). *Emperors and Biography*. Oxford: Clarendon Press.

(1969). "Pliny the Procurator." *HSCP* 73: 201–236.

(1968a). "People in Pliny." *JRS* 58: 135–151.

(1968b). "The Ummidii." *Historia* 17: 72–105.

(1964). "Senators, Tribes and Towns." *Historia* 13: 105–125.

(1962). "Missing Persons III." *Historia* 11: 146–155.

(1960). "Pliny's Less Successful Friends." *Historia* 9: 362–377.

(1958). *Tacitus*. 2 vols. Oxford: Clarendon Press.

(1957a). "The Jurist Neratius Priscus." *Hermes* 85: 480–493.

(1957b). "The Friend of Tacitus." *JRS* 47: 131–135.

(1956). "Missing Persons." *Historia* 5: 204–212.

(1953). "Reviews and Discussions." *JRS* 43: 156.

(1949). "Personal Names in *Annals* I–VI." *JRS* 39: 6–18.

(1939). *The Roman Revolution*. Oxford: Clarendon Press.

Talbert, R.J.A. (1984). *The Senate of Imperial Rome*. Princeton: Princeton University Press.

(1980). "Pliny the Younger as Governor of Bithynia-Pontus." In *Studies in Latin Literature and Roman History II*, ed. Carl Deroux, 412–435. Collection Latomus 168. Brussels.

Tassaux, Francis (1982). "Recherches sur une famille sénatoriale d'Istrie." *MEFR* 94: 227–269.

Temporini, Hildegard (1998). "Frauen und Politik im antiken Rom." In *Imperium Romanum*, ed. Peter Kneissl and Volker Losemann, 705–732. Stuttgart: Franz Steiner.

(1978). *Die Frauen am Hofe Trajans*. Berlin: de Gruyter.

Thomasson, Bengt E. (1975). *Senatores Procuratoresque Romani*. Göteborg: Struves Boktryckeri.

(1969). "Praesides Provinciarum Africae." *OpRom* 7: 164–211.

(1960). *Die Statthalter der römischen Provinzen Nordafrikas von Augustus bis Diocletianus*. Lund: Gleerup.

Torelli, Mario (1982a). "Italia: Regio IV." In *Epigrafia e Ordine Senatorio II*, Colloquio Internazionale AIEGL, 165–199. Rome: Edizioni di Storia e Letteratura, Tituli 5.

(1982b). "Italia: Regio VII." In *Epigrafia e Ordine Senatorio II*, Colloquio Internazionale AIEGL, 275–299. Rome: Edizioni di Storia e Letteratura, Tituli 5.

(1971). "Per la Storia dell'Etruria in Età Imperiale." *RFIC* 99: 489–501.

(1969). "Senatori etruschi della tarda repubblica e dell'impero." *DArch* 3: 285–363.

Tracy, Valerie (1976). "The Leno-Maritus." *CJ* 72: 62–64.

Traub, Henry W. (1955). "Pliny's Treatment of History in Epistolary Form." *TAPA* 86: 213–232.

Treggiari, Susan (2007). *Terentia, Tullia and Publilia*. London: Routledge.

(1991). *Roman Marriage*. Oxford: Clarendon.

Trexler, Richard C. (1994). *Gender Rhetorics*. Binghamton, NY: Medieval and Renaissances Texts and Studies.

Trillmich, Walter (1978). *Familienpropaganda der Kaiser Caligula und Claudius*. Berlin: de Gruyter.

Tzounakas, Spyridon (2007). "'Neque enim historiam componebam': Pliny's First Epistle and His Attitude towards Historiography." *MH* 64: 42–54.

van Bremen, Riet (1996). *The Limits of Participation*. Amsterdam: Gieben.

Vasaly, Ann (1993). *Representations*. Berkeley: University of California Press.

Veyne, Paul (1978). "La famille et l'amour sous le Haut-Empire Romain." *Annales ESC* 33: 35–63.

(1967). "Autour d'un commentaire de Pline le Jeune." *Latomus* 26: 723–751.

Vidén, Gunhild (1993). *Women in Roman Literature*. Göteborg: Acta Universitatis Gothoborgensis.

Vidman, Ladislaus (1982a). *Fasti Ostienses*. Prague: Academiae Scientiarum.

(1982b). "Osservazioni sui praefecti urbi ne primi due secoli." In *Epigrafia e Ordine Senatorio I*, Colloquio Internazionale AIEGL, 289–303. Rome: Edizioni di Storia e Letteratura, Tituli 4.

Vielberg, Meinolf (1988). "Bermerkungen zu Plinius d.J. und Tacitus." *WJA* 14: 171–183.

Vogel-Weidemann, Ursula (1982). *Die Statthalter von Africa und Asia in den Jahren 14–68 n. Chr.* Bonn: Rudolf Habelt.

von Fritz, Kurt (1957). "Tacitus, Agricola, Domitian, and the Problem of the Principate." *CP* 52: 73–97.

Walker, B. (1952). *The Annals of Tacitus.* Manchester: Manchester University Press.

Wallace, Kristine Gilmartin (1991). "Women in Tacitus, 1903–1986." *ANRW* II 33.5: 3556–3574.

Wallace-Hadrill, Andrew, ed. (1989). *Patronage in Ancient Society.* London: Routledge.

(1981). "The Emperor and His Virtues." *Historia* 30: 298–323.

Wardle, David (1996). "Vespasian, Helvidius Priscus and the Restoration of the Capitol." *Historia* 45: 208–222.

Waters, Kenneth Hugh (1974). "Trajan's Character in the Literary Tradition." In *Polis and Imperium: Studies in Honour of Edward Togo*, ed. J.A.S. Evans 233–252. Toronto: Hakkert.

(1964). "The Character of Domitian." *Phoenix* 18: 49–77.

Watt, W.S. (1990). "Notes on Pliny *Epistulae* and *Panegyricus.*" *Phoenix* 44: 84–87.

Weische, Alfons (1990). "Plinius d.J. und Cicero. Untersuchungen zur römischen Epistolographie in Republik und Kaiserzeit." *ANRW* II 33.1: 375–386.

White, John L. (1984). "New Testament Epistolary Literature in the Framework of Ancient Epistolography." *ANRW* II 25.2: 1730–1756.

White, Peter (1975). "The Friends of Martial, Statius, and Pliny, and the Dispersal of Patronage." *HSCP* 79: 265–300.

Whitehead, David (1993). "Cardinal Virtues: The Language of Public Approbation in Democratic Athens." *C&M* 44: 37–75.

Wilkes, J.J. (1979). *Dalmatia.* Cambridge, MA: Harvard University Press.

Williams, Gordon (1958). "Some Aspects of Roman Marriage Ceremonies and Ideals." *JRS* 48: 16–29.

Wistrand, E. (1979). "The Stoic Opposition to the Principate." *StudClas* 18: 93–101.

Wolff, Étienne (2004). "Pline et Cicéron: Quelques remarques." In *Epistulae Antiquae III*, ed. Léon Nadjo and Élisabeth Gavoille, 441–447. Louvain: Peeters.

(2003). *Pline le Jeune ou le Refus du Pessimisme.* Rennes: Presses Universitaires de Rennes.

Woodman, Anthony J. (1998). *Tacitus Reviewed.* Oxford: Clarendon.

(1988). *Rhetoric in Classical Historiography.* London: Croom Helm.

Woodman, Anthony J., and Jonathan Powell (1992). *Author and Audience in Latin Literature.* Cambridge: Cambridge University Press.

Wyke, Maria (1992). "Augustan Cleopatras: Female Power and Poetic Authority." In *Roman Poetry and Propaganda in the Age of Augustus,* ed. Anton Powell, 98–140. London: Bristol.

Zanker, P. (1988). *The Power of Images in the Age of Augustus.* Ann Arbor: University of Michigan Press.

Zelzer, Klaus (1964). "Zur Frage des Charakters der Briefsammlung des jüngeren Plinius." *WS* 77: 144–161.

Zevi, Fausto (1979). "Un frammento dei *Fasti Ostienses* e i consolati dei primi anni di Traiano." *PP* 186: 179–201.

Zucker, Friedrich (1963). "Der jüngere Plinius und die Familie des Konsulars Q. Corellius Rufus." *Das Altertum* 9: 37–34.

Index Locorum

General Index